Making an American Family:
A Recipe in Five Generations

Janet Rodriguez

Making an American Family: A Recipe in Five Generations
Copyright ©2022 by Janet Rodriguez
ISBN: 978-1-889568-12-6
Prickly Pear Publishing & Nopalli Press Santa Fe, New Mexico 87505
pricklypearpublishing.com

All rights reserved under International and Pan-American Copyright Conventions. No part of this publication may be reproduced without prior written permission from the publisher. Please Contact: pricklypearpublishing.com

First Edition, Printed in the United States of America
Library of Congress Control Number: 2022936272
Rodriguez, Janet.
Making an American Family: A Recipe in Five Generations/Janet Rodriguez
ISBN 978-1-889568-12-6 (pbk.)
I. Title.
Memoir, Oral History, Family, Mexican-American, Central Valley, California, Identity:

Para mi familia
For my Family

Especialmente Mario

Table of Contents:

Family Tree 1

Introduction 2

Part One: Seeds 5
    1. Pictures 6
    2. Dear Classmates 14
    3. Where Do We Begin? 19

Part Two: Gardens 23
    4. Lorraine Road 24
    5. Grandpa: A Man Called Nacho 30
    6. Grandma: The First Juana 36

Part Three: Champurrado 39
    7. Familia Avila 40
    8. Life Before the War 46
    9. The Mexican Revolution 50

Part Four: Beans 55
    10. Tía Maria – Filling the Gaps 56
    11. Leaving the Ranch 60
    12. Crossing Over 64

Part Five: Tortillas 71
    13. Fresno or Malaga? 72
    14. The Notes Under the Cup 74
    15. Lone Pine 82

Part Six: Chili de Puerco 87
    16. Malaga, California 88
    17. The Time 92
    18. The Babies 98
    19. The Home 106

Part Seven: Salsa 111
    20. Pneumonia 112
    21. What Is a Sense Memory? 118
    22. Relief Christmas 125
    23. Changes 131

Part Eight: Enchiladas 135
    24. Tracy, California 136
    25. El Ranchito 140
    26. Gender Roles 145

Part Nine: Mexican Rice 153
    27. School Days 154
    28. Addition and Subtraction 162
    29. Sepraration 169
    30. Becoming "American" 173

Part Ten: Meatloaf 181
    31. The Way Things Are 182
    32. Seven Questions—Dorothy 185
    33. Seven Questions—Terry 195
    34. Seven Questions—Mildred 204
    35. Seven Questions—Lucy 216
    36. Seven Questions—Jennie 226
    37. Seven Questions—Emily/Emmy 240
    38. Seven Questions—Molly 249

Part Eleven: Dessert 261
    39. Third Generation Immigrants 262
    40. The Challenge 267
    41. The Way Things Were 270
    42. The Baton 275
About The Author 285

Family Tree

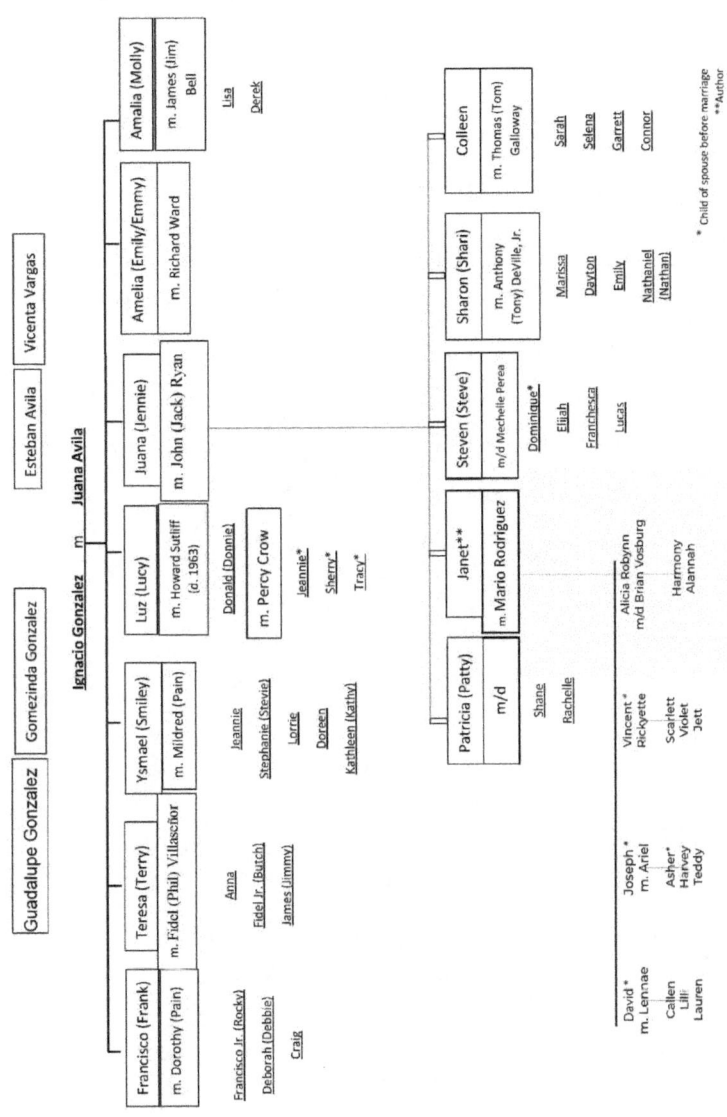

"When Mexico sends its people, they're not sending their best. They're not sending you. They're not sending you. They're sending people that have lots of problems, and they're bringing those problems with us. They're bringing drugs. They're bringing crime. They're rapists. And some, I assume, are good people."

~ Donald Trump, presidential announcement speech,
June 16, 2015

"You might be poor, your shoes might be broken, but your mind is a palace. It's lovely to know that the world can't interfere with the inside of your head."

~ Frank McCourt

"To be just, no one could be blamed...the transition from the culture of the old world to that of the new should never have been attempted in one generation."

~ José Antonio Villarreal

"Pinto flores así no mueren"
I paint flowers so they will not die.

~ Frida Kahlo

Introduction
(or why I started this swirling vortex of a project)

My grandma, Juana Gonzalez, used to make masa for flour tortillas in a big yellow bowl, mixing it with her fingers, even after her knuckles had become gnarled by arthritis.

"That's about six cups," Grandma said, tilting her head. I was eighteen years old when Grandma taught me how to make tortillas, and I didn't write anything down. I believed her measurements, especially about the pile of flour in the middle of the bowl. Grandma made tortillas every day, and rarely measured ingredients. Measurements, in her world, were handfuls of this, and pinches of that. The only thing in Grandma's kitchen that was ever measured was the bouillon cube, or "boiling cube," as she used to call it: a small block of compacted spices, wrapped in foil. Grandma's recipes were mastered through years of practice.

Preserved in a similar way, our family stories were usually told and retold around a table, where we celebrated and feasted together. If there was a generation gap, or a culture gap, Grandma's food closed it. Memories of her are still attached to taste and smell. The fragrance of molasses cookies, Christmas tamales, or the smell of lard, frying potatoes, beans, or chile rellenos, can summon Grandma's stories immediately.

Memories are powerful things. They bear the tales of family connection and survival. The oral tradition, how our story survived, eventually needs to be written down to become history, or even better: literature.

Ignacio and Juana Gonzalez, my grandparents, came from Mexico, the place where story rose from the ground and took flight. Grandpa is from Sinaloa; Grandma, from Michoacán. They never met in their home country, since they were born 988 kilometers (614 miles) away from each other. It was the early 1900's, and Mexico was in turmoil. My grandparents belonged to a people who had no written history, no rights, no deed or title to their land. As sustenance farmers, they grew up working hard, and on more than one occasion, had to scratch the ground in order to find little bits of food. They both narrowly escaped death and starvation. They crossed into this country, separately, each carrying a flimsy work permit to allow them to enter the legendary land of plenty. They worked the fertile soil; they made the soil fertile. Neither had much formal schooling, but they were expected to know everything. Their language and traditions weren't tolerated in the new land, but because of the tenacity of story, they persevered. They are here, alive in this story.

Five generations later, my grandchildren carry hand-held computers to school, live in nice houses, sleep in their own beds, have nice clothes and shoes, and are guaranteed an education by the U.S. Constitution. My grandchildren are rarely hungry for long, but like most children in the U.S.A., they're in danger of health concerns associated with a high-calorie, high-fat diet associated with processed foods. Everything is vying for their attention: cell phones, apps, video games, social media, on-demand everything. Filled with conflicting messages about God, family, work, and education, my grandchildren are swimming in information, much of it contrary to the values my grandparents tried to preserve.

Before they left this world, Grandpa and Grandma charged their children to keep the family together. Have we been successful? With every privilege we've inherited, is our collective family happy? Better off as U.S. Citizens? Have we attained the American Dream? Are we content among California's native children? No amount of research could ever answer these questions. Moreover, these weren't the most important questions.

How had our family survived in the United States when so many others had floundered? How did Grandpa and Grandma preserve family unity? Why were their children so happy? Were my siblings and I, the new family leaders, as successful? In my late fifties, I still felt childish when standing next to the generation before me. Their generation was truly unique and beautiful. I was determined to find out why.

In the process of compiling this memoir, I saw my family as a historian, and removed the rose-colored glasses I preferred to wear when I looked at them. I saw every wart and limitation, but I also noticed the understated beauty of their optimism, faith, and grace. I still have very limited perspectives of the battles they waged, just to keep our family together. This is our bloody, breathing story, a recipe for making an American family. Our collective voices have the shared flavors and aromas that unite us in the first place.

Grandma taught me to make these recipes, which survived assimilation, like hidden jewels in a secret trunk. Somehow, food is connected to our story, and bears our story. It's the way we became American—the way the U.S.A. defines American. These recipes and these stories solidify our place in the history of California and United States.

They are true and real and worthy of literature.

Part One: Seeds

"Life without love is like a tree without blossoms or fruit."
~Khalil Gibran

"Once you find yourself in another civilization, you're forced to examine your own."
~James Baldwin

Roasted Pumpkin Seeds

Pumpkin seeds from inside of pumpkin
olive oil or vegetable oil
salt and pepper
cumino chili powder
Mexican oregano
garlic salt

Scoop out pumpkin seeds and pithy parts from pumpkin, separate seeds and wash them with water. Lay them out on a cookie sheet to dry a little.

When you're ready to start, heat oven to 350 degrees and put seeds in a bowl. Line the cookie sheet with foil, and spray it with nonstick cooking spray, or drizzle oil and spread around.

Put seeds in a bowl and drizzle them with some oil. Put in seasonings. I use salt and pepper, garlic salt, cumino, Mexican oregano, chili powder, but use whatever you want (It's messy, but stir with a spoon or your hands, so they all get covered with spices). Spread the seeds on the foil so they all lay flat. No piggy-back rides! Bake seeds in the oven for about fifteen minutes (you can stir them halfway through, if you want). When the buzzer goes off, bring them out and see if they're ready. If you like them darker, roast a little bit more. Set out for people who come over and want a little snack.

1. Pictures

Imagine your most treasured family picture, the one that portrays everyone in their glory. As time passes, the picture becomes even more valuable than the day it was taken. Imagine now, that someone breaks in to your home, and steals that picture. It's gone forever— something you cannot replace.

Pictures, like memories and stories, are a sacred part of our legacy. We pass them down to the next generation, preserve them in frames, and remember what life was once like.

Family portraits convey what we value. In some cultures, photographs are forbidden. The Amish believe they are graven images, unholy and proud. The Maasai, in Kenya and Tanzania, hold fast to traditional lifestyle and culture, and refuse photographs. My maternal great grandmother, Vicenta Vargas, used to believe that someone would use her image for witchcraft, to have power over her. Our family has no photographs of Vicenta.

I'm part of a family that *loves* photographs. My father, Jack Ryan, grew up in Brookline, Massachusetts, the only child of Patrick and Alice Ryan. My mother, Jennie, grew up in the farming community of Malaga, California, the fifth child of seven, born to Ignacio and Juana Gonzalez. My parents still live in the house where I grew up, a middle-class home that has always been filled with family pictures. My sisters' old bedroom, now my parents' guest room, has a wood dresser with a mirror on top, framed with snapshots of Mom and her four sisters, standing in a row, from eldest to youngest: Terry, Lucy, Jennie, Emily, and Molly. In most pictures, the sisters are either laughing or smiling. Over the years, they've learned how to pose: one leg forward, slightly bent at the knee, toes pointed to the camera, shoulders back, chin down, head slightly tilted.

Only one professional portrait of them, taken in 1952, stands alone on the dresser. It's a black-and-white picture, still in its original studio frame. My twin aunts, Emily and Molly, are standing behind their seated sisters, Lucy, Terry and Jennie. Their father, Ignacio Gonzalez, brought his daughters into Tracy to properly capture this moment in time. Grandpa worked hard, as an agricultural laborer, but only made enough money to cover his family's basic necessities. During the winter, Grandpa didn't make enough money for that. This professional portrait is an example of Grandpa's extravagant tastes.

The girls are dressed in matching dark sweaters, with white, crocheted collars positioned on top. Each girl has an understated smile, symmetrical features, and a peaceful expression. They look as if they have everything they want. They look *happy*.

I grew up seeing this portrait, but only after I came home in 2013, after spending seven years in sub-Saharan Africa, did I start asking questions about the women in it. Mom and her sisters look peaceful and content, and pretty as a picture. I knew them as women, as leaders of their families. Their joy was genuine, permeating every aspect of their lives. Where did they get it? They had grown up poor, as children of agricultural laborers, who traveled with the harvests. They finally settled in Tracy, where the girls attended a country elementary school. They started school with only a few items of clothing, and sometimes shared these with each other.

As adults, the sisters remained close, and *genuinely* happy. I wanted to know which seeds they had sown to reap this. Hadn't they faced racism? Didn't they get in fights with each other? Feel deprived? Have bitter rivalries? What were their hopes and dreams? What was the secret behind those Mona Lisa smiles? The questions grew, like a vine in my head, until the biggest question blossomed: Why didn't I know more about my mother? Her family?

I started interviewing Mom and her sisters when they were in their eighties, but they still remembered the day their father took them to the photography studio to have this picture taken.

"Look at us in our angora sweaters!" Auntie Terry said, leaning closer to Mom. "Those collars were very popular back then, and I would say those crocheted collars were very flattering to our faces. One of our aunts made them for us."

Auntie Terry picked up the picture and examined it closely. The eldest Gonzalez sister, Auntie Terry was born Teresa Gonzalez in 1930, one year after my Uncle Frank. She has a reputation with her sisters for being gentle and kind—a second mother to them. My siblings and I know her as our funny aunt. She loves to laugh, and can find humor in most situations.

She married Fidel Villaseñor—who we call Uncle Phil, rather than Tío Fidel—right after she graduated high school. Today, Terry Villaseñor wears her brownish-grey hair pulled back, away from her face. She still resembles the Auntie I knew in my youth.

"How old were we here, Jennie?" she asked Mom.

Mom leaned closer to examine the picture, her short, curled hair, glittering in the sun. After marrying my father, Jack Ryan in 1960, she became Jennie Ryan. Mom still looked graceful and stunning, even at eighty-two. I grew up with her, a loving woman, clothed in dignity. She kept methodical, disciplined routines. Born with a strong conscience, logical mind, and a desire to help other people, Grandma once told me that Mom was her easiest child to raise. Grandma said she never talked back or disobeyed.

"I think I was a sophomore in high school here," Mom said. "Maybe fifteen-years-old?"

"I wasn't married yet," Auntie Terry said. "That's what I remember."

Mom smiled and turned to me. "It was our dad's idea to have us photographed by a professional photographer," she said. "He took pride in the way we looked, almost like we were his bevy of beauties that he wanted to parade. That day, Daddy got us together, like a beautiful bouquet of flowers. It was like he thought, 'These are mine, and I want to save them for posterity, so I'll have them photographed.' He wanted us to wear something nice, so we wore those matching sweaters with knitted collars."

Mom turned to Auntie Terry, and nudged her, playfully. "If you look closely, I'll show you the 'something extra' about this picture," Mom said. "Lucy, at a later date, drew eyeliner on herself. If you look closely, you can see it."

Auntie Terry leaned in. "I see it," she said. "Lucy was such a glamour girl!"

Mom laughed. "None of us wore eyeliner in those days," she said. "One day, when we were all still living at home, I caught Lucy taking the *original* picture out of the frame, and drawing eyeliner on herself with a pencil! I said, 'Lucy! What are you doing?' She said, 'Oh, I don't like my eyes in this picture, so I'm putting some eyeliner on myself.'"

"I was so vain!" Auntie Lucy said, laughing. "I did something with my bangs there, too. Do you see? I didn't like how I looked, so I changed it."

Auntie Lucy, born three-and-a-half years before Mom, and three-and-a-half years after Auntie Terry, has the same physical features as her sisters, but has always been different from them. Independent and outspoken, Auntie Lucy wanted much more than the life she had growing up. My siblings and I always called Auntie Lucy "Vickie Vogue," because of her designer clothes, shoes, and bags. She was never without a tube of red lipstick. Her short brown hair, teased up high, showed off her earrings and make-up. Auntie Lucy smoked Benson and Hedges 100's, which she kept in a red leather cigarette case with a gold clasp. Her laugh was an explosive, raspy blast that filled the house. When I was very young, she married Percy Crow, and moved to Los Angeles. They visited us only once a year.

"I like this picture of us," Auntie Lucy said. "It hung in the window of the photographer's studio for a long time."

"Daddy never took Frank and Smiley to have their picture taken at a portrait studio," Mom said. "They took pictures when they went into the service." She turned to Auntie Terry. "Remember that professional family portrait we took? All of us were in it? We have to find that picture."

My Aunt Dorothy, the woman who married my Uncle Frank, searched through boxes of photos in her house, and finally found the missing portrait.

It was taken in a studio in the 1940's. The photographer tried to fit them all in the frame, against a white backdrop. Each Gonzalez family member looks stoic in front of the camera, a Mexican-American Gothic. It was before color film or outdoor portraits were popular, so different from professional portraits taken today. Now photographers stage color coordinated family members around hay bales, or pumpkins. Families are photographed while walking in a field, holding hands, looking over their shoulders. Couples in rolled-up jeans and bare feet stroll on a sandy beach. Today, family portraits are digital, posted on Instagram. No one has to search through boxes of photographs to find them.

The Gonzalez Family approx. 1947. Back row: Ismael (Smiley), Luz (Lucy), Juana (Jennie/Mom), Teresa (Terry), Francisco (Frank); Front row: Amelia (Emily), Juana (Grandma), Ignacio (Grandpa) and Amalia (Molly).

"How sad we look!" Auntie Terry said, laughing to herself. "The photographer made Emily stand on one side, and Molly stand on the other. They weren't used to being separated, so they started crying, and Daddy corrected them. Remember, Jennie?"

"I don't remember that," Mom said. "But looking at this makes me wish we had more pictures of Mama and Daddy when they were really young."

"I only saw one picture of Mama as a young girl," Auntie Terry said. "She was wearing an apron. She was already working at the boarding house, making tortillas for the men who stayed there."

"Maybe our cousin, Esther, has some younger pictures of Mama," Mom said. "Tía Maria had access to a camera back then, but Mama didn't."

"Who is Esther?" I asked. The sisters looked at me, like they just noticed I was there. "Esther was Tía Maria's daughter," Auntie Lucy said to me, as if she were translating. "Maria was my mother's older sister. Their last name was Avila, but Tía Maria married Monico Ruiz. He was no relation to Mr.

Ruiz, who used to employ our father all those years on the ranch. Anyway, Tía Maria and Tío Monico lived in Malaga, a town near Fresno, and ran a boarding house, where Mexican laborers stayed. Tía Maria was able to buy property and build little houses on it, pretty close together. Our family moved to Malaga, and lived in one of those little houses, close to hers." Auntie Lucy laughed into her hand, as if she were remembering something funny. "It was sometimes a little too close, wasn't it?"

"Daddy didn't like our house being so close to Tía Maria's!" Auntie Molly said, trying to suppress laughter.

"Tía Maria was a toughie," Auntie Emmy said. "Even her husband seemed to get bossed around a lot."

Auntie Molly laughed out loud, and Auntie Emmy joined her. The youngest Gonzalez sisters, Emily and Molly are identical twins. They sometimes still behaved like young girls, sharing a private joke or planning mischief. At just five feet tall, the twins are still referred to as "cute." They always seem ready for a party, and look years younger than their real age.

"Daddy didn't like Tía Maria," Auntie Lucy said. "She was a big lady, definitely the boss of her house, the boarding house, and the whole property! She never took no for an answer." Auntie Lucy leaned closer to me. "In other words, Tía Maria was everything that our mother wasn't! Mama was a small woman, very timid, and she was married to a very domineering husband."

"And Tío Monico did anything Tía Maria asked him to do," Auntie Emmy said. "Because that was his boss! He worked for Tía Maria in the boarding house."

"Yes," Auntie Lucy agreed. "She knew all the farms around Fresno employed Mexican workers. Those workers needed to eat, have a clean place to wash, a bed to sleep in. Tía Maria was a great businesswoman and cook. Migrant farm workers stayed at her boarding house, and paid her in cash. She was the one on our property who always had money." Auntie Lucy paused, and then smiled. "She was my Godmother, so she spoiled me."

"Did she ever!" Mom said. "She *really* spoiled Lucy."

"Tía Maria had a big bosom," Auntie Lucy said, stretching her arms out in front of her. "She kept a handkerchief down there, filled with paper money and coins. When she would come over to our house, she would single me out. She'd say, 'Ven aquí,' and stick her hand down her big bosom and pull out some money for me. Spending money! I would go to the store and buy chocolate. My family could never afford to buy me candy!"

"I always wished she was *my* godmother!" Auntie Emmy said, laughing.

"Yeah," Auntie Molly said, leaning forward and pretending to search Tía Maria's cleavage. "You got any money in there for us?"

Auntie Terry interjected: "Not just Lucy, but Tía Maria brought things for our whole family, remember? Big bags of bread, tortillas, tamales…she'd bring us a lot! When you're a child, and hungry, you like all that food…" She stopped talking, as if she just remembered something. "But Daddy didn't like her doing that."

"No, Daddy didn't like that at all," Mom said. "He didn't like Tía Maria's pushiness. I think he probably felt insulted, or accused of not being able to provide for his family." Mom puffed out her chest and pretended to be her father. "'Hey, I'm the bread-earner here. Who are you? Coming in here with groceries, trying to make me look bad.' It made him feel like less of a man, but there were times in the winter when he wasn't working. We were struggling. A kid doesn't question where food comes from, and Tía Maria just wanted to help."

"She helped our family a lot," Auntie Emmy said. "She helped our family survive in California, where we put down roots. If you think about it, every family has a Tía Maria: the person who goes first, and makes it easier for the rest of the family."

"Family was important to them," Mom said. "The most important thing. Remember Mama's last words, don't you? She said, 'Keep the family together. Don't let the family fall apart.'"

"I do remember," Auntie Emmy said, solemnly. "That's the last thing she said."

***

"I feel bad that I never knew Tía Maria," I said to Mom, once we were alone.

"Tía Maria died when you were pretty young," Mom said. She told me the basics of the separation, the way she and Grandma spent most of their lives in different cities. Grandma and Tía Maria regularly talked on the phone, before Maria died. They were traditional Mexican women, neither had learned to drive. They relied on their husbands to take them anywhere, and the four-hour round trip from Tracy to Fresno grew longer as they got older.

"Why didn't we ever go to see her, as a family?" I asked Mom. "I don't remember visiting the Ruiz family, or offering to take Grandma."

"We didn't," Mom said, unbothered by her admission. Then, she suddenly asked me a question I wasn't expecting. "Did you ever go to any of the Ruiz family reunions with us?" She was referring to the Ruiz family gathering, hosted by Tío Monico and Tía Maria's children, a biannual feast and celebration. Our entire family, and our children, were always included in the invitation. Mario and I never went. Mom knew this.

"No," I answered. "I guess we were…busy."

I hated my answer.

Mario and I had just returned to the United States, after living in South Africa for seven years. We had been on a different continent, working alongside local churches and faith-based ministries. We made significant friendships with people, and through their eyes, I could see the United States, and its people, with a different lens. Over there, folks rarely used the word busy to describe life. Over there, busy, was a transient adjective, not a permanent state of being. Over there, everybody always had time for a "quick cup of tea," or a shared meal, or a spontaneous gathering. Over there, people who were busy—constantly occupied with work, having no free time for fun—were rare, unbalanced, and maybe even weak individuals.

When Mario and I moved back to the United States, I got back on the treadmill. I became busy again.

2. Dear Classmates

Mario and I lived in Johannesburg, South Africa, for seven years, working with an international ministry team. For lack of a better description, we were what Americans call "missionaries," even though we weren't that at all. Our team had relationships with other churches, all over the world, and we were a support couple, helping in various ways.

As soon as we moved to Johannesburg, I noticed a remarkable change in culture. Despite being an economic capital, the people seemed friendly and welcoming. New friends, regardless of socioeconomic status or culture, were curious about our life back home. They asked questions about our families, children, and the origin of our last name: Rodriguez. A first, I explained our cultural heritage with the same language I used in the United States:

"Mario is half-Spanish, and probably Germanic—his mother was adopted. I'm half-Irish, half-Mexican."

Our friends seemed nonplussed. "Hold on," they'd say. "We thought you were both *American.*" I hadn't realized, until then, that we *were* American—as homogenized as a gallon of milk.

After years in full-time ministry, Mario and I returned to the United States. We poured our energy into two things: reconnecting with family and finding a new home. Mario started working again, with the State of California, like he had never left. I continued writing, but also decided to go back to school.

Returning to college at the age of fifty-two is both exciting and scary. I didn't relish the idea of being "the old lady in the classroom," but was excited about the intellectual stimulation.

One of my upper-division English classes, "The Modern Short Story: Mixed-Race Authors," was led by a professor who asked every student to write a letter to our classmates.

"Explain your cultural heritage to them," she said. "And try to uncover at least two false assumptions you have about the issue of race."

I was surprised at the contents of my letter. Here is the beginning:

Dear Classmates,

My name is Janet Rodriguez, and I'm of mixed race.

I grew up Janet Ryan, the daughter of an Irish-American father and a Mexican-American mother. I married my husband, Mario Rodriguez, and proudly took the surname that I felt I deserved my whole life. I wouldn't have to explain to others that I was a Latina; they would know because now I had a label. My husband and I don't bear the classically bronzed skin of traditional Latinos—we look pretty white. I inherited my Irish-American father's sun-sensitive skin. My husband's father was a light-skinned Spaniard; his mother was white. Nevertheless, I wore my Spanish surname like a badge of honor.

The Ryan Family, on the front lawn of Grandpa and Grandma's house, 1970. Back row (l to r): Nana (Alice), Dad (Jack), Mom (Jennie); Front row: Patty, Colleen, Steve, Janet, and Shari (in front of me).

I grew up in a small town in the San Joaquin Valley of California, heavily populated with farms and farm workers. My Irish-American father worked as a Correctional Counselor at DVI, the local State Prison. He had grown up in Boston, so when he took the job in Tracy, he brought his mother, my Nana, to live with him. Dad and Nana were separated from their family, who still lived back East. My mother's family lived here, so they were the family we felt closest to.

My father tells the story of meeting my mom with the flair of a rom-com screenwriter: "I went to a church youth group meeting and saw the most beautiful woman I had ever seen in my life." Mom always told us that when she passed my father, she could literally feel sparks flying madly between them. They married, merging their cultures. Catholicism became their shared cultural identity, an equalizer and bonder that held them together.

My parents had five children: four girls and one boy. We looked charmingly biracial, but not <u>too</u> biracial. Our hair and eyes were brown, but we had relatively light skin and dimpled faces. When summer came, my pool-side complexion became darker, and I casually bragged this was because I was half-Mexican. My surname was Ryan, so I escaped racist labels applied to most Mexican kids. Because of the distance between California and Massachusetts, we rarely connected with my father's side of the family. Nevertheless, we celebrated our Irish-American culture. My mother's Mexican-American parents lived close by: Ignacio, my grandfather, was a farm laborer. His wife, Juana, stayed at home. Grandpa and Grandma were our connection to Mexican culture, expressed mostly in food. They spoke their secret language with my mother; my siblings and I never learned Spanish.

In our small town, I didn't look like "the real Mexican kids," whose mothers came to church wearing dark lace veils, carrying heavy rosaries. Compared to them, I was white, with a surname to prove it. Even Grandpa and Grandma dressed differently from the people who had just arrived from Mexico, as if they had "evolved" into what immigrants were supposed to look like. When our entire Mexican-American family was together, we posed for pictures in the backyard, looking like a picture from Sunset Magazine. <u>This</u> was our happy, American family.

Now I realize that my grandparents had to follow unwritten rules for "becoming American." There were rules of assimilation, where compliance meant leaving their culture behind. The family model was pitched to every immigrant family: Americans look a certain way, act a certain way, and speak perfect English. Grandpa and Grandma raised their children, keeping these rules in mind. Their kids grew up patriotic, speaking English, doing well in school, and excelling in sports. My mother and her sisters graduated high school and started working in government offices. My uncles served their country in the Korean Conflict; one was awarded the Purple Heart. They were grateful Americans, and raised us to be the same.

When I was a freshman in high school, race riots broke out on campus. White and Mexican Cowboys, whose parents were either landowners or laborers, had terrible brawls. Tensions had been brewing for years, and the violence was only a symptom. One morning, as my class lined up for P.E. attendance, two of my Chicano friends, Raúl and Steven, were talking about the riots in Spanish. I wanted them to shut up, and said so. Before they stopped, Steven mumbled an insult about me in Spanish. I turned around and answered him in English:

"Oh yeah? It's <u>you</u> who has nothing in y<u>our</u> head." Both Raúl and Steven were dumbfounded.

"You speak Spanish?" Raúl asked.

"I'm half-Mexican," I said, flatly. Most of the P.E. class turned around and looked at me. I knew they had thought I was white.

"Then why don't you look like half a Chicana?" Raúl asked.

"I'm half-Mexican," I said. "I never said I was a Chicana."

Even in my teenage cluelessness, I understood I wasn't one of the loud and proud Chicanas, who unapologetically celebrated their heritage. In my mind, I was <u>half</u>-Mexican and <u>half</u>-Irish, a mixed identity that has defined me all of my life.

Our professor asked us to uncover two of our false assumptions about race or ethnicity. I quickly uncovered mine. The first one is, "Real Mexicans look a certain way, and because of this, I am not a real Mexican." The second one is only a little less painful: "White people have no idea what it's like to be Mexican." Based on both of these assumptions, I think it's fair to say that I am at war with myself. If I'm not a real Mexican, I must be white; if I'm white, I have no idea what it's like to be a real Mexican.

My professor loved this essay, and asked me to read it aloud in class. As I did, I started crying and couldn't stop. If you're a college student in your fifties, trying to blend in, it's not a good idea to break into tears while reading aloud in class.

3. Where Do We Begin?

I always thought our family story began in Malaga, California, a town just south of Fresno, in the agriculturally-rich Central Valley. This was the place Grandpa and Grandma met, in a boarding house for Mexican farm laborers. Grandma worked there, making tortillas, serving food, and cleaning up after the paying customers. Grandpa was one of these men, a handsome, hard-working laborer. They noticed each other from a distance, exchanged secret love letters, until one day, without the knowledge of Grandma's family, Grandpa whisked her away to get married. It all sounded so romantic and dangerous—the perfect place to begin.

Grandma would often visit me as I organized this book. Sitting in a straight-backed Danish chair, in front of Mario's desk, she crossed her legs at the ankles, arms folded over her chest. A tiny woman, Grandma's feet, in fuzzy pink slippers, or *pantuflas*, barely touched the ground. Grey bobby pins, crisscrossed in the hair above her ears, kept her salt-and-pepper curls in place. I could feel her eyes watching me, high-powered lasers behind her wirerimmed glasses. One night, I finally acknowledged her.

"What is it?"

"Nothing," she said, laughing. She uncrossed her arms. "I'm not saying nothing." She tried to be silent, but couldn't resist. "It's just that so much happened *before* Grandpa take me to get married." She waved her hands in the air, as if erasing what she had just said.

"Nevermind. You are writing this. You decide where to start."

I sighed. It was useless to ignore her. "Where would you start?"

"Well," she said, leaning forward. "Me and Grandpa grew up in Mexico, and in those days, our families had a hard time. A *real, bad, hard* time! That's why we had to come here."

"I know," I said. "But I never recorded your stories."

Grandma shrugged. "Doreen recorded me," she said. "With my little tape recorder. It's gotta be around here somewhere." She looked around, as if the tape recorder could be found in the boxes of photo albums and family records on the floor of my office.

"*Doreen* recorded you?" I asked. "Do you think she still has those tapes?" I knew I was talking to an empty chair, having another imaginary conversation with my grandmother, who had passed away nearly thirty years before, but on that particular night, I felt Grandma nudging me. My cousin, Doreen, had interviewed her, and I had to get my hands on those tapes, for posterity, for the book, for our story, which was rapidly becoming an obsession. I made plans to go to Oregon, where Doreen and her family were living.

Seeing my cousin, Doreen, was wonderful. After hugs and a visit, she handed me a green drawstring bag, with a micro-tape recorder and five small tapes inside: Grandma's recorded interview, the equivalent of solid gold. The fourth child of Uncle Smiley and Auntie Mildred, Doreen is a few years older than I am, but her pixyish face and athletic build make her look much younger. She has vivid memories of interviewing Grandma.

"I helped take care of her, after she broke her hip," Doreen said. "I stayed in Tracy right after she got out of the hospital, to help. Grandma kept getting up to cook and clean."

"Of course," I said, smiling. Doreen and I knew Grandma as the one serving food to everyone around, or cleaning house, or hanging out laundry on the clothesline, or canning, or baking cookies. Grandma was always in motion.

"I had to figure out how to make her stay in bed," Doreen said. "One day, I said, 'I'm going to interview you! Tell me your life story.' That made her stay still, at least for a while."

That night in Oregon, I recorded the microtapes with a digital app on my phone. When I returned to Sacramento, I began the work of transcribing. Grandma was elated.

"It's a good thing you find those tapes," she chuckled. "I was afraid you were gonna start our family story in Tracy. For you, *everything* starts in Tracy."

"I know, Grandma," I said, whispering, so my family wouldn't hear me. "I know."

***

Tracy, California, near the center of the state, is my home town. I've lived in Sacramento for most of my life, but when someone asks me where I'm from, I say Tracy, California.

Only after I moved to Johannesburg, did I really understand the importance of a physical hometown. Family and friends had always defined *home* for me, rather than a place, a house, or land, but when we lived in South Africa, our kids, parents, siblings, and grandchildren were eight time-zones away. Two long plane rides away. The United States, our homeland, was where our family was. The food, the soil, the touchstones of growing up, were there.

In 2013, after seven years away, Mario and I returned to the United States. Our families, like our homeland, had changed significantly. Mario's brother had died. Four of our grandchildren had been born. Our adult children, with children of their own, expressed mixed emotions when we returned. They shared feelings of abandonment, which didn't disappear right away. My extended family had weathered incredible storms, changes that actually threatened their foundations. My parents were adjusting to the physical challenges of aging: medications, grief, and the loss of close friends.

After seven years, our country had also endured agents of change that threatened its foundations. An incredible economic recession, with immeasurable fallout had made many in the U.S. lose their homes. Politics and dramatic news had become table conversation. Citizens were even more polarized in what they believed. The subject of immigration, especially from Mexico and Central America, was one of these polarizing issues. While we were away, the U.S. had erected camps at the U.S./Mexico border, where undocumented women and children were housed in jails or camps. Donald Trump became the 45th U.S. President, and made good on his promise to erect a border wall. From this side of it, my family, including the children of immigrants, had ceased identifying with immigrants. Like most people, they were dealing with their own personal battles. They had become what immigrants wanted to be: U.S. Citizens.

Grandma nods as I type this. When I look up, she smiles, sadly.

"It's easy to forget, mija," she says. "It's easy to forget that people are dying."

"It *is* easy to forget," I repeat, contemplating the weight of this.

"You know, right?" Grandma says, pulling her cable-knit sweater tighter around her. "In Africa, you saw the poor people there? That's what it was like for us."

"I know, Grandma," I say, but I really don't know.

"Now, you come home, and you got everything," she says. "Don't forget."

Grandma is right: it's easy to forget. When Mario and I came home to the United States, re-entry proved to be harder than we imagined. No one seemed to be interested in the years we spent over there, the ministry we were a part of, or how we survived. No one asked us about anything, and no one seemed to care. Now and then, we had shallow conversations with friends and family.

"So, are you happy to be home?" our friends would ask.

"It's complicated," I answered. I was coping with homesickness for my other home. "But you're happy to be home now, right?" they would ask, not expecting an answer.

In some ways, returning felt like relief, and life felt wonderful and familiar. In other ways, *home* felt strange, and I felt strange in it.

Mario and I came back, and started over in a fragile economy that had been turned upside down. We purchased a small fixer-upper of a house, and began the work of making a home again. Every day, my fifty-two-year-old body ached in different places. I found pictures of my grandfather, Ignacio Gonzalez, who built his first house on Lorraine Road when he was fifty-two. This similarity made me smile, but I had to remind myself that Grandpa started from scratch.

He built his house on a concrete-slab foundation, making sure it was solid. Every other house he had lived in was a temporary, pieced-together, impermanent dwelling. This one would be able to stand the test of time—he made sure of that.

The home on Lorraine Road redefined Ignacio Gonzalez. He was now able to plant his own garden on his own land. He would make the leap into permanency.

He was now an American homeowner.

Part Two: Gardens

"Let us not forget that the cultivation of the earth is the most important labor of man. When tillage begins, other arts follow. The farmers, therefore, are the founders of human civilization."
~ Daniel Webster

"Our ambitions must be broad enough to include the aspirations and needs of others, for their sakes and for our own."
~ Cesar Chavez

Grandma's Salad Dressing

One part vinegar (I use white)
three parts oil (I use vegetable)
about 1/4 cup grated hard cheese (you can use parmesan)
garlic, chopped up fine (about 2 cloves)
1/2 white or yellow onion, chopped up fine
pepper
garlic salt

Shake ingredients up in canning jar. If it stays in the refrigerator overnight, it will really have flavor, but if not, it's still good.

Serve at room temperature

4. Lorraine Road

In the early 1950's, Ignacio Gonzalez bought an acre of land—nothing more than a dirt plot—just outside of Tracy's city limits. Lorraine Road was the site of the first and only house he would ever own. He hired electricians and plumbers to do contracted work, but most of the manual labor he did himself. Friends, mostly people he knew from work, and his sons, Frank and Smiley, helped him. Everyone admired Ignacio's mission to build his first house. They helped transport bricks, pipes, and cinderblocks with various vehicles. They set up parking areas. They dug through the hardened dirt to help establish the gardens.

I'm part of a large family, one of five children, one of twenty grandchildren. My siblings, cousins, and I remember Lorraine Road as the place we saw Grandpa and Grandma. We all have flashes of memory (kisses, hugs, aromas, flavors, songs) attached to this place. To us, the house on Lorraine Road is more than a structure—it's a delicious connection to family, celebration, and love. Our grandparents were celestial bodies we orbited, as fixed as the stars. They never raised their voices, weren't hurried or angry, and—possibly most important—always had time for us.

Their house was twenty minutes, and worlds away, from the Ryan house. My siblings and I called it "the country," even though it was a street of homes on one-acre plots. The house itself had a sweet, white-brick exterior and a red tile roof, and stood on the southern portion of the rectangular acre, close to the street. It had a detached, double-car garage, where Grandpa parked his pickup truck, used for work, and their Dodge Colt, used for everything else. The front yard had two postage stamp lawns, lined by roses on each side, and divided by a cement walkway, which led to a long, red porch. Two oak doors faced the street, but only the one closest to the garage was used.

Grandpa's roses, lining the front yard on Lorraine Rd.

Grandma would greet us at the door, kissing our cheeks as we came in. She smelled of masa (tortilla dough) or soap, or sometimes a combination of both. She wore a house dress, a cobbler apron, and pink pantuflas, or house slippers.

Their house was always spotless, but warm and functional. As soon as we walked in the door, we were standing in their living room/dining room combination, decorated with simple mid-century furnishings. Three bedrooms were off the hallway, to the right, and each one had its own double bed, with bedspreads that never looked wrinkled. There was only one bathroom, at the end of the hall. It had a blue toilet and bathtub. Grandpa had his own separate shower room.

The utility room, a bedroom that served as a breezeway between the hall and the kitchen, had a bed, an ironing board, a crib, a rack to dry hand-washable clothes, and above the doorway, a picture of Jesus carrying a lamb on his shoulders, as other sheep followed. I loved that picture.

Next to the kitchen, a narrow passageway served as pantry and laundry room. Her washing machine and canned goods shared the same space. The door to the backyard was in the pantry, so traffic was nonstop.

Grandma's kitchen, in the center of the house, was where everything happened. Food was prepared, conversation flowed, people gathered like chickens, in the warmth of tantalizing aromas. Two big windows, one over the sink, one near the breadbox, ushered in natural light. Grandma's gas stove was a large, white, shiny, enamel mother-of-appliances, usually with two or three simmering pots on top, next to her comal. Tortilla production began as soon as we arrived, the singular blessing of our lives. Sometimes, I'd sit at the chrome and Formica table, just to observe Grandma and her daughters as they talked. Sometimes Grandma put me to work, while I sat there, sorting beans, or shelling walnuts, chopping vegetables.

"She was a good Grandmother," my sister, Colleen, remembered. "She was always cooking, always in the kitchen."

Grandma cooked everything from scratch. She canned seasonal vegetables and fruits regularly. She made three kinds of cookies: molasses cookies, snickerdoodles, and Russian tea cakes. If we came over on baking day, the whole house smelled like cinnamon and sugar.

"I loved Grandma's cookie jar," my cousin Kathy remembered. "Sometimes, it was bulging with cookies, and the lid wouldn't close."

"I loved spending the night there," my cousin, Debbie, said. "I'd sleep in the utility room, and wake up to the smell of bacon. I could hear Grandma humming while she cooked the most amazing breakfasts. She'd serve skinny fried potatoes, Mexican hot chocolate, and a fresh stack of tortillas."

Outside, the fresh air was filled with the fragrance of surrounding farms: soil, manure, grasses, and fruits. A covered patio, with two, long, wooden picnic tables was where our family gathered and feasted on bar-b-que chicken, beans, rice, green salad, fideo, and strawberry shortcake. Grandpa and Grandma sat at the head of the first table, surrounded by their children. We, the grandchildren, sat at the second table, where we tried to eat without laughing too much, or fighting too much, depending on the day.

Just beyond the patio, the backyard stretched from west to east, the length of their house. To the west, a row of willow trees lined the fence, a drinking fountain, nearly hidden in their shade.

"I loved that drinking fountain, made of rock-and-cement, by the willow trees, covered in ivy," my sister, Colleen said. "Grandpa made that drinking fountain by hand."

The disciplined backyard was surrounded by a boxwood hedge, a green wall that marked the end of cultivation. Inside its borders, smooth cement pathways framed five lawns. The walkways met in the middle of the yard, in a large, cement circle. An arial view would look like the sun, rays stretching through a sky of lawns.

Grandma (in pink pantuflas) holding Jason, my cousin, Kathy's baby. Behind her (out of frame) is the cement/rock drinking fountain

An ash tree, to the north of the center circle, provided generous shade for Grandpa, who staffed the barbeque with most of the men surrounding him. Sometimes a transistor radio, wedged into the Y of the two main branches, broadcasted the tinny sounds of San Francisco Giants' games. To the east of the circle was Grandma's clothesline—she never owned a dryer—which she used only on laundry days, never when she had company.

Beyond the clothesline was a horseshoe pit. Grandpa, Dad, and my uncles would throw real iron shoes at iron stakes, and sometimes a loud clang, followed by cheers, would cause everyone to look over at them.

Dad and Uncle Rich at the horseshoe pit, approx. 1980

Towering over the horseshoe pit was the apricot tree, which produced more fruit in season than any other I've seen before or since. Next to the tree were five disciplined rows of chiles, which grew without the whisper of a weed. Grandpa's chili plants radiated an unholy heat. Even when slightly touched, the oil they transferred to our fingers burned our faces, eyes, and lips. From these five rows, Grandpa raised an enormous crop. Whatever Grandma couldn't use or can, Grandpa would sell to independent grocers, who paid him in cash. With the proceeds, he was able to take Grandma to Stockton, for dinner and a movie.

The rest of the acre was a flat, level field, an open invitation to run free. When we were very small, our parents would play games of baseball there. The men would hit the ball over the wire fence sometimes, or into the orchards, beyond the acre plot.

On the western part of the dirt acre, Grandpa erected a wooden shed to hold his garden tools. Later, he built a large chicken coop, near the fence, but their disobedient rooster, Lee, never liked it. Instead, Lee strutted around the dirt acre, scratching and crowing like he owned the place. When Grandma would carry him a plastic pail of kitchen scraps, Lee would run to her, lunging at the bucket, too impatient to wait for her to dump them on the compost heap. Grandma would swat him back with her wooden spoon, like a lion tamer with a whip. She'd say, "Your mother! Your mother!" which we thought was hilarious. Grandma had taken our slang, "Your mama," and made it her own.

Grandpa (Ignacio) and Grandma (Juana) approx. 1981

"I once spent a week at Grandpa and Grandma's house, when I was in college," my sister, Patty said. "Every day, Grandpa would get up early in the morning, go out to work in his garden, and stay out there until noon. He would come in, have some lunch, and then go back out again. He'd be out there until late in the afternoon. I was really impressed with this. At that time, Grandpa was older, and I thought, 'Wow! He's still working, even though he doesn't have to! He could be inside, relaxing, like most men do in their retirement.' Grandpa wanted to work. He had a strong work ethic."

"Grandpa was known for working hard" my cousin Debbie, said. "I loved how he sat down and told us his stories, a mixture of English, and Spanish, and somehow, we'd understand him."

"He would say, 'Ho-kay, ho-kay,'" Colleen, said. Grandpa often peppered his stories with *Okay*—which sounded like, *HO*-kay—when he had established a foundation, and was moving on. "Sometimes, Grandpa would take our fingers and massage them as he told us a story. That's what I remember about him most. He was very loving."

Grandpa's stories were gifts for his grandchildren, for whoever wanted to listen. It was one of the ways he showed love for us. He shared about growing up in Sinaloa, Mexico, on his family farm, and about coming to the United States, by train.

He played Spanish guitar, and shared his music in the same way, the way of letting himself be known, a deeper soul beyond the man we could always see, working hard. When I learned to play guitar, in the most elementary way, I began to see how music could translate something deeper, even beyond words. I could relate to this part of Grandpa.

He dreamed of living in the United States, owning his own farm, and making music for the rest of his life. He fought for everything he had, just to partially realize these dreams. The house on Lorraine Road was the fruit of these dreams.

Many of the men who worked with Grandpa, helping him build the house on Lorraine Road, labored without financial compensation. It was their way of showing honor to the man they called Nacho. The patrón called Nacho *the foreman*, a bilingual liaison who made sure the work was done. Nacho could make an old truck run again, hook-up a trailer, and help the men understand what was expected of them at work, church, and in their community. Because he could read and write in English, Nacho could help them fill out an important form, and not make them feel *tonto*. If it weren't for Nacho, they'd still be moving with the harvests, clipping grapevines, or doing odd jobs. Because of Nacho, they kept their heads down and worked locally. Their families had a place to call home. They were fiercely loyal to him, the man they called Nacho.

5. Grandpa: A Man Called Nacho

On July 31, 1900, Ignacio Gonzalez, my grandfather, was born near the city of Guamúchil, about sixty-two miles northwest of Culiacán, in Sinaloa, Mexico. Ignacio was the sixth of ten children, born to Guadalupe and Gomezinda Gonzalez. They had even more children that died. The Gonzalez family were sustenance farmers, working the same communal land that their family had been farming for generations. Without aqueducts, reservoirs, or irrigation systems, rural farmers were dependent on good weather and hard work. In the time that Grandpa was born, the state of Sinaloa was one of the more prosperous states in Mexico, according to national records. For the rural farmer, however, there was no share in this wealth.

Porfirio Díaz, the president of Mexico, had been in office for sixteen years. While publicly lauded for modernizing the country, Díaz was a master manipulator, running Mexico like a dictator. He changed land laws to profit himself. The hacienda system, in place since Spain colonized Mexico, was growing instead of shrinking. If private owners could not prove ownership through title, or if ejidos, the communal farmlands, had no documentation, their land was taken over by companies run by wealthy families. Díaz ruled Mexico this way, and showed no sign of giving up control.

At the Gonzalez farm, a small holding, Grandpa's family of origin lived in a small house. They had a barn for their farm animals, a few acres of corn, beans, and fruit trees. They had no deed or title to their land, and were therefore, vulnerable.

A few years before he died, my cousin, Doreen, interviewed our grandfather.

"In my family, we had ten kids," Grandpa said. "So, with Mom and Dad, we were twelve. Okay. The oldest [of my siblings] was Abel, then Miguel, then Jesus—I don't want to speak about the one that died—then Emiliana, then yo, Ignacio, then Pedro, Petra, Francisca, Guadalupe, and the baby, Dolores. Tenían una familia muy grande—diez hijos (They had a very big family—ten kids). Siempre tratamos de vivir lo mejor que pudimos, y lo logramos (We always tried to live the best way we could, and we succeeded). We made it, because we grew up together, without making any big mistakes.

"In Mexico, we worked the farm for ourselves," Grandpa said. "There's a different planting time over there, a different green time. We planted in July; that's the green time over there. In September, we don't have to do anything except go back and forth and see how the plants are doing. In October, we pick the crops and take them home. We didn't measure things by acres. If a piece of land was farmed by my great-grandfather, then by my grandpa, and then my father, it would go to me, or my brothers and sisters. On that land, if I wanted to farm one piece, I had to prepare it, clear it, chop the wood, work the land. Only then I can say, 'It belongs to me.'

"We raised chickens, cows, hogs, and a donkey. We don't have too many animals, but they have a lot of little ones. We were busy taking care of them. Nobody can say, 'Why are you doing things this way?' It's very different here."

Grandpa came to the United States to work when he was nineteen. He crossed the US/Mexico border three times, to help support his family, who desperately needed money. His first crossing was in 1919, when he came to Southern California with his uncle. They each had a work permit, which expired in six months. They worked a sugar beet harvest, and went home by train. When Grandpa returned to his family, he told them about the fertile land of el norte. Maybe one day, he told them, he would plant his own garden there. Who knows?

The second time Grandpa crossed, he did it without a work permit. He crossed into and out of the United States without documentation, but I don't remember him talking about it.

The last time Grandpa crossed the border, in 1920, he did so by train again, but this time he was alone. He bought the only ticket he could afford, a three-day journey on a rickety freight train meant for cargo, not passengers. He slept in a small area, essentially lying down on the bare floor of a boxcar. Grandpa's space was so compact, he would bump against the walls when it swayed or turned. When the brakes were pressed, the train stopped suddenly, and made a loud, screeching noise. The train passed through many cities, where passengers got off, but Grandpa stayed until they reached the northernmost point: Fresno.

Grandpa's last journey on that cramped rail car changed him, especially the way he approached travel. My father, Jack Ryan, told me a story Grandpa shared with him.

"Your grandfather was a man with first-class tastes," Dad said. "Ignacio and one of his friends were going to Colorado, for work, and Ignacio paid for first-class tickets on a passenger train. After that ride to Fresno, he couldn't ride anything but first class. When he walked up to the conductor, he handed him the first-class tickets. The conductor said, 'No, no! You two have to ride back there....' He pointed to coach, or second-class passage. Your grandfather showed him that he paid for first-class tickets, but the conductor still refused. He said, 'No Mexican is going to ride first-class on my train!' The way Ignacio handled this was interesting. Instead of confronting the conductor, which probably wouldn't have done any good, he took his tickets back and walked away. Grandpa's friend wanted to go by coach, but Ignacio wouldn't do that. Instead, he rented a hotel room for the two of them, where they spent the night, and took the next train for Colorado in the morning. He boarded the train and traveled first-class, with his first-class ticket."

Dad got quiet after telling me this, and shook his head. "Your grandpa had to live his life as a man," Dad said. "He went through things like that all the time. He always had to skirt around issues like that."

He had to live his life as a man, Dad said. Grandpa was polite, looked nice, and wasn't going to be treated like a dog or an animal, just because the conductor was a bigot. Grandpa probably faced many instances like this, but the train was the only one he ever told us about.

Ignacio Gonzalez, work permit picture 1920

In the United States, Grandpa worked the fields, just like he did in Mexico. In the United States, however, the landowners told him what to do and how to do it. He worked hard for others as a trabajador, or farm laborer, to produce a crop that would belong to someone else.

Grandpa had a temporary work permit, set to expire in six months, but this time he decided to stay in the United States. He made friendships with other agricultural laborers, who traveled the circuit—the seasons of harvests through the American West—a loop from Fresno, to Colorado, to Arizona, to Southern California, and back again. Many land-owners took advantage of Grandpa's undocumented status. He was paid almost nothing, while they got wealthy. For Grandpa, working for someone else was the most bitter pill he was forced to swallow.

"When I came here [the United States], I had to work the farm for someone else," he said. "Uncle Pedro, back home, was not working for anybody. He's working for himself because it's his land. But me?" Grandpa exhaled. "I know those ways." It was a sigh that possibly only another agricultural laborer could understand. He was an older man, telling the story of his life of hard work, to build an empire for someone else.

***

After he had lived in the United States for many years, Grandpa helped other Mexican immigrants navigate the complicated legal requirements of staying in the country. He would also encourage them to make an informed decision before settling in the United States.

"I ask them, 'Why you want to move over here?'" he said. "I try to tell them, 'Your people were not born here. You'll be far away from your home. You can't see family when you want.' That's the hardest part, coming from

Mexico. Nobody knows what it's like until they get here. I stayed gone twenty-five years before I go back to Mexico—that's a long time! When I go back, my mother was still alive. My father passed away in 1924, but when I go back, Grandma was still alive!" On tape, Grandpa made an impressed noise. "When I went back, my grandma was ninety-six years old, and she was still working the land by herself. I see her in November, and she passed away seven months later," he said. "Oh, Mama was happy to see me! I told Mama that my sons, Smiley and Frank, left for the service, but she didn't say anything." He paused at this point, and laughed at the irony. He had been missing his two sons, who had left for Korea, both in different branches of military service. Instead of offering sympathy, his mom only looked at him.

"I told her, 'Mamá, ¿no me perdonas?' (Mama, won't you forgive me?) She said, '¿Por qué?' ("For what?" or "Why should I?") 'Porque estoy muy lejos' (Because I am far away). She said, 'Sí, ¿por que no?' (Sure, why not?) Quiero hacerte una pregunta: ¿Cómo se siente el padre de sus hijos cuando los hijos estan lejos?' (I want to ask you a question: How does the father of his children feel when his children are so far away?)"

"Oh, I had no answer! I hold my head like this," Grandpa bowed his head so his chin touched his chest. "Big shame, huh? Because Mama waited twenty-five years for *me* to come home! My mother was that kind of lady—strong! I never see her cry. I didn't see her cry when my brothers, my dad, or my sisters died. With my dad, I didn't go to the funeral. I was over here, and she was there, but I know she didn't cry when my dad died."

Grandpa was silent for a while, then summed up his mother's strength: "My mama don't cry. She don't know how to cry!" Grandpa became quiet and solemn, and for a while said nothing. "I think we were better in those days."

Whenever Grandpa talked about his mother, Gomezinda Gonzalez, he spoke with love and respect. I didn't know my great-grandmother, but I had seen her picture, in a round frame, hanging on the wall of Grandpa's room. My brother and sisters used to be afraid of her face, even though she had been dead for years. We would pass by in the hallway, and catch her glaring at us. She looked angry enough to smack us from the grave.

"In those days, people didn't smile for pictures," Mom told us.

"That woman never smiled," Grandma said in a low voice. "Never, never." I believed Grandma about most things, and this time was no different.

I now see Gomezinda, and her portrait, differently. The same picture I avoided in my childhood, now hangs on the wall in my office. Gomezinda's expression, unchanged after all these years, matches Grandpa's description of her: strong. Who knows if this woman ever felt love from her husband? Grandpa never said. She was a poor woman, who stayed alive in Mexico during a time of outrageous violence and poverty. She was a woman: little more than property. No one cared if she complained—so she didn't. She buried at least three children, her husband, and lost my grandfather to the United States. She wasn't a woman who would smile, just because a photographer brought out a camera and told her to do it.

In fact, he had no right to ask her.

Gomezinda Gonzalez, my paternal great-grandmother

6. Grandma: The First Juana

My mother's name, like the names of her siblings, was chosen because of a Catholic saint. Born on March 8, Mom shares the feast day of St. John of God (Juan de Dios), so she was christened Juana Gonzalez. She had the same first name as her mother, so her family called her Juanita. When she started school, Mom's name was changed by her teacher, and Juanita became Jennie in one day. The only place Mom ever heard her given name was at home, where Grandma was still Juana and Mom was still Juanita.

I first heard this story in 1988, when I was twenty-five, and pregnant with my daughter, Alicia. The subject of names came up in a conversation with Grandma.

"How did you choose your children's names?" I asked.

"In Mexico, we let God name them," she said. All of Grandma's children were born in the United States, but she and Grandpa were faithful to keep this particular tradition. "The day a child is born, we name them after the Catholic Saint on the church calendar."

"Really?" I asked. "What if a Saint had a weird name you didn't like? Would you choose another?" I laughed, but Grandma didn't. She seemed uneasy with my humor.

"No," she said. "Because they're really God's kids. In fact, every day, I pray, 'Please take care of these kids. They're yours, not mine.'"

I thought of Vince, my three-year-old son, the light of my life. I was about to have another baby, and I desperately yearned to keep them safe in this world. I didn't want to make any mistakes, but I had a reputation, even with myself, for messing things up.

"I pray, 'Please take care of them,'" Grandma repeated, as if she were reading my mind. "They're your kids, not mine.'" Then, she looked at me, and said, "You should pray that, too."

"I will," I said. And, to this day, I do.

***

Maria Juana Avila was born on October 31, 1906, just outside of the city of Coeneo de Libertad, in the state of Michoacán in Mexico. Grandma's parents also named their children for Catholic saints, but their calendar listed October 31st as the Feast of All Souls. Because of this dilemma, her mother chose to name her after Coeneo's patron saint: John the Baptist, or San Juan Bautizado.

The City of Coeneo de Libertad still celebrates San Juan Bautizado on his feast day, June 24, with a street party. Musicians, dancers, and every citizen of Coeneo parade through the streets, lifting up an ornate shrine of San Juan, John the Baptist. The town's most special residents follow the shrine, anyone named Juan or Juana—*los Juanes*. As they advance, the crowd sprinkles them with water, from hand-held bottles or rattles. Grandma would glow as she told us about this parade. She lamented the loss of this celebration.

"Where I came from, they always celebrate San Juan," she said. "And everybody with his name—todos los Juanes! But here? *Nobody.*"

***

I knew Juana Avila Gonzalez as Grandma, an affectionate, servant-hearted, apron-wearing, tortilla-rolling, salsa-canning, cookie-making, feast-producing, cleaning machine. Grandma also believed that any cat, wild or domestic, was possessed by demons, and therefore should be shunned. If she saw a cat around her house, she would chase it away with a broom or a stick. "Cats look for babies," she'd tell us. "They suck the breath out of them, and then, sometimes the babies die."

As much as she hated cats, Grandma loved gossip. She would listen to friends and neighbors retell a juicy story, with her hands folded on her lap. As the gossip got juicier, her thumbs would twirl around each other. Most of this gossip was in Spanish, so I used to watch her thumbs. The better the gossip, the faster the thumbs would twirl.

Stories made the world go around for Grandma. In every generation, there is a storyteller—the bearer of family story, as accurate as it can be—and Grandma was that person. She told us about growing up in a little village in Michoacan, Mexico, a place she remembered in living color. She would recreate it in her stories, painting glorious pictures of her green birthplace, vividly depicting its lush landscape.

We were able to see the Mexican Revolution through Grandma's eyes. To her, Pancho Villa and Emiliano Zapata were not brilliant or enigmatic leaders fighting for Mexico's independence, they were marauding horsemen who raped young women and held them hostage. Scaling the precarious ladder of memory, she recreated the dangers she faced, mostly because she was born female. Grandma proved to us how ten years of civil war did more than devastate the country, it changed it forever. It changed her.

Most poor farmers, like Grandma's family, were destroyed by the Revolution. They were written off as collateral damage, even by the revolutionaries, who trampled over them in the name of victory. The farmers, who had been in place for generations, were starving, and caught in the crosshairs of power-hungry men. Grandma's family was forever trying to avoid these crosshairs.

Part Three: Champurrado

"And whoever gives one of these little ones even a cup of cold water because he is a disciple, truly, I say to you, he will by no means lose his reward."

~ Matthew 10:42 ESV

Champurrado

6 cups milk (use whole milk for creamiest texture)
1 piloncillo cone (cane sugar used in Mexican baking) or 1 cup brown sugar.
1 round of Mexican chocolate (from Abuelita stack)
1/3 cup masa harina (softened in enough warm water to look like porridge)
Cinnamon sticks, Vanilla, salt (all for flavor as you prefer)

Heat milk in a saucepan on medium heat. Put piloncillo and Mexican chocolate into the milk, stirring gently until they start dissolving. Add the cinnamon stick and bring it to a simmer. Lower the heat.

Add a drop of vanilla extract and a pinch of salt to the masa harina (softened in water) before adding to the saucepan. Add to the chocolate mixture and whisk it together until it looks smooth. Taste hot chocolate. Cook and whisk until the champurrado is thick, creamy, and smooth.

Pour a large mug full of the finished champurrado.
Champurrado can be cooled down on the stove until kids wake up.
Reheat on the stove top. Whip up with a hand-held whisk for foam on top, which is really nice.

7. Familia Avila

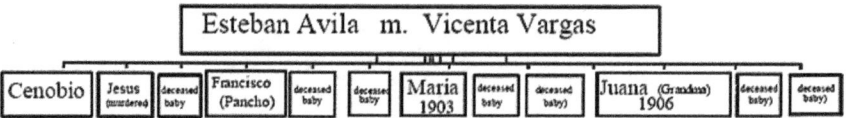

When Maria Juana Avila, my grandmother, was born in 1906, Mexico was in turmoil. Porfirio Díaz, the president, had been in office for twenty years, significantly longer than anyone else in its history. He and his oppressive government earned the nickname, *el Porfiriato*. The ones who suffered most under Porfirio Díaz's rule were Indigenous farmers, the working poor. Díaz was Spanish, and knew the European demand for sugar. His idea to make Mexico a garden of sugar beets, the most profitable crop, robbed the Indigenous sustenance farmers of their land. Most farmers who worked the rural lands in Mexico had no deed or title to it. When Díaz's government began to require proof of land ownership, the land was taken from the farmers, and run by hacienda managers. The sustenance farmers who had been living there, were "contracted" to farm sugar beets, but paid very little, not even enough to buy food or essentials for their family. Despite working long hours, and doing hard work, they were little more than slaves. Hacienda managers carried out Díaz's plan to enslave the poor, which profited only the rich.

Two miles north-east of Coeneo de Libertad, in the eastern part of Michoacán, the Avila family lived in a little village, one my grandmother called San Isidro. A collection of small family farms, named for the patron saint of farmers, San Isidro was surrounded by woodlands, a neighboring mountain range, and a sea of fruit and pine trees. Flowering manzanita, assorted vines, and ground shrubs adorned the rolling landscape. Several running creeks provided drinking water for the cattle and sheep, who grazed on the hills. Butterflies and birds of every kind nested in the trees. Grandma's favorites were the tiny hummingbirds that glittered as they buzzed past her, a brilliant yellow and green light. San Isidro had a pastoral setting, but the place was not peaceful.

By the time Grandma was born, her father, Esteban Avila, understood the precarious hold his family had on their property, and the stress was beginning to overwhelm him. Like most of their neighbors, the Avila family had no deed or title to their farm, but it had not yet been commandeered by the hacienda system. Whispers of a revolution had been circulating, and the farmers in San Isidro discussed rumors of agrarian reform, and a possible change in government. These men kept constant vigil, especially over the community well, their shared horse corral, and a nearby venero, a natural spring, where the young women, including my grandmother, would draw water every morning. Like all villages, there were rich and poor residents, friends and enemies, heroes and villains, harlots and saints, and plenty of gossip. Grandma's parents, Esteban and Vicenta, lived on the farm with his parents, until they passed away.

There are no surviving pictures of Esteban and Vicenta, but Grandma described her father as a strong, dark man with the classically chiseled features of his Indigenous Mexican people. Grandma's mother, Vicenta, was a mestiza, or woman of mixed-race, with light skin, jet-black hair, and more European features. Grandma also described her mother's temperament as angelic, almost otherworldly. Vicenta gave birth to twelve babies, but only five of them survived their infancy. Grandma wasn't sure about the birthdates of her brothers, or the babies who died, but she knew her sister Maria was born in 1903, and she, in 1906.

Grandma's brothers, Cenobio, Jesus, and Pancho were born *many* years before her sister, Maria. To illustrate how far apart they were in age, she told us the story of how her sister-in-law remembered her birthday.

"Cenobio got married the day I was born," Grandma said. "My sister-in-law, who eloped with him, used to say, 'I know how old you are, because you were born the day I ran off with your brother, Cenobio!'"

The Avila family worked together to run a successful farm, raise their animals, and keep their stables. The family had earned the respect of their community. Nevertheless, Grandma's father, Esteban, seemed plagued by self-hatred and insecurity. Grandma witnessed his abuse of Vicenta, her mother, on more than one occasion. Esteban loved and hated his wife's beauty, a constant reminder of the conquering Spaniards, and his own oppression. He seemed especially jealous, and preoccupied with thoughts of Vicenta being unfaithful to him. This seed had been planted by the senior Mrs. Avila, Esteban's mother.

"I didn't used to like my Grandma Avila," Grandma said. "My father's mother was really mean. She used to make my Daddy hate me. Even before I was born, she told my Daddy, 'That's not your child. That's somebody else's child!'

"Back then, the mans used to believe their mothers, even more than their wives. It didn't matter what my mother said, my daddy believed his mother. When I was going to be born, his mother told him, 'I don't want her in here. Take her! Throw her under a tree or whatever, but I don't want her to have that baby in here.' So, he did. My dad took Mama to this old lady's house. She didn't have nothing, so she used to wash dishes for other people, just to feed herself. Daddy took Mama there. I was born there.

"That old lady said, 'I don't have any food. I don't have nothing.' My Dad didn't care. He left Mama there for three days.

"Mama told me she got so hungry, but had nothing to eat. The old lady's neighbor had a peach tree outside, so Mama said, 'I'm going to see if there's any peaches that fell to the ground, so I can eat them.' She went outside and found some peaches on the ground. She ate them, and went back inside to nurse me. She said, 'If I die, then my baby will die, too.'

"A friend of Mama's came to see her at the ranch, to see if she had the baby. She found Mama, at the old lady's house, very weak. I was crying. The old lady said, 'Vicenta's been here three days, but nobody has brought her any food. She hasn't eaten anything for three days. The baby is crying all the time because Vicenta doesn't have any milk.' Mama's friend said, 'I'm going to go home right now and bring you some food.' She came back with a big pile of tostadas and a pitcher of champurrado."

Champurrado, the warm drink that Grandma was talking about, is a frothy, thick, hot chocolate drink, flavored with vanilla and cinnamon, so rich it can take the place of a meal. Grandma craved this when she was pregnant with her own children, and used to give it to us, her groggy grandchildren, for breakfast, when she watched us early in the morning.

"Mama's friend told her, 'Honey, don't drink all of this, even if you're hungry,'" Grandma said. "She warned her. 'If you do, you'll die.' But Mama told her, 'Well, I'm gonna die then. I'm going to drink it all.' Mama drank all the champurrado down. She ate all the tostadas, but she didn't die. She didn't even have one cramp." Grandma laughed, quietly. "Mama wanted to die. I don't blame her."

Grandma wasn't sure of the reason Vicenta reunited with Esteban, but she knew he needed his mother's permission. "One day, Daddy's mother said to him, 'Go ahead! She's ready to fix your lunch. You can bring her back.' So, Daddy went to the old woman's house and got her. Pretty soon, Mama was sick with double pneumonia.

"Mama's friend came back to check on her and the baby. They find her unconscious in bed. My grandma didn't take care of her, didn't take her food or water—nothing. They had to feed me with a bottle because Mama didn't have any milk, she was so sick. Mama's friend went to talk with my Grandma Avila. They say, 'Vicenta, Mama?' My grandma acted innocent. 'What? I don't know about her...' Mama's friend said, 'What do you mean, you don't know about her? She lives in your house! She's your daughter-in-law!' My Grandma acted like it was none of her business. She said, 'It's not my job to feed someone who is not related to us.'"

Stories like this, surrounding Grandma's birth, are heartbreaking. Unfortunately, they were followed by stories of Esteban's subsequent rejection. Her sister, Maria, resembled Esteban, so she was his favorite. Juana, light-skinned and small-boned, favored her mother, and therefore, was subject to her father's anger.

"I grew up knowing Daddy didn't like me," Grandma said. "He liked my sister, Maria, who was two years older, but not me. I used to see Daddy bring her things, like candies and fruits, but he didn't bring nothing for me. She would sit in his lap, and he would say nice things, *'So and so and so.'*" Grandma's imitation of her father saying sweet things to Maria, in a sweet voice showed how the words didn't matter. The nearness and tenderness he gave Maria did.

"But Maria liked me a lot," Grandma said, brightening. "When Daddy would buy things for her, she always used to save me some. She never ate them without me. She would say, 'Juana! Come here!' and she would sneak me some candy or sweet bread or whatever. Sometimes, she'd say, 'Juana, I put something for you in the barn.' We had a big barn and she would hide the candies or sweet bread there. She would say, 'Eat it right there. Don't bring it out because Daddy's going to get mad.' So, I used to eat it right there, whatever she saved for me."

Grandma laughed at the end of her story, as if she and Maria had outsmarted their father. She felt joy at the memory of Maria's provision, making sure her sister wasn't slighted.

Nevertheless, Esteban made sure Juana knew that Maria was his favorite, even the way he assigned chores.

"We used to raise pork, and Daddy got a new pig every two months. Every day, he used to make me feed the pig. It was *dirty* work! One day, I thought Daddy went to the mountains to get some wood. One day, I came back from feeding the pig, and I said to my mom, 'I don't like feeding that pig. I don't want to do it anymore! Why doesn't Maria ever have to feed him?'

"I didn't even know my Daddy had come home and was in the house. He came out, carrying a big quince branch. The quince tree has a stem you can peel, so it's like rubber. Parents used to use it for spanking their kids. Daddy came out of the house and hit me with it, right across my face. I got a bloody nose and a swollen eye.

"People used to ask me, 'What happened to your face?' I didn't want to tell them. Even Mama told me, 'Don't tell anyone what happened. Say you hurt yourself another way.' So, I told people, 'Well, I was swinging from a tree branch, and then I hit into one branch of the tree,' but that was a joke."

Grandma's voice trailed off at the end. The last part of her story loses something in translation. Grandma was young when this happened, a small girl who didn't like feeding the pig. She was hit in the face with a rubbery tree branch, by her father. It solidified her feelings of being unloved. Having to lie and cover up the abuse was no joke—it made it worse.

"I didn't know what I did to make my Daddy not like me," Grandma said. "I hear him say things to Mama, but I didn't want to believe that she had taken another man and then had me. I wondered—because he didn't like me—maybe he *wasn't* my dad.

One day, something happened. We had a work porch, and it was my job to wash the porch with water and keep it clean. You know how I have my toes? Two little ones and the rest are crooked? Well, Daddy say to me, 'Why don't you put on your shoes? Cover your ugly toes!' I said to my dad, 'Well, God made my toes, so what do you want?' He took his belt off, like he was going to spank me, but I ran inside the house, away from him." Grandma took a break here, to laugh.

"Oh! He got so mad at me! I stayed inside, and listened to see what my parents were going to say. Mama said, 'I don't know why you tease her. She's got your same toes!' I was listening to them, thinking: *Really?*

"I never saw Daddy's toes, so I started planning on ways I could see them. I thought maybe I could go in his room, when he was sleeping, and offer him a cold drink of water. Then, maybe I can see his toes. One day, I did this. I say, 'Dad, do you want a cold glass of water?' He said, 'Sure!' I take him the water, and when I was there, I looked there at his toes. *Oh, Yeah! He got my toes! That's where I get my toes—from my Daddy!* Oh! On that day, I knew I belonged to him, because my toes are like him."

Grandma laughed when she told this story. She seemed so happy to remember her discovery, with her child-like ingenuity. Grandma's toes, always covered up by shoes or slippers, looked tangled or misshapen. These toes became the symbol of her validation and belonging. It also validated her mother, Vicenta, in her daughter's eyes. The toes were proof that Grandma's mom had never cheated on her husband.

"Mama was an angel," Grandma said. "I never see other wives like her. It was my Daddy who used to have other women. He would bring his girlfriend to our house really early in the morning, and he used to wake Mama up.

"'Get up! Squeeze up some orange juice for us!' he would say. My mama would get up from bed, and say, 'Okay, I'm gonna make your favorite right now.' Then she would get up and wait on them."

On the recorded interview, Doreen asked Grandma if she ever cried, or felt rejected when her father would favor Maria over her. Grandma was quick to answer.

"No. I never used to cry about that because my sister used to like me a lot! She used to bring me anything that my Daddy gave her. Candies or sweet bread or anything. She used to save me something of everything."

Grandma's convincing tone was clear: Maria made up for the disapproval of her father. Even when Juana knew Maria was his favorite, there was no blame there because the sisters were close, and knew the truth. Maria protected Juana, shared with her, and treated her like she was a special girl, worthy of love. The sisters learned to rely on each other, even as the whole country sailed into the stormy waters of the 1910's.

8. Life Before the War

Grandma always seemed happiest in her kitchen, cooking, baking, or canning. Memories of her are attached to familiar tastes and smells: ketchup beans, spongey strawberry shortcake, egg burritos with chopped tomatoes and bell peppers, lettuce and cheese enchiladas, quesadillas, tamales, and her omnipresent tortillas. All of these had the calming, soothing effect of opium on us. Grandma was the best cook, and she knew it. She learned from Vicenta, in Michoacán. As soon as she was old enough to be near the chimenea, Grandma cooked alongside of her mother.

"Every day, Daddy used to go up into the mountains and bring down some wood, which we needed because we had a lot of stoves—we call them chimeneas—made of adobe. We made tortillas on these big, round plates, made from mud. Underneath, there was a fire burning, burning, until the coals turned red.

"Mama used to make the tortillas, and cook our food all day long, little by little. She had a lot of patience, sometimes staying near the chimenea all day. We cooked beans a lot. Daddy planted black, red, and pinto beans. We used to cook the black ones first, then the red ones. Mama would say, 'Okay, the beans are ready. Come and eat!'

"In the summertime, Mama used to cook big pots of everything: corn, sweet potatoes, zucchini, and pumpkin. Daddy used to grow corn, garbanzos, sweet potatoes, and pumpkins. The small, orange pumpkins have hard skins, as hard as a coffee cup. You can't just break them with a knife, so Daddy used to have a little axe to cut them. He would cut it in half with the axe, and my mom used to cook them just like that. That's what we used to have for breakfast in summertime. We would eat it, like a little bowl, and I used to put milk and syrup with the pumpkin. We called that *manácata*. Oh, we used to love it! It was so good.

"Then Mama used to cook, all together in a big, big pot, sweet potatoes, sweet corn, pumpkin, garbanzos, and sweet peas. That's what we used to eat in the summer. Pumpkin, milk, and sweet potatoes. Whatever was growing, that was our breakfast.

"In wintertime? That was different. In the morning, Mama used to make a big pot of porridge and that's all we had for breakfast. Porridge and sometimes brown sugar. The porridge was good with brown sugar in it. We used to take one or two cups, until we had enough of it. In the winter, at night, we would eat just beans. Yeah, in wintertime we were as poor as we can be."

Grandma never forgot how poor she was growing up. She considered herself lucky to have food. She treasured her gas stove with a flame she could turn on and off. She had a comal to make tortillas, and a big oven for baking. These luxuries were never taken for granted.

a small cantaro for drawing water

"Our farm was a lot of hard work," she said. "My Dad never let us go visit *nobody*," Grandma said, emphasizing the last word very strongly. "He used to say, 'You got lots to do at home and you got to stay home!' I had to sweep the whole patio with a short broom made of weeds. Daddy would always check it to make sure it was done just right. It was my job to carry the water from far away, to home," she said. "We had a venero, a spring, where I'd go to get water, in a little jug about this big. We used to call them cantaros, the pitchers we used to collect water. We had to fill them up with water, carry them on our shoulder, and then bring it back home. I had to fill four or five barrels each day.

So, every morning, I used to go back and forth, back and forth, bringing the water. My Daddy used to wake me up really early and say, 'Get up! Start getting the water, before it gets too hot!'

"One time, I fell in the venero!" Grandma said, laughing. "I was so scared!

I came back and told Mama. I had to change my clothes and start again. I asked Mama, 'Why doesn't Maria have to go and get water? Why is it always just me?' I didn't even know that my Daddy was there. He said, 'You don't have anything else to do, and you have to go and bring the water, and you better do it, and you better keep your mouth shut!'"

Grandma's imitation of her father, Esteban, in a sing-song voice, made it seem like he scolded her often. Her father ruled his home like a king, and wanted to make sure his daughter worked hard. He succeeded in that way, but failed to set more important examples.

"On Sundays, we had a day off," Grandma said. "We didn't work at all. Mama took us to church on Sundays, and Daddy used to go with his friends. He didn't like to come to church; he liked to go out and have a good time drinking. Mama and Maria and me would go to church. After that, we come home, or maybe we buy a little bit of groceries. We never got to go any places, just to church and then to the store. Daddy spent all day with his friends, drinking and having a good time."

While the Avila family kept up the small farm, on which they lived together, Maria and Juana were significantly younger than their elder brothers. Cenobio and Pancho, part of their daily lives, were men. They shared most of the work responsibilities with Esteban. Grandma's brother, Jesus, was a different story.

"Jesus came to the United States before I was born," Grandma said. "He was lost to our family for years. We didn't know nothing about him—nothing! He didn't used to write, even to let us know how he was. Mama used to be so worried about him. One day, she was crying and crying, and she said, 'Maybe he's dead now.' Cenobio said, 'No, he's not dead, Mom. If you let me go to the United States, I'll bring Jesus back.' Back then, even if a man marries, he still does what his mom and dad tells him to do. Cenobio said, 'If you give me the money, I'll go find Jesus.'

"So, Mama gave him the money and Cenobio went to the United States and came back with Jesus. He was married. I don't remember if he had children or not, but he came back to the ranch and we were so happy!" Grandma told the story with relief and happiness, which quickly drained from her voice.

"Three days later, there was a wedding in town. We went to the wedding, and Jesus was killed there. My brother, Cenobio, who was drunk, got in a fight with another man. Jesus went to defend Cenobio, and the other man had a knife. He said, 'If you want, I have some for you, too!' That man stuck the knife into Jesus' side, just as Jesus was running away. He ran over to a little rock fence, tried to jump over it, but he fell. He was on the ground, bleeding and bleeding."

Grandma told this part of the story slowly, especially when she described how everyone was running in different directions. It was like she was watching the chaos in the foreground, while Jesus fell behind the stone fence, out of sight, and bled to death.

"My father was there, and he was looking for Jesus, but Daddy couldn't see him behind the fence. Later, he say, 'If I saw him there, I would have tied up his wound, so he wouldn't bleed anymore.' So, Jesus died." Grandma's voice got very quiet. I could feel the pain in her words, not just for Jesus, but for her long-suffering mother, Vicenta.

"Imagine that," Grandma said, sadly. "After all those years in the United States, Jesus comes back to Mexico, and he's killed after three days? Oh, Mama got so sick! She used to suffer attacks of epilepsy, one after another. She was happy to see Jesus, and then, he's killed."

Vicenta suffered from ill health, probably epilepsy. or some kind of neurological disorder. She experienced high fevers and seizures during stressful times. She had no medicine, other than her rosary. Prayer was Vicenta's medicine of choice.

Grandma's stories of Vicenta were always told with the same, reverent tone she used for the Virgin Mary. Grandma seemed in awe of her mother, so I listened to stories about Grandma's love and devotion for her mother with particular fascination.

"Did you really love your mother more than anyone?" I asked. "Even more than Grandpa?"

"More than anyone in this world," she said, waving her palms in the air.

"More than your children?"

Grandma laughed. I was her daughter's daughter. She should have known better than to answer my question, but she did.

"More than anyone! My mama was an angel. A *saint*." Grandma dropped the highest praise she would ever give a person. A devout Catholic, Grandma didn't use the word *saint* lightly.

9. The Mexican Revolution

In July of 1910, Grandma was four-years-old, too young to realize that Mexico was on the verge of a full-blown revolution. All around her, starving farmers were joining Mexico's militia, ready to evict the stubborn Porfirio Díaz and his oppressive government. Social Revolutionaries in Mexico, young men who left their farms to join makeshift armies were a big part of the Mexican Revolution, like the Minutemen we learned about in U.S. History class. In the Northern states of Mexico, the charismatic Pancho Villa had amassed an arsenal of guns and artillery, as well as an army of fearless men, the Villistas, who would follow him anywhere. In the Southern states, the enigmatic Emiliano Zapata, and his Zapatistas, had been advocating land reform for years. Zapata opposed foreign ownership of Mexican land, and demanded agrarian reform. His men, loyal foot soldiers, were armed to the teeth and ready for battle.

Díaz promised to vacate the office of President as soon as his term finished in 1910. He swore he'd never run for president again. At the last moment, he changed his mind, declared himself the winner, and threw himself a party. This was the last straw for the revolutionaries. They declared war on Díaz and his totalitarian government. What followed was ten years of civil war, now known as The Mexican Revolution.

It wasn't until July of 1914 that this Revolution touched the Avila family. Venustiano Carranza had taken the presidency, and was beginning to show his true colors. Agrarian reform was not happening, as Carranza had promised. His Constitutional government seemed to be protecting the hacienda managers more than farmers. In October, the Convention of Aguascalientes was held in Mexico City, 204 miles east of Coeneo de

Libertad, where Carranza, Villa, and Zapata discussed peace and power-sharing in Mexico. It was a disaster. In Aguascalientes, Villa, and Zapata realized the war was not over, and made an alliance. Almost as soon as they left, battles erupted all over Central Mexico, including Michoacán. Including San Isidro.

In her recorded interview, Grandma revealed her childlike innocence and limited perspective. She remembered how soldiers, or horsemen, were suddenly surrounding them on all sides, raiding farms, taking what they wanted: food, horses, animals, women. Sometimes Grandma called them "Pancho Villa y todos," but in reality, she never knew which side "they" were on. She referred to the soldiers as "the horsemen," or just "them," because she didn't know who "they" were, or which army "they" represented. Nameless, faceless horsemen kidnapped girls for sexual pleasure and terrorized farmers without conscience. Her family was forced to hide anything of value.

"During the war time, my Daddy hid the best corn," Grandma said. "He grew real good corn, the best of the harvests, but he made us eat the bad corn first. When the horsemen came to our ranch, they got all the sacks of corn from Daddy's hiding spot in the barn, and dumped it outside. What they didn't take, they left for their horses to eat. The horses stepped on it and peed on it. It was the best corn, but we didn't want that corn anymore.

"Daddy told Mama, 'Oh, if I knew this, we would have been eating our best corn.' Mama told him, 'Didn't I tell you? You were saving the best corn and you didn't even know who would be eating it!'

"When Daddy thought the horsemen were going to hit our ranch, he told Mama, 'I think you better go up to the mountains.' Mama said, 'We've got to eat something.' So, Daddy went and picked some of that corn out of the ground, where the horses had stepped on it. We washed it real good, and Mama made a few tortillas for us. Then, we went to the mountains. "My mama and daddy never used to sleep through the night," Grandma said. "They were watching and listening for them to come. Pancho Villa y todo was against Carranza's army. Carranza was camped on that side, and Villa on that side, and they was always fighting!

"Pancho Villa y todo was terrible! They used to break into a house, and if they don't find anybody in that house, they used to burn whatever they can't take. They burned all my Mama's important papers, and all our birth certificates. They put them in a pile in the middle of the yard, and they burned them there.

"In all of the wars, the horsemen would knock on doors and see if there were any girls in the house. If they couldn't find young girls, they would take any woman—even an old lady. [The horsemen] had guns and machetes. They used to pick and stab at the adobe walls, because in the capital of Michoacán, they found girls hidden inside of the walls. Daddy told us how the people fixed their walls so they were hollow, and they hid their daughters away in them, but the horsemen found them.

"One time, the horsemen came to San Isidro and they couldn't find any girls, so they took an old woman, who was about ninety, and they killed her. The village men found her dead in the big corral there. They couldn't save her.

"Every night, we would go to bed, and Mama told us, 'Just leave your clothes on and lie down.' We never took our clothes off when we sleep. Sometimes, Daddy would wake us up in the middle of the night. He would say, 'Wake up! Hurry! Let's go, let's go, let's go!' We had to wake up so fast. It was cold and dark, but we had to hurry up and run. 'Get up! Get up! Let's go to the mountains!'

"There were caves in the mountains by our house, where people would hide when the Spanish came the first time. Daddy used to take us there. He'd tell us, 'Stay there! Stay there!' Oh, that cave was cold! It was only about this high." Grandma held her hand out, to show how the cave was not much more than two feet from the ground. "We used to crawl in there and I used to ask, 'Mama, what if the wall comes down on us and it's gonna bury us?' Mama said, 'Don't think about that. Just pray to God that we're gonna be safe. Come on, let's say the Rosary.' So, we would say the Rosary there in the cave. Oh, my poor mom! That's all she used to do. Pray and pray. She always held a Rosary in her hands. She prayed all the time."

Grandma shook her head, remembering the cruel reality of those times. She treasured her kind, pious mother. She hated the invading horsemen.

"Sometimes, all the women around our ranch had to stay in the mountains all day," she said. "Oh, we were so hungry! One of my little friends said, 'I'm so hungry,' and I said, 'Me, too. Let's eat some grass, like the cows.'" Grandma stopped to laugh at this memory. "So, we started eating grass. We did it, and... Oh, it tasted so good! But my mama said, 'Don't eat that! You're going to get sick! Do you have a cud? Grass is only for cows and sheep.' I said, 'It tastes good, Mama! It tastes good!' She said, 'You're not gonna have any more of that!'" Grandma paused and then she'd look up at us. "You see? We was so hungry, we would eat anything."

The mountains proved to be the best place to hide for the women and their daughters. Sometimes the men on horseback came too quickly for them to run there. The men in the villages had to make a plan and think of new places to hide, especially when horsemen surprised them.

"Sometimes the horsemen would come in at twelve o'clock at night," Grandma said. "We would run to the big river, in back of where we used to live. My Dad would walk out far, carrying me on his neck—I never learned how to swim, not even doggie-paddle—and he would walk out to the deep water and stay there. We didn't used to make any noise, because Daddy didn't want them to hear us. One time I looked down and I saw the water was up to here on my Daddy," Grandma held her hand under her nose, illustrating the water level. "I screamed, 'Daddy, you're gonna drown!' but he covered my mouth with his hand, so I would stop screaming. I didn't want him to drown in that river."

The seasonal river provided help in the summer, but during the winter, the sparse landscape forced the Avila family to build another fortress for the women.

"My Dad had to dig a hole in the ground," Grandma said. "Then he put a lid to cover that hole. When we got in, he put the lid down and then spread around some grass on top of that. It looked like nothing was there. He told us, 'Honey, when they come, you get into the hole if you don't have a chance to run away to the mountains.' Sometimes the horsemen came too fast. Sometimes there was no time to get away.

"One time, we hid in that hole all night. They came to the ranch and we stayed there until they leave. When Daddy opened up the lid, he said, 'Come out, everybody's gone.' We came out. Mama started looking for food, but there was nothing. They took everything and left us with nothing.

"So, my Daddy said, 'Well, I'll go see if I can find us something to eat.' and he left. We were so hungry! He came home later, but he didn't have anything. We were so disappointed. I asked Mama, "Didn't he get anything?' She looked sad, but she said, 'Well, honey, he couldn't find anything. What can we do?'

"We were always hiding from the horsemen. Hiding in the mountains and in the river and in that hole."

On the recording, Grandma lowered her voice and said something quietly to Doreen: "One time, we didn't have a chance to hide. They came and took my sister. They take her away. Poor thing."

Grandma rarely talked about the circumstances surrounding her sister, Maria's kidnapping, but she always told us it happened, the most painful proof of the war. When it was time to share details about her sister's abduction, she stopped talking. Even on her recorded interview, she offered only one sliver of information: *One time, we didn't have a chance to hide. They came and took my sister. They take her away. Poor thing.*

I wanted to know more about the details of what happened to Maria. The recorded interview was exactly like the story I remembered Grandma telling. Even after Maria had passed away, Grandma withheld missing parts. She clammed up, in unaccustomed fashion.

I was determined to find out what really happened.

Part Four: Beans

"Beans are so like us... they have a soul."
~ Pythagoras, Ancient Greek Mathematician

"Poor Mexico, so far from God, and so close to the United States."
~ Porfirio Diaz, as he left Mexico

Grandma's Beans

2 lbs beans, cleaned and sorted
1 onion, chopped fine
Salt to taste
2 cloves garlic, minced
1/2 cup lard or oil (I use lard)
1/2 cup ketchup

- Step one: cooking the beans

Clean and rinse beans thoroughly. Allow beans to soak for at least 8 hours. Re-rinse. Place beans in pot with water about ½ inch above the top of the beans. Add chopped onion and some salt. Boil. After boiling point is achieved, set to simmer and set the timer for 1 ½ hours. Do not strain the beans. You'll need the juice.

- Step Two: frying

In a separate large pot, heat lard to frying temperature. Add minced garlic. Swish garlic around in lard to allow the lard to absorb the flavor. Slowly add beans and water into the pot with the lard and garlic. Simmer. Add ketchup. Stir and add more ketchup until desired color and taste is achieved. Keep warm and serve

10. Tía Maria – Filling the Gaps

Tía Maria, businesswoman, approx. 1945

I was a very young girl when Mom told us that Tía Maria, Grandma's only sister, was dying. Grandpa drove Grandma to Fresno, where Tía Maria lived, to take care of her in her final days. Grandpa went back home, and waited for Grandma's phone call, which came one day, telling Grandpa that Tía Maria died. Grandpa went to Fresno for the funeral, and returned with Grandma to Tracy. Tía Maria was gone, and Grandma was back home.

As I put this book together, I openly lamented the loss of a woman who had died so long ago, and who I'd only just met. How could I have known so little about her? A sister so important to Grandma that our family story was incomplete without her.

"Why don't you talk to my cousin, Esther?" Mom said. "She might be able to help you with more of that story."

"Will she talk to me?" I asked. I had never met any of Tía Maria's daughters, even though Esther and Mom had grown up together.

"I'll give her a call and ask her," Mom said.

Esther, one of Tía Maria's younger daughters, remained in close contact with Mom. She had become a successful real estate agent in the Fresno area, and was really busy. I was glad when Esther agreed talk to me, but I was nervous before calling. When Esther answered, she set me at ease right away. We fell into a natural conversation about family, and the missing pieces.

"My mom, Maria, to tell you the truth, was not one to sit down and talk to us," Esther told me. "I'm one of her younger daughters, and she didn't really share things with me unless I pulled it out of her. I made her tell me things, but she always acted like she didn't have time to sit down and talk."

I shared about Grandma's quiet confession on the recording: *One time, we didn't have a chance to hide. They came and they took my sister.*

"Oh, yeah," Esther said, with such light in her voice, I got chills. "That was during the Mexican Revolution. Tía Juana and my mom were really young, about nine and eleven years old. Their dad and brothers were off somewhere, I don't know where, but they weren't at home. Their mother, Vicenta, got really sick with a fever. The only way they could make the fever go down was to put wet towels on Vicenta's head. All day long, Mom and Tía Juana were doing this, but Vicenta's fever wouldn't break. Her temperature was so high she was getting delirious. Mom said they used to live in a little house, like an adobe shack, with no amenities, and they were running out of water. Neither of them were supposed to go out, because of Pancho Villa's revolutionaries. My Tía Juana—I loved her so much, but she was nothing like my mother—was so scared. She knew she couldn't go out and get more water, because the water source was half a mile away. My mom decided she would go to the well, in the village. Mom was a great protector of Tía Juana, so she went to get water."

I groaned. This had to be why Grandma used to get so quiet when she told the story. She probably blamed herself for her sister's kidnap. It was Grandma's job to carry the family's water, and that day, there wasn't enough.

"Mom ran to the well," Esther said. "It was getting dark, and while she was getting the water, she heard the sound of hoofbeats. She knew the horsemen were coming, so she hid behind the well. Of course, the men found her there. There were about six or seven revolutionary soldiers, who grabbed her up and took her." "Oh no," I said, feeling darkness descend.

"You didn't know that part, did you?" Esther asked. "That really happened! I once verified this story with my Tía Juana, just to make sure Mom told me everything. Tía Juana said it happened just like that. 'Oh, yes. I begged Maria not to go to the well, but she said, *¡Ahorita vengo!* (I'll be right back!) Then, she ran off to get water.' She left Tía Juana with Vicenta, and ran to the well. The horsemen took Mom away, and didn't bring her back. Her family didn't hear from her, couldn't find her. Can you imagine? She was lost to them for at least *six or seven months*! Everyone knew she had been taken, or kidnapped. When she didn't come back, they thought the worst."

"This is awful," I said. "Did your mom ever tell you what happened when those horsemen took her?"

Esther sighed. "My mom told me that she was afraid of the horsemen," she said. "She thought they were going to rape her, but she said they didn't. Instead, they dumped her at a little house, way out in the boonies. The horsemen knew this old man who lived there and since they were on their way to fight, they left her there. That old man was the one who took advantage of my mother. My poor mom. She told me, 'I didn't know much of anything, back then. I hadn't even started menstruating.' Anyway, that's how she got pregnant with my step-brother, Ezequiél."

Esther was quiet for a while. "In six or seven months, my mother got to town, somehow. She was only about twelve or thirteen years old, but when she saw her family again, she was pregnant."

The next time I listened to Grandma's recorded interview, I could hear the grief in her voice, telling only a fraction of the story. I can only imagine how she felt, knowing her sister had gone to fetch water, which she was responsible for collecting. Grandma probably blamed herself.

Tía Maria's kidnap and systematic abuse was not uncommon. Yolanda Chávez Leyva, a professor of history at the University of Texas at El Paso, writes about the palpable terror for women living in the Mexican countryside during the revolution in her paper, "'I Go to Fight for Social Justice': Children as Revolutionaries in the Mexican Revolution, 1910-1920:"

> Narratives of the Mexican Revolution are replete with stories of rape and the 'robbing' of women and girls, although the discussion at times becomes euphemistic, clouding the reality of sexual violence. Historian Luis Gonzalez records that 'parties of rebels often came to visit their friends in San Jose, either to rescue the girls from their virginity, or to feast happily on the delicious local cheeses and meats, or to add the fine horses of the region to their own.'[1]

---

[1] Yolanda Chávez Leyva. 1998. "'I Go to Fight for Social Justice': Children As Revolutionaries in the Mexican Revolution, 1910-1920." *Peace & Change* 23 (4)

History of the Mexican Revolution includes the brutalities against women, often regarded as the spoils of war. To say Maria was kidnapped and dropped off with a strange man is almost a euphemism. Maria was an eleven-year-old girl, abducted by soldiers with guns, who probably abused her, then gave her to another man. No one thought of returning her to her family, until she got pregnant.

Victims of sexual assault survive. They often carry the children of their abusers. During the Mexican Revolution, the families they returned to were usually poor, religious, downtrodden people. If a pregnant daughter returned home, the shame and reminder of being violated was always before them. Some of these women married their abductors, and joined the Revolution. Some, like Maria, went home. In her case, she was returned to a family with a mother who loved her, and a father who once favored her. Could they return to the way it used to be? Could anything?

11. Leaving the Ranch

The Avila family waited for Maria to come home. She didn't. Sleepless nights became worse, and turned into sleepless months. The family continued to hide from marauding horsemen, but with crops destroyed, their daughter gone, and the family still in danger of being killed, Estevan made a terribly hard decision to leave. Without hope, and little chance of finding any scrap of food, the family decided to make a run for the nearest city.

"We was so hungry!" Grandma said. "My dad finally said, 'I can't take this anymore! We're moving to town.' We'd been living on the ranch all our lives, and we only left because the horsemen were hitting the farms all the time."

Like most of their neighbors, the Avila family decided to abandon their farm and take refuge in the nearest city, where there was protection. Coeneo de la Libertad was about two and a half miles away, but for starving, sleep-deprived people, traveling this distance on foot, carrying any possessions through dangerous territory, it was a marathon.

"I was about ten years old when we make a move to town," Grandma told us. "I had an aunt, named Marcelina, who lived half-way to town. Mama kept saying, 'If we can just get to Auntie Marcelina's. I hope we can get to Marcelina's!' We made it, but when we got there, Auntie Marcelina told us the horsemen hit that place, too. They took everything. Everything. All the food they found? They gave it to their horses. My aunt said the horsemen were mad because they couldn't find girls.

"Mama asked her, 'Don't you got anything to eat? They're dying! They're starving!' My aunt said, 'I haven't got anything, except a few garbanzo beans for roasting.' So, she roasted them. We each had four garbanzo beans." Grandma purred as she remembered. "Oh! They was sooooo good! I ate three of them right away. I didn't want to finish that last one. I thought, 'Shall

I save it? Shall I eat it now? No, I better eat it.' That was all we had, all day. Four garbanzos. That helped us make the walk into town."

Grandma loved that story, of how simple garbanzos saved her. She added that her Auntie Marcelina, a country woman, fiercely independent, stayed behind on her ranchette. Even with no food, Marcelina didn't want to move to town.

"We made it to town, to my aunt's house," Grandma said. "We made it. When we get there, my sister, Maria, was there." In the recorded interview, Grandma whispered the next part to Doreen: "But the men had abused and raped her."

Grandma left out any details about reuniting with her beloved sister. Instead, she talked about food.

"We got to my aunt's house," Grandma said. "She was Maria's Godmother, that aunt who lived in town. We found Maria there. Maria's Godmother fed us. My Aunt told Mama, 'I'm going to feed you, but don't eat too much right away. It's two days since you ate food and you might get sick if you eat too much.' We was so hungry! She made some *fideo* for us, and Oh! It was so good! She gave us a little plate about this big, but we didn't eat it all. It was two days since we had a regular meal. Then, my Aunt said, 'I got a loaf of bread.' She brought it out. The people that live in town, they don't have to make tortillas because they buy bread at the store."

Grandma's recollection of this, as an adult, still have the sense memories of her ten-year-old self. Grandma talks about the fideo, coiled wheat pasta, thinner than angel hair, cooked with chicken broth and tomato sauce. After months of eating almost nothing, a weak and starving girl near death was revived by a plate of fideo. It brought her back to the world.

Grandma didn't talk about reuniting with Maria, but if seeing Maria for the first time in months was a celebration, she would have talked about it. She would have included all the exciting details, the family's reaction, the tears of joy she shed. Instead, we heard about fideo.

It's very possible that the Avila family left their farm and came to town because Maria's Godmother sent word to them that Maria was there, and she was pregnant.

By all accounts, Esteban was a proud and controlling man. He wouldn't have been happy to see his daughter, maybe twelve or thirteen years of age, pregnant. His rage might have expressed itself as blame, or shame. He might have erupted, or hit something, or got drunk. By that time, Esteban was a defeated man. He had left his family's ranch and come to Coeneo, filled with rage, fear, and uncertainty. His favorite daughter stood before him, no longer a girl, but a woman with child, and he was powerless to do anything about it.

***

"We lived in town for a while," Grandma said. "We didn't have to hide because the horsemen couldn't get past the watchmen that guarded the town. They had really good watch stations."

The Avila family stayed in the same, small house where Maria's Godmother's family lived in Coeneo. It was crowded, but safe. Food was available, but still restricted.

"Me and my sister thought maybe we would get to start school," Grandma said. "My sister's Godmother told my dad, 'Maria has to go to school. I'm going to take her to town and she's going to go to school.' So, Maria's Godmother took her to school, but Maria had to quit. While she was there, Maria learned how to write the alphabet, she used to teach me handwriting, and pretty soon, my handwriting was better than hers. I practiced all the time. I wanted to learn how to write with pencils, because it was hard for me to write with pens. Guess what we used for a pen? Chicken feathers!" Grandma laughed. "We used to make the ends of the chicken feathers real pointy and then dip them in the ink, but it was hard for me. It was easier to use pencil."

Despite the opportunity to go to an organized school setting, Grandma and Tia Maria practiced writing the alphabet, mostly behind their father's back. This was hard to do in town, because Esteban was always around. There was no ranch to take care of, no animals to corral, no crops to tend. He was unemployed and restless.

"Back then, people didn't used to believe in school," Grandma said. "In those days, parents didn't send their children to school. My daddy didn't even know how to write his name. Mama couldn't read or write, either. I think Mama was fourteen-years-old when she got married. They used to think a girl doesn't have to read or write to get married. That's the way it was then.

"Daddy didn't want me to go to school, or learn how to read or write. Mama wanted me to have school. She used to say, 'Why don't you let Juanita go to school? She has to learn. I don't want her to grow up like me. I don't even know how to write my name.' But Daddy used to say, 'No, she don't need to learn anything.' Daddy didn't want me to go to school."

Grandma hated her father's fierce control over her, especially when it came to keeping her uneducated.

"The poor people in Mexico were poor, and we were meant for something, but not for school. None of my family went to school. That's why a lot of people, they don't know how to read. They don't know how to write."

***

Grandma grew up to be a woman who loved learning new things, especially English vocabulary and idioms. She was constantly learning. Most of my memories are of Grandma in the kitchen, the warm, magical place where dough balls were rolled into circles, and became tortillas once they hit the hot comal. The tortilla would be slathered in butter, folded into a triangle, put into a napkin, and placed in your hand. Love.

One day, as I waited for my tortilla, I saw a wooden clothespin by Grandma's bread box, standing on its legs, pinching an index card in its mouth. Written in Grandma's careful cursive was a single word: *bashful*.

"What's that?" I asked, pointing to the card.

"That's *bashful*," Grandma said. She handed me a buttery tortilla. "Bashful means shy." I smiled. "I know what it means, Grandma. Why did you write it on that card?"

Grandma closed her dough drawer and smiled. She looked a little embarrassed as she wiped her hands on a dish towel.

"I'm trying to remember how to say that word," she said. "I always say *vegetable*."

We laughed together. This memory seems so fragile, and so strong at the same time. Grandma was uneducated by most people's standards, but she was incredibly curious, and determined to learn things she thought were important.

Language was important to Grandma.

12. Crossing Over

In January of 1917, as Mexico was engaged in Civil War, most of Europe was fighting in WWI. Germany's foreign minister, Arthur Zimmerman, chose this time to send a secret message to Venustiano Carranza, President of Mexico, to propose an alliance against the United States. Germany's intention was to keep the United States from entering the Great War. The telegram, however, was intercepted by British Intelligence, and made public. It incited global furor, and acted as a catalyst for the United States to enter the war.

In April of 1917, the U.S. Congress voted to declare war on Germany and join the Allied troops in Europe. The Zimmerman telegram, even though it failed, put Mexican President Carranza in a precarious position. He couldn't afford to alienate the United States, but he didn't want to anger Germany, either. So, Carranza did nothing. No reply, just silence.

In February of 1917, Carranza's government ratified the Constitution of 1917, the most important document in the nation's history. The Constitution defined Mexican citizenship, as well as mandating land reform. Article 27 declared that any land taken from "the peasantry" during the Porfiriato be returned, even if the farmers didn't hold a deed or a title. All of this needed to happen in order for Mexico to have peace and prosperity. Once this was done, he asked Villa and Zapata, his main opposition, to surrender to a new and just government. Villa and Zapata, instead, formed an alliance against Carranza, who they didn't trust.

In May of 1917, in the neighboring United States, the Bracero Program was established. Despite strong anti-Mexican sentiments, the US government invited Mexican workers to fill seasonal jobs, left vacant by men who had gone to fight overseas. The Bracero Program marked the first formal working relationship between the United States and Mexico. Most Braceros (laborers) were brought in to work the fields, especially to tend and harvest sugar beets. Employers who wanted to hire Mexican Braceros were required to follow protocol and provide workers with written contracts. Employers were required to pay Braceros the same wages they paid U.S. Citizens, at the same rate, for the same number of hours. Braceros, in turn, received work permits, which they could renew only once. They had to leave the US at the end of their contracts, "at no cost to the US government," with a train ticket purchased by their employers.[2] Many employers didn't like these conditions, or refused to pay for a Bracero's return ticket to Mexico. As a result, many Braceros stayed in the United States.

This chain of events in 1917 catapulted Mexican citizens into a different world. Suddenly, displaced farmers were getting permits to enter the United States, hoping to earn a fortune in six months. Esteban Avila, Maria and Juana's father, only thought about going back to his ranch to farm again. Mexico was his home, and despite the setbacks, he wanted to stay. Despite this desire to return, he wasn't exactly sure when the revolution would be over.

As much as her father wanted to stay in Mexico, fourteen-year-old Maria wanted to leave. She was tired of being treated like the bearer of family shame, and something in her hungered for something more. She believed the rumors about jobs in *el otro lado*—the other side. Since minors were not allowed to cross the border unaccompanied, Maria had to think outside the box. If she went without her family, it might be dangerous, but she told her sister, Juana, that she was planning on crossing anyway, just as soon as she had the baby. Soon afterward, Ezequiél, whose name means "God will strengthen," was born.

Maria left Mexico in 1918, a full year before her family. Ezequiél would be the first in the Avila family to be more American than Mexican, the forerunner of a new generation.

When I talked to Esther, she clarified her mother's plan to come to the United States.

"My mom really wanted to come to the USA," Esther said. "She made a

---

[2] Martin, Phillip. "Mexican Braceros and US Farm Workers." Mexican Braceros and US Farm Workers, Wilson Center, 10 July 2020

plan to cross the border with some other people, but Tía Juana was not with them. Mom swam the Rio Grande, and stayed with the other people. They were coming into the U.S. without permission, but they all stayed together, and went to Colorado."

"Wait a second," I said. "Your mom swam the Rio Grande?"

"Yes," Esther said. "What happened is that she strapped my brother, Ezequiél, to her back and she swam across."

"She swam across with *her baby* on her back?" I asked, trying to get my bearings.

"Yeah, apparently, she was a very good swimmer," Esther said. "My mom was a tiny girl back then. You wouldn't know it from all the pictures of her. Everyone remembers my mom as a heavy-set woman, but there was a time when she was fit..."

As Esther continued, I could feel the story rising all around me, like the Rio Grande. Its lost pieces rising, and clicking together. Maria went first into the country, crossing the milky, blue-green water that lapped at her chin and ears, and threatened to pull her under. The weight of her new baby on her back, his little hands flailing, her heart beating wildly. Surrounded by a group of strangers, she kept swimming, to the end of herself, to the edge of reason, to the border of her sanity, into a land that didn't know her. She focused on the other side. There had to be a better life over there. She had to get to it. She had to keep going. *She had to keep going.*

***

Maria was the first in, and probably found work tending or harvesting sugar beets. Sugar beets were a cash crop that performed well, even during the Great War.[3] After sugar beets, many Braceros took the train to Fresno, where there were grapes. Maria sent word to her family that she was safe and living in Fresno, and added that her father might actually like working the railroads here. Maria would meet her husband, Monico, in Fresno, and together, they would make a home with Ezequiél.

Maria became the family's bridge between Mexico and the United States. The rest of the Avila family would cross the border together in 1919, including Grandma's eldest brother, Cenobio, with his family. They traveled by train, carrying simple suitcases, packed with clothes and shoes. They had

---

3 "Prosperity for the Beet Growers." *Oxnard Courier*, 14 March 1919, page 2.

left most of their possessions at Maria's Godmother's house, thinking they would one day return. Grandma remembered the crossing, passing checkpoints and answering questions. They each were given a six-month work permit. Grandma stuck close to her parents, and kept her eyes down. They were finally here, to work long days, doing hard work. This was nothing new for the Avila Family. The living arrangements were.

"We were contracted to come and pick beets for six months," Grandma said. "They had farm camps where we stayed, so we slept close to other families in the same place. They came over, just like us."

"We were supposed to go back after the six months were over," Grandma said. "But when the work contract was finished, my Daddy's boss took him to the side. He said, 'You work hard. Where do you want to go? Back to Mexico? Or some other place in here?' Daddy asked him, 'Can we go someplace in here, if we want to?' The boss said, 'Yes, I'll buy the tickets for you, just tell me where.' So, Daddy tell the man that Mama had a sister in Fresno, and she wanted to see her. So, the boss bought train tickets for Fresno, not Mexico.

"We went to Fresno, and there was Mama's sister! Daddy got a job at the round house in Fresno, where all the trains stop. He used to work there at night." The family was also reunited with Maria. They met Monico, Maria's future husband. For a while, everyone was happy. No one expected trouble, or tragedy.

***

"When we were in Fresno, I finally got to go to school," Grandma said. "But I only got to go for two or three years. My dad stopped me from going to school, after Mama died. He told me, 'You're not going to school anymore.' I couldn't believe it. I said, 'I have to, I have to.' He said, 'No, you don't have to.' I said, 'If I don't go, the cops are gonna come to this house and force me to go.' Daddy didn't care. He just said, 'Don't you worry about that. I know what I'm going to tell them." I was crying, but he was mad. He said, 'What do you want? You went for two years.' I told him, 'What can you learn in two years? Nothing.'

"One day, the police came to our house," Grandma said. "Daddy told them I eloped with a boyfriend and went back to Mexico. The police believed him, and never came back. I didn't go back to school."

As heartbreaking as this story is, I wondered if I missed something in the recorded interview. *Did she just say, 'My dad stopped me from going to school, after*

Mama died'? I listened to this portion of the recorded interview over and over. I wondered if I had missed something. *Vicenta died? When?* Grandma's recorded interview with Doreen is about two and a half hours long. I listened to every part closely. Grandma only mentioned her mother's death twice: when she talked about going to school in Fresno, and when she describes her mother's beauty, never photographed.

"Mama was *beautiful!*" Grandma said. "She had light skin and thick black hair that she wore in long braids. I don't have any pictures of her, because she never let us take her picture. When she saw a camera, she would say, 'Get out of here! Don't take my picture!' People in those days used to believe that somebody could hurt them if they had their pictures.

"The only picture we ever had of Mama was when she was dead in her coffin. I let my brother take this picture with him when he went to pick cotton in another place. One day, there was a hard rain. He was living in a basement and everything was flooded. Everything was spoiled. Mama's picture and everything."

When did Vicenta die? It was a mystery how Grandma's beloved mother died. In Grandma's stories, she was alive one moment, and in the next, in a coffin, getting her picture taken. Like the subject of Maria's kidnap, Grandma never elaborated. When she was alive, Grandma spoke about her mother's health concerns, her beauty, the devout life she lived, filled with love for God and her children, but never how she passed away. *Why not?*

***

One night, at my parents' house, as I sat around the dining room table with Dad, Mom, and Auntie Emmy, I heard the story of how Vicenta died. At the time, Dad and Mom were in their early eighties, and Auntie Emmy, in her late seventies.

We had just eaten dinner, and were all sitting back in our chairs, considering if we should move to the living room. I had a cup of tea in front of me, and for a brief second, I didn't want anything more from life. We talked about recording interviews. I decided to ask about Vicenta.

"Why didn't Grandma talk about her mother's death?" I asked, to no one in particular. "It was a painful subject for her," Mom said.

"Do you know the story?" Dad asked. "Of how she died?"

"No," I said, surprised. "Do you?"

"Yes," Dad said. "It wasn't openly discussed in Grandma's neighborhood, but most of the adults around there knew about it." I remembered Grandma's stories of the close-knit community where Esteban and Vicenta lived when they first arrived. It was a place where everyone knew everyone else's business.

"It was a painful subject," Mom said, refolding a paper napkin in front of her. "When I think about my poor mother and how she carried this pain all of her life...." Mom's voice trailed off, but then she looked at me. "Do you want to know the story?"

"Yes," I said. I tried not to sound as desperate as I felt. "What happened?" Mom leaned forward in her chair and looked at me.

"Janet, I did not learn this story until I was working for Jim Stroup, in the 1980's."

Jim Stroup was Mom's friend, a tax attorney who employed Mom for many years. "We always knew that Mama's mother died young, right Emmy?" Auntie Emmy nodded, yes. She seemed to be listening as attentively as I was.

"It never occurred to me to ask her about it," Mom said. She looked at Auntie Emmy again. "Did it ever occur to you to ask Mama how her mother died?"

Auntie Emmy shook her head. "No, never."

"One morning, I went to Mama's house to have coffee," Mom said. "I had taken the kids to school, Dad was at work, and I just asked her, 'Mama, how did your mother die?' She answered me. 'It was a very bad accident and it was all my fault.'"

"What?" I asked, almost involuntarily.

"Exactly," Mom said. "I had the same reaction, and then I asked her why she thought that. She said, 'I was about fifteen years old, and I was in the confirmation program at church. I needed to go to confirmation class one night, and my dad wasn't home to drive me there.' Vicenta told her to go across the street and ask the woman for a ride to class. She had a son in the same confirmation class. She gave her a plate of food, and said, 'Here, I made a little dish of something. Go take it to her, and ask her if she can give you a ride to tonight.' But Mama had a crush on that woman's son, so she was embarrassed. She said, 'No, Mama! Don't make me do that! I don't want to take it because he's over there.' Her mom, Vicenta, said, 'It won't even take a minute. You need to go!' Mama kept begging her, 'Please, don't make me go!' Mama asked so much that Vicenta finally gave in. She said, 'Alright, give me the dish!' She took it from my mom and said, 'I'll go over there and ask her myself!' Vicenta went across the street with the dish to ask the woman to give Mama a ride. They lived on a street with a sharp corner, and as Vicenta was walking back, she stepped into the street, and a car came around the corner and mowed her down. Killed her."

I gasped. We were all silent. I felt like I just watched it all happen in front of me.

"Your Grandma lived with that guilt for all of her life," Dad said.

Auntie Emmy was pale. "Oh, my goodness!" she said, shaking her head slowly. "I *never* heard Mama talk about this!"

"No," Mom said. "She didn't *ever* talk about this. Never. Why didn't we ever ask her about it? I never knew how her mother died, or her father, for that matter. I never asked her!"

"Neither did I," Auntie Emmy said.

"It's a heartbreaking story," Mom said. "But I was a married woman with teenagers the first time I heard it."

"Well, I heard it for the first time tonight," Auntie Emmy said.

"Really?" I asked, looking at Auntie Emmy. She seemed deep in thought. She looked at Mom.

"Molly and I regret not asking Mama and Daddy more questions about their background and upbringing," she said.

Mom nodded. She sat back in her chair. "I regret not asking her, too, Emmy."

I didn't say much more at the table that evening. I wondered if Grandma had been able to grieve her mother properly. Did she ever visit her mom's grave? Grandma was always visiting graves, as if it were her right and privilege. She would pull blades of grass away from their headstones, or admire their flowers.

I looked up at my father and mother, sitting next to one another. Dad yawned, and smiled at Mom.

It was getting late.

Part Five: Tortillas

"When you've got nothing else, you'll always have at least a tortilla to get you through."

~Carribean Fragoza, "Tortillas Burning"
Eat the Hand that Feeds You

Flour Tortillas

5 to 6 Cups flour
1 ½ tsp. baking powder
2 tsp. salt
1/3 to ½ cup shortening (Grandma used lard)
warm/hot water

Mix dough in large bowl until soft ball forms. Make small balls of dough about the size of a golf ball. Roll ball flat into a circle, and cook on comal or griddle. Store leftovers in securely closed plastic bag.

13. Fresno or Malaga?

Grandma is here again, watching me type, sitting in the same straight-backed chair in my office. With her arms folded, and legs crossed, she's bobbing one leg. One pink pantufla dangles from her legendary toes. I want to ask, *What the hell, Grandma?* but I remember to treat her with respect.

"Why didn't you tell me about your mom, Grandma?" I ask. "Or about Maria's kidnap?" Grandma uncrosses her arms and folds her hands on her lap. She looks at me.

"I didn't want to talk about it."

"I know it's sad," I say. "But I wish I would have known, because I love you. It would have helped to hear these stories from *you*. I think I knew how much your mom meant to you. She was the most important person in your life, right?"

"Yes," Grandma says. "Her and my sister, Maria. They both liked me a lot." Grandma's expression softens. She's not sad, and I'm sure she can see them both now, just as easily as she can see me. We're quiet for a while. When I realize she's not going to say anything else about it, I sigh and move on.

"Why did you *stay* in the United States?" I ask. "Didn't you want to go back home?"

"After Mama died, my Daddy wanted to go back to Mexico so he can marry again," Grandma says. "I was only fourteen, so I don't know what to do. Cenobio lived in Fresno, with his wife and children, and Maria got married with Monico, and they stayed in Fresno. I didn't want to go back to Mexico with my dad. I said, 'What am I going to do in Mexico?' Daddy said, 'You can marry a man from your own country.' I said, 'I'd rather not!' He asked me, 'Why would you say that?' I just looked at him and said 'Because of the way you used to treat my mom!' He said, 'How did you know about that?' I said, 'Ah, Daddy, you don't think I knew that, did you? But I knew the whole story about you, Dad.' He didn't say nothing to me after that."

Grandma laughs softly and crosses her arms again. "No, he didn't say nothing to me after that. He just went back to Mexico." Still smiling, Grandma is looking straight ahead, as if she's remembering. Suddenly, she turns to me. "There was plenty of work for us here," she says, and makes sweeping gestures with her arms. "The camps were everywhere around Fresno! There was grapes, fruits, lots of orchards, and vineyards. The Mexican workers were all over Fresno, and they need a place to stay. That's why I work for a boarding house."

"That's where you met Grandpa, right? At Cenobio's boarding house in Malaga?"

"No," she says. "I met your grandpa in a boarder house in Fresno, when I was working for my cousin."

"Your cousin?" I ask. I search my desk for my spiral notebook, which holds all my notes. I find it under my water bottle, and flip to the page about the notes in the cup.

"Look," I say. "This says you were working for your brother, Cenobio, in Malaga." When I show Grandma, she smiles.

"I don't know why they told you that," she says, laughing at my nonplussed expression. "¿Ves? I have to tell you what happened, really. I *sure am glad* you found those tapes of me. Now you're gonna know."

Grandma emphasizes each word: *sure am glad*. I sigh and put the spiral notebook back.

"You're right," I say. "Without the recordings, we would be the unreliable narrators of your story. We each heard such different versions, didn't we?" Grandma nods, and pulls her sweater tighter around her.

"Yeah, I *sure am glad* you find those," she says.

14. The Notes Under the Cup

The notes under the cup makes my grandparents' love story as delicious as champurrado, topped with foamy bubbles. We grew up hearing this story from Grandma, Mom, and our aunties, but since her death, Grandma's story got jumbled, and no one told it the same way.

On a visit to Oxnard, I sat with Mario, my mom, and Auntie Terry, with cool drinks, at the Villaseñor picnic table in their backyard.

"So, you want me to tell you about Grandpa and Grandma meeting?" Auntie Terry asked. "Don't you know their story?" She tilted her head to one side. Auntie Terry is our funny Aunt. She loves to make us laugh.

"Okay," Auntie Terry said, leaning forward, as if she were speaking into a microphone. "I'll tell you everything I know." Mom and I laughed, while Auntie Terry found the perfect place to start.

"Mom had a box. Remember, Jennie?" she asked, looking at my mom. Mom nodded, one hand over her mouth. I could tell she was covering a smile, trying not to laugh. "She kept the box under her bed, covered in newspaper, and she never opened it. I never questioned what was in it because I knew it was her secret. She kept it in that dark place, hidden from us."

I looked at Mom to share a giggle, but she was listening carefully to her sister.

"One day, as I was approaching the date of my own wedding," Auntie Terry said. "I decided to ask my mother about that box. 'Mom, since I'm going to get married, can I see your wedding dress?' Instead of answering me, Mama looked at me and made an X over her lips. So, I thought something was wrong."

"She made an X over her mouth?" I asked.

"Yes!" Auntie Terry said. "Like 'Be quiet!' So, that scared me. Why would she do that? I asked her again. 'Don't you want to show me what you have in that box under your bed?' Mama said, 'Okay, you want to see what's in there? Okay.' She took me there. I could tell she was a little angry. Mom got the box from under her bed and put it on a table. Dust came up as she opened it."

Mom couldn't hold it in anymore. She laughed. Auntie Terry was supposed to be telling her version of our grandparents' story, but it was morphing into something else.

"My mom showed it to me," Auntie Terry said. She mimicked Grandma, holding up a dress. "It was a beautiful wedding dress, but it was falling apart. In fact, it was dissolving right before our eyes. It was a 1930's dress..."

"It was like a flapper dress," Mom said. "With a drop-waist."

"Yes," Auntie Terry said. "Mama said, 'Look! Is this what you want to see? This is what happens when you want to get married!' I asked her, 'What happened, Mama?' She told me the story.

"Mama was living in Malaga, working as a kitchen helper, cooking for her brother, Cenobio, and his wife. My dad ended up in that boarding house. Cenobio always made sure his wife and sister never ever spoke with the men. Daddy noticed Mama and he wrote little notes to her. Then somebody would hand them to her...."

Mom leaned forward and touched Auntie Terry's arm. "No, Terry," she said. "Don't you remember? He put them under the cup, remember? That was the best part of the story!"

Auntie Terry looked at Mom. "What?"

"Yeah," Mom said. "Daddy folded the notes first."

Auntie Terry looked impressed that Mom remembered this detail. "Look at you, Jennie!"

Then, Mom sat up straight, as if she were taking the wheel of a car. "Our mom used to tell it this way...."

Among her sisters, Mom is known as the one with the best memory. I found out, through the retelling of this story, this was true. It's nearly word-for-word like Grandma's recording.

***

14-year-old Juana at work. The youngest picture we have of Grandma. 1919

"I was living in Fresno," Grandma said. "I worked at my cousin's boarder house, where there were sixty or seventy men to feed every day. We made flour tortillas *every* day. Fifty pounds! Those darn Mexicans didn't want bread! They didn't like bread. One day, my cousin said, 'Don't make tortillas today! They're going to eat bread whether they like it or not!' They didn't want to eat the bread; they got so used to tortillas.

"I used to make the tortillas and wash dishes. I would start tortillas at two o'clock in the morning, because we used to feed all those people at five o'clock. They had to eat before they go to pick grapes, really early in the morning. I used fifty pounds of flour every day! I make so many tortillas.

"Then, one day, your grandpa comes in. He was a boarder there. Oh! He was a *handsome* man! His eyes used to have long eyelashes, almost up to his eyebrows. Yeah, he used to have big eyes, and eyelashes, and a lot of hair. Not curly-curly, but thick and wavy hair."

The way Grandma told the story, it was like she was seeing young Ignacio, my grandfather, for the first time. Ignacio paid Juana the same attention most young men usually pay a young woman at an all-male boarding house. He saw her for the rare beauty she was. Later, Grandpa told us that Grandma worked harder than any other woman he had seen in this new country. This mutual admiration, combined with the forbidden eye-contact, eventually led to a bold action.

"We couldn't talk," Grandma said. "Cenobio was watching me all the time. One day, as I was cleaning up, and Grandpa asked me, 'Can I have a cup to drink water?' We used to serve drinks in coffee cups with saucers. I say, '¿*Por qué no*?' (Why not?) I took a cup and give it to him, and then watched him. He didn't drink anything, but he put a letter in there, folded up, *real cute*. He gave it back to me and said, 'Here's your cup. Thank you very much.' So, I look under the cup and I take that letter out. I knew I can't read it in the kitchen, so I went to the toilet to read it." Grandma laughed at herself, embarrassed by the fact that her only privacy was in an outhouse.

"The letter he wrote me said, 'I like you. Do you want to be my girlfriend? I really like you since I saw you the first time.' I decided to write back. I say, 'Yeah, I want to be your girlfriend, but I can't go out on dates, because my family is really strict. Don't even talk to me with them around.'

"One day, he came into the kitchen, like he was going to get something," Grandma said. "He came closer to me and said, 'I'm leaving tomorrow to go pick cotton at another camp.'" Grandma laughed. "So, we decided to go get married.'"

Grandma used to tell us the story of her elopement like it was love at first sight. In her mind, Cenobio didn't consent to their union, so she had to sneak out of the boarding house and run off with Grandpa to be married. To hear Grandma tell it, the romance was palpable.

The truth is less romantic. After Grandpa's awkward proposal, Grandpa and Grandma went to the Fresno courthouse, on Monday August 13, 1928. Grandma didn't consider this an official wedding, even when the county recorder issued their marriage certificate. In Grandma's mind, the license was only a document that gave Grandpa permission to marry her in a Catholic church so the priest would know they had no other legal attachments. The license, issued at the peak of cotton season, was given to Grandpa just before he left for Lone Pine, to pick cotton.

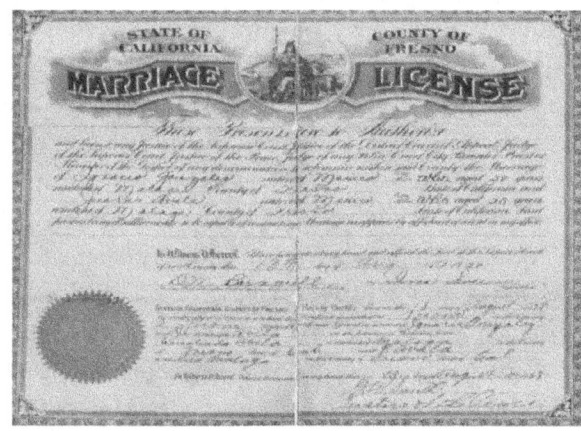
Grandpa and Grandma's Marriage Certificate, dated August 13, 1928

Of course, Grandma's brother, Cenobio, found out about their clandestine relationship. According to Grandma, Cenobio was determined to block the *real wedding*, in the Catholic church, with a priest performing the Sacrament.

"My brother, Cenobio, didn't like Grandpa," Grandma said. "When I was getting ready to get married in the Catholic Church, Cenobio said to me, 'Why are you getting married to that man? You don't even know him!' I said, 'I don't care. I can tell he's a good man. He's a hardworking man, and that's why I like him.' Cenobio wouldn't stop saying, 'You don't even know him a year.'

"I said, 'I don't need too much time to know him. I like him. He's a good, hard-working man.' This made Cenobio angry. He knew I wasn't going to listen to him. The same week I was supposed to get married, he told me to pack a bag and get ready to pick cotton. Every year, we go to pick cotton in Visalia, but I didn't want to go. I told Cenobio, 'I'm going to stay with my cousin, right here in Fresno, because I'm getting married this Sunday.' Cenobio didn't let me. He told me, 'No. You have to come with us.'"

At this time, Grandma was twenty-one years old, certainly of the age where she could make up her own mind. As a traditional girl, living in a patriarchal society, however, Cenobio had the final say, just like her father. Everyone around her would have listened to him over Juana—even the cousin who employed her.

"I asked Cenobio, 'Who's going to bring me back to get married on Sunday?'" Grandma said. "He said, 'I'll bring you back on Sunday,' but I didn't believe him. I knew he was lying. I said, 'Are you going to drive all the way back here, with the whole family? My sister-in-law and your kids, too?' Cenobio says, 'You never mind about the family. I'll bring you.' So, I went with them.

"When it was Friday, I ask Cenobio to drive me back home. I had my dress, my veil, my shoes, everything! Cenobio said, 'Later, later.' He didn't take me back that day. The next day, on Saturday. I said, 'You said you were going to take me back to Fresno!' He said, 'I'll take you tomorrow morning.' I said, 'I'm not going to have enough time to dress myself and get ready for the wedding.' He said, 'You will. I'll take you early.' Early on Sunday morning, I said, 'Cenobio! It's time for me to go!' He said, 'Don't worry, I'll be right back.' I said, 'You're going to pick cotton first? Then you're going to take me?' He said, 'I'll be right back. I just want to drop off my wife and kids and let them start picking.' He never came back. He didn't take me." Grandma's voice got very quiet, still reeling from disappointment and betrayal.

"I started crying," Grandma said. "My sister-in-law, Cenobio's wife, came over to me and said, 'Don't cry, Juanita.' I said, 'Don't you think I have a good reason to cry? He should take me yesterday, not today! He didn't take me. Everything was made, the food, and everything was ready. He didn't take me.' I was crying and crying. Another lady heard me and came over. She whispered to me, 'Don't cry, Juanita! My husband is going to Malaga today. Do you want to send Ignacio a message?' I said, "Yes." I hurried up and wrote to Ignacio and told him what happened. I wrote down the name of our camp and gave a mail box address to write back. So, that lady gave the letter to her husband. He took it to Malaga.

"Once Grandpa found out what happened, he started looking for me. He went to Visalia to see where we were, but he couldn't find us. He didn't know which camp where we were staying, and didn't find that camp. Grandpa was looking for me for a whole week he. He finally gave up and went back to Lone Pine, where he was picking cotton. He was so mad that he left.

"From Lone Pine, Grandpa wrote me a letter. He said, 'If you still want to get married, go over to your cousin's and I will pick you up from your cousin's.' I went to Cenobio, crying. I told him, 'If you're not going to take me to our cousin's, I'll look for somebody else to take me.' Cenobio said, 'Okay, if you are gonna do this no matter what, I'll take you.'

"He took me to my cousin's place. Grandpa had left them money to put me on the train to Lone Pine. They took me to the train station, I said goodbye, and I got on the train."

Grandma had not been on a train since she came to this country, from Mexico. Back then, she was with her family. The journey from Fresno to Lone Pine took nine hours by train back then, with stops. Even at twenty-one years old, Grandma looked more like a sixteen-year-old, and wasn't used to being by herself, let alone on a train. She had never been to Lone Pine, and had nothing more than a train ticket, with "Lone Pine" written on the top. As she told the story, she laughed at her innocence.

"It was the first time I traveled all by myself. Oh! I was so nervous, I was shaking! I thought, *What if I'm going to get lost?* I asked the people next to me, 'Where are you going?' They said, 'Lone Pine. Why?' I was so relieved. I said, 'That's where I'm going, too.' When the train pulled into the Lone Pine station, I got off. There was no town, no nothing. I saw all these people who were meeting their parents or relatives, hugging them. I looked around for Ignacio and I couldn't see him. I thought, *What shall I do? What shall I do?* There was nothing but fields all around. *What shall I do? Where am I going to go?* And I started shaking again, because I don't see your Grandpa."

Juana searched the surrounding fields for any sign of Grandpa. The panic of displacement overwhelmed her. She had a small suitcase, and was dressed for travel, but felt like a child. She saw the woman who sat next to her on the train, and asked her a question.

Lone Pine Train Station, 1918

"I asked this lady, 'Where is the town?' She answered me, 'Oh, the town is two miles from here.' I thought to myself, *Oh my Lord! How can I walk two miles?*

"Then, I saw Grandpa! He was with one of his friends, and they were walking toward me. Oh! My head came back to my body again. As soon as he was close to me, I said, 'Where were you? All the people had relatives here, waiting for them....' Grandpa said, 'I wasn't too sure that you was going to come.' I said, 'You should be here anyway! I got real nervous. Look at my hands! I'm perspiring. I was so worried!' Grandpa was quiet, but he said, "Well, I wasn't so sure that you were going to be here. That's why I didn't get closer.' Oh! I said, 'Oh well, I'm here now! Let's go!' And so, we went to the camp where he was working."

As if the train ride were not enough of a traumatic experience, Grandma went straight to the work camp, with her little suitcase and her box of wedding clothes. It was the same box she would later show to Auntie Terry, years later. In it, her wedding dress, veil, and shoes were packed, ready to be worn. They never were. Grandpa and Grandma were later married by a priest in their Sunday clothes, after church one Sunday. The next few years would contain the bleak reality of marriage, to match Lone Pine's stark landscape.

15. Lone Pine

Lone Pine, the place where Grandma first lived with Grandpa, is situated in the Owens Valley, between the rugged Sierra Nevada Mountains on one side and the Inyo Mountains on the other. It's still considered a frontier. The echoing canyon used to have a massive pine tree guarding its entrance, hence the name Lone Pine. The windswept, dry landscape provided the perfect climate for growing the country's new cash crop. When Grandma first arrived in Lone Pine, in 1928, it was a sea of cotton, as far as she could see. Most farm laborers were Braceros, recruited from Mexico, but many Filipinos were living and working there as well. Slavery had been abolished, but cotton picking was the closest thing to it. Braceros worked long hours, for very low wages, and were given substandard accommodations. In his book, *North from Mexico*, Carey McWilliams documents the economic politics of cotton growers in California:

> Commanding a premium price, with a yield-per-acre twice the national average, cotton soon became a $40,000,000 crop in California. Largely produced on high-priced irrigated lands which had been capitalized on the basis of cheap labor, the expansion of cotton in California was premised upon the availability of a large supply of low-cost labor exclusively earmarked for cotton growers.[4]

Despite the huge profit margin, living conditions were terrible for cotton pickers. The typical laborer was a single male, between the ages of eighteen

---

[4] McWilliams Carey, *North From Mexico: The Spanish-Speaking People of the United States* (New Edition, Updated by Matt S. Meier, Westport: Praeger Publishers, 1990), 161.

and forty. They slept in wooden barracks, or bunkhouses, hastily constructed by speculators, most without proper ventilation. Camp managers leased workers with families the cottages across from the bunkhouses: boxy, one-room cabins with the same shoddy construction. The family units at least had access to better water taps and ablutions: one outhouse to two cabins, compared to one outhouse per bunkhouse.

The cottages and bunkhouses were separated by a common area, with picnic tables for the workforce to eat. After a day of grueling work in the sun, groups of men gathered to play music, or cards. Workers shared campfires, and talked into the night. The threat of violence was always lurking, just beneath the surface. Some less-scrupulous workers would gaze at the wives in the cottages, remembering the women they left behind. This is the environment where Grandma found herself, without friends or family for the first time in her life. She had been raised in poverty, but always had family around her. These rustic conditions were a shock.

"When we get to Lone Pine, Ignacio brought me to the cabin," Grandma said. "We had no bed, but Ignacio had bought a mattress, so the first night, we sleep on the floor. The house had no stove, no sink, no place to cook. Ignacio only had one frying pan, two little pots, and a coffee pot. He told me, 'I'll take you to go shopping for dishes, because I don't know what you need. I haven't got a car, but I can rent one, or somebody can take us to town.'

"I say, 'What I really need is a big pan to make the masa for the tortillas, and another pot to cook beans, and a camping stove.' So, Grandpa asked the boss if he could borrow a truck. The boss let him take a pickup truck. So, he took me shopping." Grandma laughs at the memory.

"We go to the fifteen-cents store, and I bought a few things. Spatulas, two more pots, a washing board, two tubs—one to wash and another to rinse—until Grandpa stopped me. He said, 'I haven't got much money, and we don't have credit here.' I said, 'Tell me when to stop, because I sure need these things.' He watched me shop, and then he said, 'Alright, that's it. You can stop buying.' So, we bought things, little by little."

Grandma laughed again, amused by their humble beginnings. All her life, Grandma learned how to live with very little, but as a new wife to Grandpa, she had to buy the same things she had always used.

"The next morning, we woke up," Grandma said. "Grandpa and I were on the floor, sleeping on the mattress. He said, 'I'll go ask the boss if we can have an old bed, because I can't afford to buy a new one.' His boss told him,

'Sure. There's two extra beds in the bunkhouse.' So, Ignacio brought one back. It was an old iron bed. It had a big arc.

"Grandpa asked, 'How do you like the bed?' I told him that I liked it, because I didn't want to sleep on the floor again. We put the mattress on it, which was kind of small for the frame. I said, 'That's alright, I'll cover it with… wait, we need sheets, we need bedspreads, we need pillows.' He said, 'Oh my gosh! I'm going to have to borrow money from friends. All my money is gone.' He borrowed money from friends, and bought two pillows, one sheet, one blanket, and one bedspread."

Grandma chuckled at the reality of how little they had. She had expected Grandpa to have the nest built, and ready for her. Instead, Grandma built the nest, and Grandpa paid for it.

"I used to wash our sheets and towels every week, and hang them out, then put them back on, right after they was dry. I had to do it, because we didn't have extras. Grandpa bought three towels—one little one and two big ones. He said, 'I can't afford more sheets this time, but maybe next payday.'

"I used to make pillows and slips from flour sacks, the cloth kind that held fifty pounds of flour. The size of that bag was just enough for a pillow, and I crocheted a border for the pillow slip to make it look better."

Grandma tried her best to accept her new place. She tried to cook good food. She tried to be pleasant to her new husband. She tried to be happy, but Lone Pine was just like it sounded: lonely. She didn't expect her new husband to wander over to the common area after supper, but he did.

Grandpa played the guitar. He was learning to play in a group, with other men who worked the fields. Together, they sang rancheros, the traditional Mexican music knew and loved from his home country. After work, he would come home, eat, and go back to the common area to practice with the band. Soon, they were asked to play music for traditional Mexican parties, in town. Soon, Grandpa's band played for weddings, dances, quinceañeras, and celebrations of life.

Before long, Grandma was pregnant with my Uncle Frank. After Frank came Teresa. Grandpa continued playing with his band in town, with his friends, in a bar that featured traditional music. Soon after Teresa, Grandma became pregnant again, with my Uncle Smiley.

"Ignacio left me all alone at night," Grandma said. "He was off playing music with the mans. I could hear coyotes howling, in the hills, and the wind would blow. Oh, I was scared of being alone in that place!"

For Grandma, Lone Pine's only saving grace was its Post Office. Getting a letter from her sister could make Grandma's week. The correspondence mattered to both sisters. Maria worried about Juana, especially when Grandma described what life was like for her in Lone Pine. Maria urged Grandma to send her a picture. *Have Ignacio take you to town and get a picture taken.*

Grandma, holding Teresa, and Grandpa, holding Francisco. Grandma is pregnant with their third child, Ismael, here.

Grandpa thought this was a great idea. He was handsome, his wife was robust and pregnant, and his two children were more beautiful than any other—the photographer even said. In many ways, this was the happiest time of Grandpa's life—you can see it on his face. He was playing music, raising a family, working steadily. Life was everything it should be.

Auntie Lucy, looking at the picture many years later, smiled broadly. She leaned closer to me.

"Look at them," she said, tilting her head to the side. "Look at Grandma's cute shoes! Look at your grandfather's hair. Don't they look like they have money?"

Part Six: Chili de Puerco

"The changes in women's lives affected gender relations. Women living without men, and women who entered the labor market had more physical freedom and increased access to economic resources... changing images of women in the United States influenced Mexican women..."

~Devra Weber
Dark Sweat, White Gold: California Farm Workers, Cotton, and the New Deal

---

Chili de Puerco (red)

4 lbs pork, cut up into cubes
1 onion, cut in half twice
1 onion chopped fine (about a cup)
12 garlic cloves (4 of them cut up in dice)
4 ancho peppers
2 guajillo peppers
2 arbol peppers
2 red, small peppers (if you want hot salsa)
9 tomatoes, cut in quarters
1 can tomato paste
1 bay leaf
1 boiling cube (boullion)
chili powder, cumino and oregano to your taste

Hydrate the peppers if they're dry: remove stems and seeds, soak in hot water for a little bit. If you have fresh peppers, remove stem and seeds and then chop finely.

Fry the pork in a little bit of oil, on high heat until browned, adding salt and pepper as you turn it. After about ten minutes, add the onion, 4 cloves of garlic. Stir around for a while, then pour enough water to cover the pork meat. Add boiling cube and bay leaf. Bring to a boil, and then sir around. Turn it down to simmer. Put in ancho peppers and chili powder, to your taste. Cook on low heat like this for 1 hour, until puerco is tender.

While the meat is cooking, make the salsa in a saucepan. Fry the tomatoes and chopped onion in oil. When the onions look a little clear, add tomato paste and a little bit of water (half cup). When the sauce makes a boil, turn down and add cumino and oregano. The sauce will look chunky at first, but it will get added to the Puerco juice, so don't worry. Bring to a boil and cook for 10 minutes. Add 4 diced up garlic cloves, the guajillo and arbol peppers and turn the heat off.

Take the ancho peppers out of the simmering pork. Put them into the salsa in the saucepan, with about a ½ cup of the juice from the pork. Pour salsa into blender. Blend a little bit, but be careful—it might jump up, because it's hot. Stop and taste. It might need salt. Add the rest of the salsa into the blender, then blend again.

Strain and reserve pork juice/broth. Return the pork meat to dry pot, and fry again, if you want (in about 3 tablespoons of oil). Stir in the blended salsa and enough of the pork juice/broth to cover meat. Bring to a boil. Season with salt to taste. Cover and reduce the heat to low. Simmer for 1/2 hour.

You can serve in bowls or on plate, with flour or corn tortillas. This is good if you have cousins coming over and they don't eat at the same time. They can always help themselves.

16. Malaga, California

California's San Joaquin Valley is about two hundred and fifty miles long, stretching from southern California's grapevine to the grape vineyards above Lodi. Its exceptionally fertile soil enjoys the temporal climate of California, and the protection of its Sierra Nevada and Coastal Mountain ranges. Fresno is located near the center of the San Joaquin, in what's commonly referred to as its Central Valley. At the beginning of the 1930's, the fields and orchards in the Central Valley supplied the country with wine, grapes, nuts, dried fruits and most green vegetables. The agricultural workforce that tended and harvested what the rest of the country ate was mostly migratory, moving with the harvests. When in the Central Valley, Mexican Braceros stayed in boarding houses run by Mexican Americans, where they could communicate with each other in Spanish and eat real home cooking. Boarding houses also proved to be one of the steadiest places for employment in the Central Valley in the 1930's. Working in one had drawbacks, however. To keep a boarding house running, meant working long hours, starting before sunrise and quitting after dark. Grandma's brother, Cenobio, still worked for his cousin at her boarding house, which provided housing for his family. Like Grandpa, he supplemented his income by working the cotton harvests, but the boarding house gave him the opportunity to stay in one place and enroll his children in school.

Tía Maria, now married to Monico, understood the potential of owning her own place. They decided to buy property in Malaga, six miles southeast of downtown Fresno.

"Somebody told Dad about Malaga," Esther said. "He took Mom to go see it, and she said, 'This is where we're going to build our home.'

"They bought a little house there, and Mom started running a boarding house." Esther said. "My mom didn't have any education, but she knew how to get things done. She was always thinking, 'There must be another way to do things, to make money the right way.' Everybody just loved her food, and she loved cooking. Once people tasted her food, they had to come back for more. That's how the business grew—word of mouth.

"Mom got up every morning and made tortillas. She got everything ready for the boarders to eat breakfast before they went out to work in the fields. She would prepare fried potatoes, eggs, bacon, beans—she always had beans going—and set the tables with coffee and sugar. Early very morning she would do this.

"At lunch time, Mom would take food to the borders who paid for lunch," Esther said. "She would prepare Chili de Puerco, or another good dish for them. Mom never learned how to drive, so Dad would come and pick her up, and drive her to the work location. She would pass out dishes to the boarders—back then, there were no paper plates—and then served them. The workers ate their food in the shade, and when they were finished, they would give her back the dishes. Mom would come home, wash the dishes, and start getting ready for dinner. When the boarders came back, she would serve dinner to them. It was hard work, but Mom loved it."

The whole Ruiz family got involved in running the boarding house. It didn't take long for Maria to start turning a profit. She saved any extra money to upgrade their property, putting extra houses on it for her extended family. Soon, even Cenobio and his family were staying at the Malaga complex.

"Mom was a very good negotiator," Esther said. "She knew how to get things done. Eventually, she bought ten acres in Malaga, near the boarding house. There were already three small homes on the ten-acre property. Mom bought two other little houses and moved them there. She fixed the houses up, and started renting them to people who needed a safe place to stay." Esther laughed a little. "Sometimes her renters couldn't pay her. Sometimes they could. Things were hard in those days, and people needed a decent place to stay.

"After she had those five houses, Mom hired some people to build other little houses on the property. She built a house for Pancho, her brother, for Jose Ruiz, my dad's brother, and then mi Tío Pedro, next door. She even built one for Tía Juana and her family."

It was Tía Maria's dream for her family to live close together again. She wanted to experience the community they once had in Mexico. The United States had a way of separating families. Working long hours, traveling with the harvests, and staying in company housing, made it even worse. The moment she and Tío Monico bought ten acres of land, she crossed a threshold into hope. Now, everybody could live closer together.

"These houses weren't mansions," Esther said. "They were little, but Mom owned them, which changed things. Our house, the one Mom and Dad bought in Malaga, had three bedrooms. After

we had been there awhile, my mother added a bigger living room in the front of the house. She would conduct business meetings there, to meet with people in that room.

"Everybody thought that Mom was the lady with the money," Esther said, laughing again. "But Mom was too generous! As soon as she had any money, she gave it away, or used it to help family or friends. Mom's fortune was found in her family and friends."

I thought a lot about Esther's synopsis of her mother. Depending on the people I interviewed, Maria was either generous and helpful or she was controlling. She was either strong and competent, or pushy and forceful. Maria represented the changing roles for women, all across cultures. In the patriarchal Mexican culture, a woman taking the lead was not necessarily a good thing. Maria didn't seem to care what people thought. She was a woman who swam the Rio Grande with a baby strapped to her back—and it only made sense that she had crossed over even greater divides. She went from renter to property owner, and from employee to employer. With power moves like this, Maria was a force to be reckoned with.

According to Esther, Maria was first and foremost a family woman. She knew her sister, Juana, wasn't happy in Lone Pine. In her letters, Maria told Juana about the changes in Malaga. She explained the plentiful jobs for Nacho, all over the Fresno area. She described the little houses she was building on their property. She promised to keep one vacant for Juana's family.

Both sisters longed to live close together, but they also knew Ignacio was a traditional Mexican man. It would have to be *his* idea to move to Central California. Nacho would have to be the person to make the decision to move his family to Malaga. *He* led his family.

Maria and Juana were practical. Short of an act of God, they would have

to wait for Ignacio to decide Malaga was a good idea.
    It didn't take long.

17. The Time

The Great Depression was the worst economic downturn in the history of the industrialized world, lasting from 1929 to 1939. It began with the stock market crash, on October 24, 1929, which caused consumer panic. Over the next several years, consumer spending and investment dropped, causing steep declines in industrial output and employment as failing companies laid off workers. By 1933, when the Great Depression reached its lowest point, some 15 million Americans were unemployed, and nearly half the country's banks had failed.

In 1933, Lone Pine, like most towns in the United States, faced economic uncertainty. Moreover, a greater scarcity threatened its economy: water. Lone Pine, located in the Owens Valley, had endured years of court proceedings and injunctions over water rights. They had just lost a long legal battle to keep its own water resources. Despite strong objection from ranchers and farmers, the California Aqueduct diverted the valley's water to the ever-thirsty, ever-growing metropolis of Los Angeles. Lone Pine's residents felt the sting. The hardware store, a grocery store, dry goods, and several watering holes, which served the mostly-male workforce, were precariously alive, but watchful. Local merchants extended credit to the working class, but only for basic food items. As farmers and ranchers faced a future with no water, land values plummeted, and leaving their farms seemed impossible.

For the first time, unemployed US Citizens were actually considering the back-bending work of miners and agricultural laborers. The Dust Bowl brought a flood of white farmers, mainly from Oklahoma and Arkansas, looking for work in the fields. California's labor force, previously only Filipino and Mexican-Americans, were suddenly in danger.

The Great Depression provided the economic conditions necessary for nativism to thrive. Suddenly, white citizens were accusing Mexican and Filipino laborers of stealing American jobs. Most laborers had been picking cotton in the valley for years. Most were unprepared for the sudden hostility of their neighbors. Lone Pine wasn't the only place looking to "send Mexicans back" to their homeland. In their seminal book, *Decade of Betrayal*, authors Francisco E. Balderrama and Raymond Rodríguez explain the climate of the 1930's:

> Americans, reeling from the economic disorientation of the depression, sought a convenient scapegoat. They found it in the Mexican Community. In a frenzy of anti-American hysteria, wholesale punitive measures were proposed and undertaken by government officials at the federal, state, and local levels. Laws were passed depriving Mexicans of jobs in the public and private sectors. Immigration and deportation laws were enacted to restrict emigration and hasten the departure of those already here. Contributing to the brutalizing experience were the mass deportation roundups and repatriation drives. Violence and 'scare-head' tactics were utilized to get rid of the burdensome and unwanted horde. An incessant cry of "get rid of the Mexicans" swept the country. [5]

Grandpa and Grandma realized the sudden hostility directed at their community. They weren't sure what to do. Grandpa's lifestyle of working hard and making music was suddenly gone. A new climate of nativism threatened his family's safety. Even fellow Mexican braceros, hoping to make enough money to survive, joined other laborers in an organized cotton strike that turned violent. In her book, *Dark Sweat, White Gold*, Devra Weber describes this:

> In September of 1933, over 18,000 cotton pickers associated with the Cannery and Agricultural Workers Industrial Union (CAWIU) went on strike. The strike marked the culmination of a wave of thirty-seven agricultural strikes in California that affected 65 percent of the state's crops. Seventy-five to ninety-five percent of the cotton strikers were Mexicans...Attempting to stop further strikes, the Los

---

[5] Balderrama, F. E., & Rodriguez, R. (2006). *Decade of betrayal: Mexican repatriation in the 1930s*. University of New Mexico Albuquerque.

Angeles Chamber of Commerce tried to deport strikers, or convince them to repatriate voluntarily to Mexico.[6]

Crossing the picket line was dangerous. Some undocumented workers entered the fields via the boss's truck, conveniently parked behind the bunkhouse every morning. This practice was discovered by the strikers, who reportedly fired shots. Grandma remembered this violence clearly.

"In those times Lone Pine was awful," Grandma said. "They were shooting at each other! I was expecting a baby, and we had three little kids. Grandpa said, 'You know what? I'm going to send you to Fresno to live with your sister. This isn't a good place for you right now. You might lose the baby.' I packed two suitcases, one for the kids and one for me, and then Grandpa take us into town."

Grandpa put his wife and three small children on a passenger train, bound for Fresno. Grandma, pregnant with my Auntie Lucy, cried all the way to the station, filled with anxiety about leaving her husband. Despite her recent feelings of abandonment, she loved Grandpa. She remembered the train ride to Fresno vividly.

"I was crying and crying," Grandma said. "Frank asked me, 'Mama why are you crying?' I said, 'Because I'm happy to go see my sister.'" Grandma laughed at this. "I wasn't happy. I just said that so he wouldn't worry. The kids kept asking, 'When are we gonna get to Auntie's?' I say, 'Pretty soon.' Grandpa put us on the train at about nine o'clock in the morning and we didn't get to Fresno until two or three o'clock in the afternoon."

Tío Monico and Tía Maria were there as the train pulled into the station.

"Oh! My sister was so happy to see me!" Grandma said. She clapped her hands together and sighed. "We all moved into her house, and stayed with her until the strike was over. Lucy was born in her house."

Grandma named her baby girl Luz Maria, after the Nativity of the Blessed Virgin Mary, the Catholic Saint whose feast day was on the calendar for September 8th, even though Auntie Lucy was born on September 9th. Maybe Grandma felt that Luz Maria was a perfect name for her baby, because it mirrored the name of her Godmother, Tía Maria. Maybe she just got the date wrong.

---

6 Weber, Devra. *Dark Sweat, White Gold: California Farm Workers, Cotton, and the New Deal*, University of California Press, Berkeley, 1996.

"Grandpa wrote to me," Grandma said. "Grandpa said, 'The strike is over. I'm coming to Fresno.' Oh, I was so happy he was coming to Malaga!"

Grandpa remembered his last days in Lone Pine. "They came to all of us," he said, possibly referring to local law enforcement, hired to enforce new policy. "They told us, 'Everyone from here to the line—back to Mexico!' I didn't want to stay there [in Lone Pine] at that time, so we moved north." Grandpa laughed when he said this, even though the subject wasn't pleasant.

Grandpa arrived at the Fresno train station in October of 1933, greeted by his wife, Juana, his children, and his baby daughter, Luz Maria. Tío Monico drove them all to the Malaga property, where Tía Maria showed Grandpa the place that had been set up for his family.

Grandpa moved his family into the small house, but secretly questioned Maria's generosity and strong personality. *Who was this woman? His wife's sister? Why was she flaunting this wealth in front of him, making him look like less of a man to his family?*

***

Esther Lango, Tía Maria's daughter, explained the layout of the Malaga complex.

"Next door to our house lived mi Tío Pedro," she said. "Pedro Ruiz, one of my father's brothers. Across the street from him, a family named Vargas lived. They were somehow related to my mom, but I don't know how. At the corner of our street was my Tío Jose's house. This was another one of my dad's brothers, and he lived there with his family. Their son, Phil, was the same age as me and your mom. Tío Pancho and his family lived right across the street from us, Mom's brother, Pancho Avila. Their daughter, Nellie, was also our age. Tío Pancho had a yard with a little pasture, and an old cow used to graze there. Through that pasture was our little shortcut to the Gonzalez house, where your mom's family lived. Mama always took the shortcut through Tío Pancho's pasture to get to the Gonzalez house, but I didn't like doing this when I was by myself. I was afraid of Tío Pancho's cow!" Esther laughed at this memory. "That cow was crazy! If I was by myself, I'd go the long way around, using the alley." Esther couldn't stop laughing. I imagined her as a girl, trying to outrun the cow.

To Grandma, living in Malaga was heaven on earth. She was surrounded by her family. Grandpa was with her, and her children, in the same house. Her beloved sister lived only a few yards away. There were plenty of cousins for her kids to play with. Grandma wasn't suffering isolation, like she had in

Lone Pine.

By comparison, the time in Malaga was hard for Grandpa. The only job he could find was trimming grapevines for a private vintner. Grandpa was given responsibility in the vineyard, but significantly less money than he made harvesting cotton in Lone Pine. Grandpa was paid in cash, but his wages were much less than what he needed to feed his family. He felt unappreciated and unrecognized, as a farmer and a man. Seeing Grandma's sister, Maria, become a successful businesswoman, made it worse. Grandpa supplemented the family income by working cotton harvests in the central valley. The work was familiar, and took him away from Malaga, where his sister-in-law was. He'd often take his sons, Francisco and Ismael, once they were old enough.

"They worked hard with me," Grandpa said. "The men in the fields called them 'los motorcitos' (the little motors)." He laughed when he said this. Grandpa taught Uncle Frank and Smiley how to work hard, from an early age. For the rest of their lives, they would work physical jobs with or for Grandpa. Whether it was the fields, around the house, or doing odd jobs, Grandpa discouraged idleness. Still, when Grandpa remembered the Great Depression, his tone changed.

"We suffered too much at that time," he said. "Everything was *hard*. It was really *hard* to make any money. We suffered much because we worked long hours for such little pay." Grandpa paused to think about this, then added his favorite saying: "But hard work never killed anybody."

Hard work never killed anybody. Grandpa always said this. He believed it. He never complained about work, especially when it came to the earth. It wasn't until much later that I realized how the hard work affected my grandfather's body. By the time he reached his sixties, Grandpa walked carefully, slightly stooped. His gnarled hands showed everyone how hard he had always worked. I recently read a medical study that proved farm laborers have an average life expectancy of 49 years, compared to the 77.2 years, for most men in the U.S. Agricultural workers face a higher disease burden than any other population, since they work in occupations with high hazard levels. In addition, their lower socioeconomic levels affect the way they feed their families, and their access to healthcare services.[7] In the 1930's, in addition to everything else, any field boss could threaten a laborer with deportation if they were late, sick, or didn't meet quota.

---

[7] Win, Aung. "The migrant worker: visible, yet invisible." *BMJ case reports* vol. 2015: bcr2014208484. 22 Jan. 2015, doi:10.1136/bcr-2014-208484

This combination was enough to wear even the strongest man down.

18. The Babies

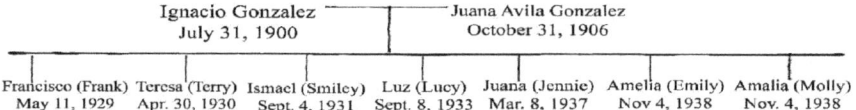

On March 8, 1937, my mother, Jennie, was born at home in Malaga, with the help of a midwife. The fifth of her parents' seven children, there are no known pictures of Mom as a baby, or as a toddler. A year and a half after Mom's birth, in November of 1938, Grandma gave birth to twins, Emily and Molly. Twins were a rarity, and drew attention from far and wide—friends, family, and strangers. People visited Juana and her twins, bringing cameras to take pictures of them. No one thought to take pictures of the other baby, just twenty months older than her twin sisters.

In 2018, on a sunny afternoon, I sat with Mom and her twin sisters, Emily and Molly, at the umbrella table in my parents' park-like backyard. We discussed birth order in a big family.

"One of my first memories is when we were in a school play together," Mom said, waving her hand across the table at her sisters. "I must have been in the first or second grade, and the twins were always one grade behind me. We were dressed in our costumes, little dresses made out of crepe paper. After the play, we were walking home, and people stopped us, just to admire the twins. They said to Grandma, 'Oh my goodness, Señora, are these twins?' She said, 'Yes, they are.' The people would 'Ooooh!' and 'Ahhh!'" Mom smiled, and demonstrated their gestures of approval. Suddenly, she let her shoulders fall. "Oh, my goodness! I felt so overlooked! I was standing there, thinking, 'Hey, somebody look at me. Isn't anyone going to notice me? Don't I look cute in *my* crepe paper dress?'"

My aunts, Molly and Emmy, broke into sympathetic groans.

"Oh no! Poor Jennie!"

"I'll always remember that feeling," Mom said. "So, whenever someone has twins or multiple births, I make a point to pay as much attention to all the other kids in that family. *All* children need to be noticed."

"To me, the saddest thing is the pictures," I said, touching Mom's arm. "There are no baby pictures of you."

"It is sad, isn't it?" Mom said. "There's a baby picture of all my siblings, but not *one* of me as a baby. I always asked Mama, 'I'd love to see what I looked like as a baby, how come there are no pictures of me? Why do all my brothers and sisters have baby pictures, and there are none of me.' She said, 'I don't know, mija, I can't remember. Probably there was no camera or no photographer who came to the house.' That was it. That was Mama's explanation."

"None?" Auntie Molly asked. "Are you sure?"

"Yes," Mom said, smiling, but firm. "Don't you think I'd know?"

"Even Lucy had a baby picture," Auntie Emmy said. "She was sitting on a big chair."

"The youngest picture we have of Mom is with you two," I said, nodding at my twin aunts.

Amalia (Molly) Juanita (Jennie) and Amelia (Emily)

The sisters continued to discuss the subject of family pictures, and the exorbitant costs associated with them. To have a picture, you needed a camera, an unnecessary expense, and the camera needed film, another expense, and to develop the film, more money. I watched Mom, using a different lens. My beautiful mother felt invisible as a child. *All children need to be noticed*, she said.

I could relate to Mom's feelings of invisibility. I was born second in our family, thirteen months after my sister, Patty. My birthday was three days after Christmas, and three days before New Year's Eve, which didn't help things. I was always longing for attention, longing to be noticed, longing to feel significant. This longing has never really left me, and even as an adult, I can feel invisible. Unlike Mom, I have baby pictures. Most of my baby pictures have Patty in them. Baby Janet, with a smiling Patty over her shoulder. Baby Janet in her walker, with Patty behind her. Patty and baby Janet on the couch.

Growing up, I would often ask Mom about this. "Where are all of *my* baby pictures? Didn't you want pictures of my face, like all these of Patty?" Mom would only shrug.

"I don't know, mija," she'd say. "I think there are plenty of pictures of you."

I now understand why Mom didn't seem concerned. There were more than a dozen baby pictures of me. There were no baby pictures of her—not one.

***

In March of 1937, when Mom was born, Malaga was a poor, farming community. Most agricultural laborers had families, and most were still trying to recover from the Great Depression. The Central Valley was suddenly flooded with people coming from states hardest hit by the Dust Bowl. People around Malaga looked like subjects in a Dorothea Lange photograph.

Most Braceros lived in temporary housing, and had families back in Mexico. Tía Maria's boarding house was always full. Most of their wages went to her.

Mom's family was comparatively lucky. They were together. They lived in a house of their own, one that Tía Maria saved for them. It was a two-room, small place with no electricity or plumbing. They drew their water from a pump outside, and used an outhouse. The conditions were poor, but the family tried to stay positive. Aunt Lucy, two and a half years older than Mom, remembered life in Malaga as very simple.

"We had a little house, shaped like a box," Auntie Lucy said. "It had one bedroom, with three beds, which we shared."

"Where did Grandma and Grandpa sleep?" I asked.

"Oh," Auntie Lucy looked at me like I hadn't understood. "They had their own room." "I thought it was a one-bedroom house," I said.

"It *was* a one-room house," Mom said, offering more detail. "When you walked in, there was a kitchen, where we ate. The rest of the house was one large room, where we all slept. One year, Daddy decided he was going to build a private area for himself and Mama, so he was sawing and hammering for a long time until he finished that project." Mom laughed. "We put up with that noise for a long time, I remember."

"Their bedroom had a door," Auntie Lucy said. "They kept it closed when they were in there. Next to their bedroom was our 'living room.'" Auntie Lucy made air quotes when she said this, and laughed. "Our living room was just a little space, with one of those roaring oil heaters. It wasn't good if that oil heater wasn't lit."

Grandma was grateful for their home, and even after having five children, she didn't want much more. In the Mexican tradition, family closeness was a blessing. Like most Mexican women who had immigrated to the United States, the new world challenged these old traditions. Even her sister, Maria, had a home that separated her children into different rooms. Grandma held firm to the old customs, including pregnancy and delivery of her babies. Every one of Grandma's children was delivered at home, with the help of a midwife—until her last two, her twins.

"I knew something was different with the pregnancy," Grandma said. "I felt something building up inside of me. I used to make the kids get out of the house, 'Okay, go play! Go outside!' I would go to my room, and scream into my pillow. My feets and hands were swelling up, like balloons.

"One day, Grandpa said, 'I'm gonna take you to the doctor, in town.' There was a doctor in Fresno who used to see pregnant Mexican women for free. Grandpa took me there and the doctor examined me. He was getting mad, and he wasn't talking." Grandma mimicked the doctor, who paced back and forth, shaking his head. "I couldn't stand it anymore," Grandma said. "I asked him, 'What's wrong with me?' He said, 'You want to know what's wrong? You're gonna die!'" Grandma mimicked the doctor's disgusted voice: "'You *Mexican* women! You never see the doctor, and have your babies at home. Now you're gonna die! What do you think about that?'

"Grandpa told him, 'We're gonna have to do something about that. What should we do?' The doctor said, 'Go home, pack her suitcase, and meet me at the hospital. If you want her and your baby to live, go do this now!' So, we left his office. I was walking down the street, crying, and your grandpa was so embarrassed. He said, 'Why are you crying, like a crazy lady? Stop it!' I try to stop crying, but I couldn't. I say, 'I'm gonna die! I have to go home and say goodbye to my kids. Who's going to take care of them?' Grandpa kept saying, 'Stop that! Stop crying!'" Grandma mimicked Grandpa's whisper-shouts. Grandma's imitation of Grandpa was convincing. Even as a child, I knew Grandpa as a proud man, very concerned with appearances.

"I packed a bag and kissed my kids goodbye," Grandma said. "Even Juanita, the baby. Maria promised to take care of them. Teresa was old enough to help, but I didn't think I was coming back. I was crying and crying.

"When I got to the hospital, they put me right into a bed. All the nurses were looking at my legs and my feets, because they was so swollen. They put an IV in my arm, and said, 'Now you're gonna sleep. When you wake up, you're gonna feel much better.' I knew they was lying, because the doctor said I was gonna *die*."

What I know now is that Grandma had pre-eclampsia, a condition that can cause serious complications, even death. The doctor could see Grandma, so close to her due date, needed to be hospitalized to get life-saving medicine and have labor induced. Grandma had never received pre-natal care, and sonograms weren't widely used, so no one knew she would deliver twins. The IV probably included something to calm Grandma's nerves—she fell into a deep sleep.

"When I wake up, it was night," Grandma said. "A nurse was there and she said, 'Oh, you're awake!' I asked her, 'Let me see my legs!' She lifted up the sheet and my legs were skinny as sticks. I ask, 'Am I gonna die?' The nurse said, 'I don't think so. We're taking *real* good care of you.' So, I went back to sleep."

The following morning, Grandpa came back to the hospital. The nurses told him the baby would be born that day; Grandma was in labor. At 8:30 p.m., Grandma delivered Amelia, my Auntie Emmy, a tiny, pink, healthy daughter. Grandpa admired his new child through a glass wall, kissed Grandma goodbye, and went home to his five other children. When he arrived home, he told his kids they had another little sister.

Back at the hospital, the doctor had left Grandma, satisfied that she would not die. As the nurses cleaned up, however, Grandma's labor pains continued.

"I tell the nurses, 'I think there's another baby coming,'" Grandma said. "At first, they don't believe me." The nurses checked her, and saw there was, indeed, a twin. Despite being exhausted, Grandma bore down and pushed.

The nurses sent for the doctor, before he went home. He returned, shocked to see Grandma pushing again. For the next hour, Grandma struggled. She lost consciousness during the last part of labor. Most of what she remembered about the birth of the second twin, Amalia, came from the nurse's recounting.

"The doctor was worried that I might die after all, so they have to pull the baby out of me with tongs," Grandma said. She held her hands shoulder length apart. "But the doctor's hands were too big, fat, and sweaty, so the nurses have to do it. They took turns pulling her out of me. They had to be careful not to hurt her head or her eyes.

"So, those nurses delivered the baby, not the doctor," Grandma said, smiling. "I wasn't even awake." Auntie Molly's head, stuck in the birth canal, took some skillful coaxing to make it through. Obviously traumatized by the process, but miraculously alive, Auntie Molly was delivered, and then whisked away to intensive care.

Grandma woke up a few hours later, in a fog of medicine and exhaustion. *Did she really have two babies?* The nurses said yes, assuring her she had twin girls, who were alive and well. They told her about the delivery, even sharing how they were the ones who delivered the second twin. Satisfied things were good, Grandma drifted back to sleep, but not before the nurses secured the names for the babies' birth certificate. The first nurse, Suzan, suggested that Grandma name one of the babies after her. The second nurse, Carmen, said that if Grandma was going to name one of the babies after Suzan, she should name the other twin after her. Grandma consented.

[At their christening, Grandpa gave the twins matching names: Amelia and Amalia. The hospital birth certificates, however, are recorded this way: eldest twin, Suzan Gonzalez, born at 8:30 p.m.; twin number two, Carmen Gonzalez, born at 11:30 p.m., three hours after her sister. Grandpa and Grandma kept the nurse's names as the twins' middle names.]

At sunrise, Grandma awoke and asked to see her babies. The nurses who had delivered them the night before had gone home. The new nursing staff seemed less than forthcoming.

"They whispered, like they were telling secrets," Grandma said. "One nurse came back with Emily, in a little blanket. She was *real* cute. I ask, 'Where is the other one?' The nurse said, 'Oh, she's asleep right now.' I ask them to bring her, later, but the nurse said, 'I can't bring her right now, I'm too busy.' All morning it was like this. I called for the big nurse, and when she comes in, I tell them, 'I want to see my two babies together, right now.' The big nurse says, 'Oh, they're both asleep.' I said, 'So what? The first one was asleep when you brought her to me. Bring them both in here, at the same time.' So, they did."

Grandma's reenactment of this scene was performed like a stand-up comic. She demonstrated the nurses' nervousness, processing into the room, eyes downcast.

"The one who had Emily walked in first, and the nurse holding Molly, behind her, like she was hiding. I said, 'Put them on the bed, so I can see them together.' They wouldn't do it. Molly's face was covered with a blanket. I tell that nurse, 'Just open up the blanket. Let me see her.'

"The nurse who was holding her was nervous. She looked at the other nurse like, 'What should I do?' Finally, she opened up the blanket like this," Grandma bent down, pretending to show me an imaginary baby. She lifted the blanket corner, flashing a glimpse of the baby's face.

"I asked her, 'Why are you doing that? Hold it open so I can see her.' So, she did. Molly's mouth was on one side of her face," Grandma said, puckering her lips and twisting them to one side. "Her head was pointy, and no hair in places. She have bruises all over her neck and her nose was smashed. Oh, poor thing!" Grandma reacted to the sting of this story, and clapped her hands together, as if it just happened. "The nurses say to me, 'Don't worry! She's gonna look normal in a few days,'" Grandma said. "But I didn't believe them. Pretty soon, Grandpa came to get us. He saw the babies together for the first time. He said, 'That one has a broken nose.' I tell him, 'They say she's going to look just like the other one in a few days, and I believe them!'" Grandma laughed. "I really didn't believe them, either, but I tell Grandpa, 'Anyway, broken nose or not, she's our baby and she's alive.'"

In a few days, Auntie Molly's swelling *did* recede. Her face matched her twin's face within a week, and her hair grew back evenly. The twins became the subject of attention. Baby Juanita, my mother, was only twenty months old when the twins were born, still in diapers, still in need of holding, attention, and care. And yet, all attention was diverted to them.

Amelia (Emily) and Amalia (Molly) 1-year old

I used to think it was poverty that kept Grandma from getting proper medical care during her pregnancy, even after Grandma explained how doctor visits and hospitals were not the way her people did things. Midwives were preferred among Mexican women, and came with a supportive community. If a woman was giving birth, the women would gather around to help the expectant mother. Grandma's own birth story includes this. Vicenta's friend, checking up on her at the time she was due, explains how she found her in the old lady's home. It explains why she brought her life-saving champurrado and tostadas.

Grandma relied on her community, but she could feel the old customs slipping away. The culture of women helping each other, pitching in, and caring for another woman's family, was lost in the new world. Even her sister, Maria, a busy businesswoman, was moving into this culture. In Mexico, according to Grandma, most of the medical care a woman received, after she had given birth, came in the form of teas, herbs, and multi-colored sopas, prepared by family and friends. In traditional culture, the delivery of the baby, like the delivery of food and medicine, was personal. Physical love and care from a woman's community helped a woman heal, in Grandma's opinion, much more than a hospital.

19. The Home

After all seven children were born, the Gonzalez family home was very full. Their house was just part of a cluster of homes, spaced very close together, on land that Tío Monico and Tía Maria Ruiz owned. For Mom and her siblings, growing up in such close quarters was poor, but acceptable.

"It's almost hard to explain," Auntie Lucy said. "We didn't know any better, so we liked it." She laughed, but I could tell she was struggling to summarize what life was like.

"Was Malaga a poor community?" I asked.

"It wasn't posh, if that's what you're asking," Auntie Lucy said. "*We* were poor, though. Our family was poor. I remember being sad about that."

"Our neighborhood had dirt roads," Auntie Emmy said. "There were no sidewalks. Whenever we went somewhere, we were walking on dirt."

"That's how it was," Mom said, turning to me. "We lived in a Mexican community, with *very* modest homes. Our houses were really close together, and no one had indoor plumbing."

"It was my job to wake up early," Auntie Terry said. "I was the oldest girl, so I helped Mama with breakfast. I had to go out, even on cold mornings, and pump water from the pump outside." She laughed. "It was ice cold. Mama heated it up on the stove, in the kitchen, so we could all use it to wash up."

"And every house had their own outhouse," Mom said. "I was small, so I hated using the outhouse! I was afraid I was going to fall in the hole..."

Auntie Emmy burst into laughter, and Mom joined her. "I always wanted someone to go with me," Mom said. Her cheeks were flushed with color, pink apples, contrasted against the dark brown of her hair. "Especially at night. I hated that outhouse!" She nudged Auntie Emmy's elbow. "Do you remember how our cousin, Nellie, used to tease us?" Mom asked.

"Yup," Auntie Emmy said. She wasn't laughing anymore. She crossed her arms.

"Nellie used to live across the alley from us," Mom said. "She would do anything to scare us. If she heard me ask one of my brothers, 'I need to go, can you take me?' she'd say, 'Don't let *la Llorona* get you! She's in the outhouse...'" Mom made sure I understood the cultural reference. "La Llorona is the...did you see *Coco*?"

"I know who La Llorona is," I said, standing up straighter. "The crying woman, right?" I felt a little annoyed that Mom thought I didn't know Mexican folklore.

"The *weeping* woman," Mom said, correcting me.

"She drowned her children and then she drowned herself..."

"And now she wanders ..."

"Wailing and crying in the dark streets," I said. Now *my* arms were crossed.

"Anyway," Mom said, realizing she had touched a nerve. "Nellie liked to scare us."

"She was so mean to us," Auntie Emmy said. "Mama and Daddy always cautioned us about strangers, too. That's what I remember. I was scared of strangers, in the street. Parts of our neighborhood had *really* rickety houses, and strange people. Mama didn't like us having close relationships outside of family."

"Mama was also scared about germs and disease," Mom said. "She hated germs!"

"Our house was always squeaky clean," Auntie Lucy said. "Because Mama *hated* germs! All of us were sandwiched into that space, so Mama wanted to keep it really clean. Next door, we had neighbors who rented a bigger home than ours, from Tía Maria. They had seven or eight kids, too, remember?"

"I do remember that family," Auntie Emmy said. "They had lots of kids, like us."

"Like Terry said, we got our water from the pump outside," Mom said. "Terry would fill up our nice, silver bucket, bring it inside, put it on the counter, and put the ladle with the long handle in it. We'd use that water for cooking and drinking. Mama let us help ourselves. We'd dip the ladle in the bucket, pour the water into a cup, and drink from the cup. Our neighbors, with all their kids, would drink from the ladle. Sometimes, when they put the ladle back in the bucket, a string of saliva would stretch, from the ladle to their mouth!"

"Ew!" Auntie Emmy groaned. "Terry would never allow us do that."

"Never drink from the ladle," Auntie Terry said, scrunching up her nose.

"I remember telling Mama about that," Mom said. "I said, 'Mama, guess how our neighbors drink their water?' And Mama would say, 'Don't drink water at that house. In fact, don't even go inside to play.'"

"And that was it," Auntie Lucy said. "Mama thought they were messy. Their father was really overweight, and their mother was lazy... all those reasons. The neighbor man had a job with the railroad, and their family always seemed to have more money than ours. Even as a child, I knew this was why my parents didn't like them. That man didn't work as hard as Daddy, and he was fat. Daddy was fit, and he worked every day of the week, rain or shine, pruning vineyards. Still, Daddy didn't make as much money as that neighbor, and this was always a source of unspoken tension.

"One of their daughters was my age," Auntie Lucy said. "We became close friends, and we'd walk to school together. After school, we'd play in the yard. One day, I was sick, so I stayed home from school. By the afternoon, I was feeling better, so I snuck off to the neighbor's house, to play with my friend. For some reason, Daddy came home early. He looked around for me, and asked Mama, 'Where's Luz? I thought you said she stayed home from school?' Mama looked around and said, 'She was just here. Maybe she went over to the neighbor's house?' This made Daddy furious. He said, 'Go get her!' Mama came and found me there, playing with my friend. I knew I was in trouble, but as we walked back to our house, she said, 'Daddy's home. You shouldn't have gone over there.' Oh! I was scared to death." Auntie Lucy looked at me, and annunciated each word: "*Scared. To. Death.*"

Mom nodded her head. "We were scared to death of our dad," she said, quietly.

"Mama brought me back to our house," Auntie Lucy said. "Daddy already had his belt off. He said, 'What were you doing over there? You know you're not supposed to go inside. I'll teach you never to do that again!' He grabbed both of my hands in one of his. With the other hand, he started hitting me. POW! POW! POW! on my bare legs. He didn't hit soft, it was hard!" Auntie Lucy mimicked the violent whipping motion. "Somehow, the belt buckle got loose. It hit me right here," Aunt Lucy pointed to a spot above her forehead, just beyond the hairline. "Oh! Suddenly, I saw red. Blood came pouring down my face, and everything else stopped. I heard Daddy say, 'Juana! Get in here!' Mama came in and saw me. Daddy said, 'Take care of her!'" Auntie Lucy paused and shook her head.

"Not, 'I'm sorry I hurt you,' or 'Are you okay?' No, Daddy *never* said he was sorry. He just pushed me toward Mama and told her to clean me up. Mama was absolutely livid, and started shouting, 'You animal! See? Your temper! Look at this! You could have killed this girl!'

"Sometimes, when I get my hair done, I remember," Auntie Lucy touched the front of her elaborately coiffed hair. "A hairdresser who doesn't know me will ask, 'What's this?' I just say, 'It's a scar I got when I was a kid,' which is the truth, but I never say where it's from."

As I listened to Auntie Lucy's story, I thought of Grandpa. I couldn't imagine anyone being scared of Grandpa, let alone *Scared. To. Death.* The Grandpa I knew was a kind, gentle gardener. He played chess and Spanish guitar. He always gave me quarters to go to the store.

And yet, Auntie Lucy had a story like the one Grandma remembered, about her father, hitting her in the face with a quince branch. Instead of the furious anger I felt toward Esteban, I was instantly overwhelmed with sadness. The Grandpa I knew, the musical, chess-playing gardener, had a violent temper that affected his family. I couldn't imagine Grandpa acting like this, at least not the Grandpa I knew.

One day, as I reflected with my own father about this dichotomy, Dad said something significant.

"You knew your grandfather at a good time," Dad said. "By then, he was mellow. No pressure to feed his family, or to prove himself. He'd already made his peace with the world."

Dad's words resonated with me, long after he spoke them. Grandpa had *made peace with the world* by the time I knew him. He had become the unhurried, kind person who tended his gardens and bar-b-qued chicken. He had *made peace with the world*. Maybe that was one of the secrets to being happy.

Maybe.

Part Seven: Salsa

"Hunger is the best sauce in the world...."
~ Miguel de Cervantes, *Don Quixote*

Tomato Salsa for Canning

2 parts chopped tomatoes (preferably Roma)
1 part finely chopped onion (preferably white or yellow)
1 part chili peppers cut up in a small dice (jalapeños, serrano, hatch, depending on your taste or desire for heat)
1/3 part bell peppers
A few garlic cloves, pressed into mince (I use 1 clove for every 2 cups of tomato)

Chop tomatoes into a fine dice and put (juice and all) into a big, super-clean pot. Dice the onion, even finer, and add to the pot. Add the minced garlic. Lastly, remove seeds and pith (membrane) from chili with a spoon (some people have to use gloves to do this). Dice as fine as the onion. Add everything to the pot and stir. Bring pot to a boil, and then simmer for about 40 minutes. Add a little salt and pepper if you want, but not too much (salsa shouldn't taste salty). Keep stirring. Cool off a bit, then add to clean, warm canning jars. Seal with brand new lids and rings.

Have two canning pots ready to boil jars of salsa. Load filled and sealed jars into pot, then add hot water, so that water is two inches above tops of lids. Bring water to boil, then reduce temperature. Water will be gently boiling. Set timer for 20-30 minutes, making sure water continues to boil gently, and covers jars.

Carefully remove jars **after** water has cooled down (some people have a jar-lifter, which is nice). It won't hurt if you keep jars in there for a few minutes. Place jars on counter overnight. When you hear a lid pop, a lid has sealed. Shout, "Atta boy!" because he's a good one.

20. Pneumonia

Illustration from the U.S. Department of Public Health brochure, 1940

In 1936, U.S. President Franklin D. Roosevelt declared that pneumonia was the nation's foremost public health concern, the leading infectious cause of death in the country.[8] He appointed a new surgeon general, Thomas Parran, to attack the problem, and develop pneumonia control programs. Parran's strategy involved a cooperative effort between federal, state and local health agencies, to reduce pneumonia-related deaths. By 1940, the United States Department of Public Health had made this concerted effort known to most residents, publishing and circulating literature, short films, and posters, in the hopes of educating U.S. citizens.

By 1940, California's Central Valley had experienced an overwhelmingly high number of pneumonia cases, especially in farming communities. Agricultural workers and their families were prone to upper respiratory infections (URI's), because they regularly worked among allergens and pesticides, lived in densely populated areas, and didn't have as much access to medical care. Not long after her sister-twins were born, my mother, little

---

[8] Podolsky, Scott H. "The Changing Fate of Pneumonia as a Public Health Concern in 20th-Century America and Beyond." *American Journal of Public Health*, vol. 95, no. 12, 25 Dec. 2005, pp. 2144–2154.

Juanita Gonzalez, got sick with pneumonia. She developed a high fever, and within hours, she was hospitalized.

"I was taken to the Fresno public hospital, or county hospital," Mom said. "I still remember my little hospital bed, or crib, lined up in a row with the others. The hospital kept all the children together, so we slept in a dorm setting." Mom paused, and laughed into her hand. "I have this memory of looking under another kids' bed, and seeing a fuzzy little rabbit, and his ears were moving." Mom laughed again. "There really was no rabbit! I had such a high fever, I was hallucinating."

For toddlers, like my mom, three-year-old Juanita Gonzalez, high fevers, chills, seizures, and hallucinations were not uncommon. Mom considered herself lucky, seeing a rabbit.

"It wasn't scary," Mom said, smiling. "Just fuzzy."

Mom's hospitalization included a new treatment: sulphapyridine, an anti-pneumococci serum. The surgeon general, driven to stop the death toll, offered federal funding for the serum, for any public health department that would comply with a strict regimen of testing, reporting, and administering serum to patients. By 1940, nearly two thirds of the United States had developed pneumonia-control programs, with federal funding increasing this number nearly sixty-fold from just three years before.[9]

"I'll always remember how strange the hospital was," Mom said. "Some things were good. I got to eat my meals in a real high chair, with a tray that came over my head and became a table. I remember that vividly!" Mom beamed, as if she were talking about her first car. "I also took baths in a *huge* tub," Mom said. She held her arms out in a circle in front of her. "I guess it felt huge, because I was so little. The nurses would wash me with *green* soap. I had never seen *green* soap before!" Mom sat back in her chair and sighed.

"My parents came to visit me," Mom said. "My mother was smiling, trying to be cheerful, but my father was a little more serious. When it was time for them to leave, I screamed, 'Don't leave me! Don't leave me!' But of course, they had to leave." Mom remembered her parents trying to console her, even as they were forced to ignore her desperate pleas. "My mother tried to make the visit pleasant, but it wasn't. I was in the hospital for two weeks, and that's too long."

---

9 Ungerleider, Harry E., M.D., F.A.P.H.A., et. al, "Public Health and Economic Aspects of Pneumonia-A Comparison with Pre-sulfonamide Years." *American Journal of Public Health*, Sept. 1943

For a three-year-old girl, who had never before been separated from her family, the worst part of pneumonia was being separated from family. Many other children, all over the United States, were being quarantined in hospitals. While stressful to families, hospitalization and sulfonamide treatments reduced mortality rates.[10]

Three thousand miles east of Fresno, in Boston, Massachusetts, a group of public health advocates had won the right to bring sulphapyridine serum out of large, metropolitan hospitals, and into homes.[11] The idea that patients, especially children, in the early stages of the disease, could benefit from private home care, was radical. The Massachusetts health advocates, however, proved that nurses who were trained to administer the drug could monitor patients in their homes, and train the patient's family to care for them. A new health care professional, the pneumonia duty nurse, became a weapon in the fight against pneumonia—just in time for little Jackie Ryan, a boy who would be diagnosed with pneumonia in neighboring Brookline.

Jackie was an only child, born to Patrick and Alice Ryan, Irish-Americans from Brookline, Massachusetts, a suburb of Boston. At the beginning of 1940, Jackie became sick with pneumonia—again.

"I had pneumonia a total of three times before I went to elementary school," Dad said. "The last time, I got *really* sick."

His parents, my Grandpa Ryan and Nana, were sick with worry. Married in January of 1921, Dad's parents struggled with infertility for twelve years. They had nearly given up hope of conceiving a child, when Nana found out she was pregnant with Dad in 1933. By then, Nana was in her forties. Her doctor warned her she could face serious health risks—if she could even carry the baby to term. Dad was born, healthy and beautiful. His parents were elated.

As he grew, Dad received all of his parents' attention. Nana, naturally overprotective, was fearful that harm would come to her only son. Extremely vigilant, she prayed for Dad as he crossed the street, went to school, played baseball with friends, slept in his bed.

Jackie's third pneumonia diagnosis, during a nation-wide pandemic, made Nana both desperate and hopeful. She'd heard about the home-health

---

10 Podolsky, Scott H. "The Changing Fate of Pneumonia as a Public Health Concern in 20th-Century America and Beyond." *American Journal of Public Health*, vol. 95, no. 12, 25 Dec. 2005, pp. 2144–2154.
11 Ungerleider, Harry E., M.D., F.A.P.H.A., et. al, "Public Health and Economic Aspects of Pneumonia-A Comparison with Pre-sulfonamide Years." *American Journal of Public Health*, Sept. 1943

program, and she begged her husband to ask for a pneumonia duty nurse to come to their house. She didn't want her only son going to a hospital and being quarantined. Patrick agreed, and made the arrangements.

"My parents set up a big crib for me," Dad said. "They put it in the dining room, not the bedroom, and I slept there. I had a plastic oxygen tent over my head area. A nurse came into our house, and she was with me around the clock."

"Wow, Jack," Mom said, marveling at the difference in their experience. "Your family probably had the money to do it."

"Yeah, you were rich!" Auntie Emmy said. She and Auntie Molly laughed, and Dad smiled, slightly embarrassed. His family was working class, just like Mom's, but Dad was an only child. In their Irish Catholic neighborhood, one child to an Irish-Catholic couple was rare.

"People called us lace curtain Irish," Dad said. "My father only made fifty dollars a month, working for the fire department, but I was their only child. That combination made us a little better off than most people in our neighborhood."

*Patrick Ryan, my paternal grandfather,
Brookline Mass. Fire Department. approx. 1918*

"When I got really sick, my mother prayed to Saint Gerard," Dad said. "That's how I got my middle name, John Gerard Ryan, after him. At my confirmation, my mother said, 'You should choose Gerard, because St. Gerard is the patron saint of children. I prayed to him when we thought we were going to lose you.'"

As a child, I had heard Nana's stories about praying to St. Gerard for a miracle, but I always thought she was talking about having a baby. Now I know Nana prayed for Dad's life.

Alice (Nana) and Patrick Ryan with Jackie on his first birthday (1935)

A picture of Dad, taken at his first birthday party, reveals the quiet confidence of an only child. He sits on his father's shoulders, looks at the camera, and plays with his birthday crown on his father's head. His parents, Patrick and Alice Ryan, are dressed nicely, and look proud of their boy. They're obviously older than the average parent in the 1930's, but share the same cautious optimism for the future of their one-year-old son. Plenty of pictures and portraits of Jackie Ryan exist. Some are even colorized, to accentuate Dad's brilliant blue eyes, and rosy cheeks.

*John Gerard Ryan, first grade 1941,
after his third bout with pneumonia*

After World War II, the widespread use of penicillin changed the way doctors treated pneumonia. Pneumonia control programs were eventually dismantled.

Despite vastly different experiences in treatment, Dad and Mom both have clear memories of surviving pneumonia in 1940. Both belonged to devout Catholic families, and both had mothers who saw their child's recovery as an answer to prayer.

Pneumonia serves as a light, the illumination of my parents' early environments and upbringings. My father was the only son of Irish-American parents, lived in a Boston suburb, and recovered at home. My mother was the fifth daughter of seven children, born to Mexican-American immigrants, and lived in a rural landscape, densely populated with agricultural laborers. She recovered in a public hospital, separated from her family. Both grandfathers worked hard, but Grandpa Ryan had job security, and only one son. Grandpa Gonzalez worked hard, but many employers took advantage of his undocumented status, and paid him ridiculously low wages. He had seven children to feed. With pneumonia as a plumbline, it was easier for me to see just how *different* Mom and Dad's early years were.

Today, when my parents talk about their childhoods, they are realists. They're quick to say that their parents did the best they could. They remember the sting of their family having expenses but not enough money. And yet, Dad has so many pictures, before-and-after pneumonia: Jackie at one-year-old, in first grade, in the park, shoveling snow.

When Mom came home from the hospital, no one took her picture for posterity, to illustrate her miraculous homecoming. It would be four more years before Mom would have her picture taken.

21. What Is a Sense Memory?

A memory, very simply put, is the brain's recollection of stimuli and information. When our brain receives stimuli from the senses—sight, sound, feel, taste, and smell—they are processed as data. Data is easier to recall when it's attached to more than one of our natural senses, especially smell or taste. If you close your eyes, it's easy to remember.

You arrive at Grandma's house, where the aroma of fresh tortillas fills your senses. This triggers memories of last week, when you walked in and smelled tortillas. Last week, you followed your nose to the kitchen, where Grandma gave you a fresh, hot tortilla, folded like a flat cone, with a paper napkin at the bottom, to catch run-off butter. You took it, bit into its warm flesh, tasted salty butter, and chewed it slowly. The tortilla made your cares and concerns fall away from you, like a heavy coat, hitting the floor. This sensory data, of the week before, took anywhere from milliseconds to five seconds to recall, but it triggered a feeling of well-being.

Your week has been filled with other memories. You've woken up early every day, showered, driven your beat-up car to a low-paying job, and sat behind a grey metal desk, and finished work that no one cares about. On Tuesday, you see your boyfriend. He suggests you try a new diet, and adds you are probably twenty pounds overweight. On Wednesday, the same boyfriend flirted with a small blonde at one of his baseball games. On Thursday, you ate nothing but celery and bologna. On Friday, your electricity gets turned off. You realize, in your young-adult cluelessness, you forgot to pay the electric bill. That night, your boyfriend takes you to his best friend's house, where you watch them play cards as you contemplate your finances. On Saturday you visit your parents, and carefully ask them to help you turn your electricity back on. It involves an extra fee, but you can't do it without a credit card. Your father is angry about this. He asks how you let this happen. He reminds you about financial responsibility and personal integrity and credit ratings. He agrees to help, but adds it will be just this once. On Sunday, you go to church, because you have to. Later, when your mother asks you what the homily was about, you can't remember.

The following Monday, you have a day off. You drive your beat-up car to your grandparents' house. It's a fifteen-minute drive from your crummy apartment, but the orchards line the road in front of you, like a tunnel into another world. When you pull into your grandparents' driveway, you see Grandpa, dressed in work pants and a plaid shirt, watering his roses. The bushes are as tall as his shoulders, erupting in giant blooms of pink, yellow, and red. Grandpa makes an exaggerated squeal when you get out of your car. Your visit surprises him, but somehow, this is a good thing. You hug, and he smells like soap and wet earth. He walks with you to the front door, opens it, and calls to Grandma. She peers around the refrigerator as you walk in, then walks over to greet you with a hug and a kiss. You both walk back to the kitchen, where she rolls a ball of dough into a perfect circle. As soon as it hits the comal, the tortilla's aroma summons last week's memory. Your brain releases serotonin, the hormone responsible for the feeling of well-being. It's been a long time since this hormone was released. Your brain remembers last week, the week before that, and the week before that. These sense memories are stacked, like tortillas, in your limbic system. They are the foundational bricks on which other memories are built: *It's always beautiful here. Grandpa and Grandma are always kind and unhurried. They're always happy to see me.* For the rest of your life, you'll equate tortillas with love. You'll spend your life chasing the perfect tortilla. You'll look for the same texture and taste of Grandma's tortillas, but you'll never find them. Nothing even close—not even the ones you make, using her recipe.

It's more than smell and taste, it's the time and place and love that went into the tortillas you ate in your grandmother's kitchen. Those will always be good. Always. *Tortillas are a big part of the way Grandma showed her love. It was a big part of the way you received her love.*

When I open my eyes, I look over at Grandma. She's sitting in a straight-back chair in my office. I long to touch her, really hug her again. I try to say this, but there's a huge lump in my throat.

"I miss you so much," I whisper.

"I know, mija," she says. Then, she adds: "Purty soon, you're gonna see me again. Right now, you be a good grandma to *your* grandkids. They'll love you the same way."

I don't know if this is possible, since I'm me, and not Grandma. Life is so different than it was when I was growing up. I start to say this, but she interrupts me.

"Pray for them, cook for them, and tell them *your* stories," she says. "All the time."

"You're right," I say. That's what Grandma did my whole life. She gave me a place in her world that didn't change. "I try to do that for them. But do you really think they'll hold me in their hearts, like I hold you in mine?"

"Yes," she says. "They will. You'll see."

***

First Holy Communion 1940(l to r) Ismael (Smiley), Teresa, Luz (Lucy), Francisco (Frank).

Mom and her sisters share sense memories of Malaga School. Most are connected to holes in their shoes.

"We had to walk to school," Auntie Lucy said. "Mama didn't drive, and Daddy went to work early. We walked on the side of the road, because there were no sidewalks."

"Mama would always caution us to stay waaay over to the side," Mom said, leaning her body to the right. "One kid had been hit by a car, and she warned us to be careful."

"We were walking on a dirt road," Auntie Lucy said. "And we always had holes in our shoes."

"We hated walking in the rain," Auntie Terry said. "Even if we had an umbrella, if the ground was wet, our socks and shoes would be soaked by the time we got there."

"Water seeped through the holes in the soles of our shoes," Auntie Lucy said. "By the time I got to school, my feet were soaking wet. I wouldn't *dare* cross my feet in class because the other kids would see I had *holes in my shoes*."

"Our family had a way of handling the holes-in-the-shoes problem," Mom said, smiling. "I mean, we couldn't go buy another pair of shoes, because we couldn't afford them. Mama would cut out a piece of cardboard and she'd put that in the bottom of our shoe. We wore those until the rain soaked them. When it wore out, we'd get a new piece of cardboard."

"When she didn't have cardboard, she used newspapers," Auntie Lucy said, laughing.

"Remember, Jennie? *La Opinión*?"

Mom laughed. "You're right," she said. "*La Opinión* was Daddy's Spanish newspaper, and there was always plenty of it around the house."

Auntie Lucy sighed. "We're laughing, but it was the first time I realized we were poor. I didn't know until I went to school."

"None of us had good shoes," Auntie Terry said. "People gave us their old ones, but the bottoms were worn. Even with cardboard, the water still seeped in. I got chilled, and sick."

"Auntie Terry was sick a lot when she was young," Mom said, reaching over to touch her arm. "Her teachers held her back, more than once, because she missed so much school. She was supposed to complete make-up work at home, but she was always busy, helping Mama. As the eldest daughter, she had a hard time getting her schoolwork finished."

"I was twenty-one when I graduated from high school," Auntie Terry said, sitting up straight, proud of herself. "I worked *real* hard to stay in school."

"At least you graduated," Mom said. "Mama went to the same school we did, but she *never* graduated. She only started school when she was fifteen."

Malaga School had a predominantly Mexican student body. It was never officially segregated, but had adopted curricula for students from Spanish-speaking families. No official school mandates required speaking English only, but the push seemed to be more urgent as time passed. Grandma attended Malaga School for two years, until her father removed her. In the 1930's, her children started attending the same school.

"Mama was fifteen-years-old in the first grade," Auntie Terry said, smiling. This concept still amazed her. "She wanted to go to school so bad. She learned English there. Right, Jennie?"

"Yes," Mom said, sympathetically. "Mama was embarrassed, because the teachers told her she tested at a first-grade level. She'd reminisce with us, about her school days. She'd say, 'At least I knew more English than my friend, who went to school with me.'"

"Mom knew a lot of English," Auntie Terry said. "Didn't she, Jennie?"

Mom looked at Auntie Terry and shook her head. "No, Terry. Daddy spoke more English in those days, for work, but Mama didn't speak much English."

"She liked to speak English with us remember?" Auntie Terry said.

"Sure," Mom said. "But I think the older kids went to school, learned English, and brought it home."

Auntie Lucy agreed. "Everyone learned English from them," she said. "Terry, Frank, and Smiley learned it in school, and then taught us."

"Oh, yes," Auntie Terry said. "Mama spoke English with us, just for practice, right? We would come home from school, and we'd talk with each other in English, so the rest of our family picked it up."

"I learned English through play," Mom said. "We added it to our language. We played our cousins and siblings, so by the time I got to school, I knew enough English to understand the teacher. Then, I learned more."

"Were you ever punished for speaking Spanish at school?" I asked.

"Of course not!" Auntie Emmy said, quickly. "No one ever *told* us not to speak Spanish. We just knew that school was a place where we spoke English."

"We weren't punished for speaking Spanish," Auntie Molly said. "The other kids were speaking English, so we did, too."

"At home, we spoke Spanish to our parents," Mom said. "Even after they were fluent in English, we spoke Spanish to them, out of respect. They would ignore us if we spoke English. It was their way of saying, 'Speak Spanish to me.'"

"That's how it was," Auntie Terry said. "Spanish at home. English at school."

"I just watched the documentary, *Stolen Education*," I said. "It's the story of a court case, where eight Mexican-American students challenged racism and discrimination in a court trial about elementary schools in Texas, in the 1950's.[12] The students came from Mexican families, and were punished if they spoke Spanish at school. Some were punished by being forced to repeat first grade, up to three times. It makes me wonder why Grandma was put in first grade when she was fifteen. That seems strange."

"She said they tested her," Mom said, shrugging. "They said she knew as much English as someone in the first grade."

"Who tested her?" I asked.

Mom laughed. "Janet, I don't know," she said. "In those days, they didn't test kids like they do today."

"Doesn't it seem unfair to an incoming student?" I asked. "So many Spanish-speaking kids were forced to repeat grades, more than once."

"Like me," Auntie Terry said, solemnly. "I worked hard, but Daddy wouldn't let me drop out of school, even when I wanted to. I got discouraged, especially when most of my friends were graduating."

"Things were different back then," Mom said. "Teachers did the best they could."

"Maybe," I said. I thought about dropping the subject, but I couldn't. "One professor in *Stolen Education* said that some Mexican immigrants raised a generation that were made to feel shame for speaking Spanish, and *they* raised a generation who are ashamed because they *don't* speak Spanish."[13]

Mom leaned back in her chair. "I know, mija," she said. "I know you feel ashamed that you can't speak Spanish." Her expression softened, a mixture of sympathy and exhaustion. My feelings were often too large for Mom. "Maybe all my kids feel the same way."

Auntie Terry smiled at me. "Why don't you *learn* Spanish?" she asked.

"I've tried..." I said.

A thousand sense memories tumbled through my brain. I remembered humiliating moments, where I'd mixed up verbs, over-rolled my r's, pronounced with gringo O's, or just froze-up completely. My Spanish-speaking friends teased me about word usage. My heart beat faster, my mouth seized, like I ate a marbles-and-peanut-butter sandwich. I've tried to speak Spanish, but I've sounded like a clueless Anglo. Maybe that's what I am, deep

---

[12] *Stolen Education* is a 2017 documentary film by Enrique Aleman, featuring Esperanza Aleman, directed by Rudy Luna, which documents the untold story of Mexican-American school children who challenged discrimination in Texas schools in the 1950's and changed the face of education in the Southwest.
[13] Ibid

down inside.

I looked over at Mom, for support, but she waited, like Auntie Terry, for my answer.

And it seemed like such a simple question.

22. Relief Christmas

One afternoon, in 2018, Mom and I sat with Auntie Terry, in her Oxnard backyard. My face was slightly upturned, toward the sun. Green plants, in terra cotta pots, decorated the Villaseñor's back steps.

"Did I ever tell you the story of my dad going to the Relief office?" Mom asked.

Mom's question barged in, like a bandit, kicking over Auntie Terry's potted plants. The subject of Grandpa going to the Relief office was one he *never* discussed. To him, it was the lowest point of his life.

Grandpa always looked nice, smelled nice, and did his best to provide for his family. His family was beautiful. Grandpa put a lot of faith in appearances, but in Malaga, appearances became harder and harder to keep. As hard as he worked, his salary as a vine trimmer was never enough to provide for his family. He never had enough for extravagances, like Christmas presents.

"In those days, welfare was called 'Relief,'" Mom said. "Tía Maria was the one who encouraged Daddy to get some help. He was always working hard, but he didn't make much more than ten cents an hour in the winter, pruning the vineyards, which was nothing. We were kids and we needed food, clothing, shoes and all that. Tía Maria told him, 'Go down to this place called Relief. They'll help you with the kids, even with Christmas gifts.'" "How do you know all this?" I asked.

"My dad told us this story," Mom said. "Everything I tell you is what he told us."

My body relaxed, with relief all its own. We had Grandpa's permission to talk about this.

"It was winter," Mom said. "For agricultural laborers, there's not a lot of work in the winter. Our father had no money, and there wasn't enough food for us, let alone Christmas presents. By the time he got to the Relief office, he was devastated. He wasn't thinking about the whole country, suffering. He only thought about how he couldn't make enough money to provide for his family. When it was his turn to be interviewed, the interviewer was officious, with her list of questions. Some of those questions were tough, and apparently, Daddy felt like the interviewer was taking shots at him. He stood up to leave, saying, 'That's enough!' The woman stopped my dad from leaving. She said, 'Mr. Gonzalez, sit down. Sit down!' Daddy said, 'No. I've had enough of this. I don't want your help.' The woman just looked at him and said, 'Mr. Gonzalez, please listen to me.' So, he sat down. The interviewer said, 'You're taking this personally. This money isn't for you, it's for your *children*. They can't represent themselves. Are you turning down an offer to help them? Are you turning down an offer to *feed them*?' Daddy said these words hit him like a ton of bricks. He realized she was right, and said, 'How can I turn down the offer of help for my children?' Then, he very humbly answered her questions. He got through the rest of the interview, somehow."

Mom and Auntie Terry smiled, softly, at each other. They realized the miracle of grace, which allowed their father to get instant perspective from a bureaucrat.

"I'll never forget that story," Mom said. "It made such an impression on me. My dad had a lot of pride, and sometimes, that pride got in the way. He had to admit he needed help."

"He did it for us," Auntie Terry said, leaning forward. "His children."

"Yes," Mom said. The sisters looked at each other and smiled again. "And those Christmas gifts were actually pretty good, right, Terry?" Mom asked. "Remember your doll?"

Auntie Terry smiled broadly, and looked at me. "I once got a doll that had a mole right here," she said, pointing to the space above her lip. "Is that the one you're talking about, Jennie? The woman who gave it to me said, 'Look, mija. Look what *Santy Claus* told me to give you.' I *hated* that doll with the mole on her face! It was made of…what is that material, Jennie? Como glass?"

"Porcelain?" Mom asked, smiling.

"Porcelain!" Auntie Terry said, snapping her fingers. "They gave me a porcelain doll, made for show, not to play with. Who would put a mole on a child's doll? I hated it, but I had to keep her."

Mom laughed. "I wasn't talking about *that* doll, Terry," Mom said. "Remember that cute one you got? The twins and I wanted it. We loved it. We never got a doll."

"No?" Auntie Terry asked, surprised. "What did you get?"

"I got a cute little piano," Mom said. "It was about knee-high, and it came with a little stool.

Daddy knew I was musical. I would sit on the stool and play it. It was really cute."

"They had nice gifts," Auntie Terry said. "But my favorite was the wristwatch."

Mom looked surprised. "You got a watch?"

"Oh yes," Auntie Terry said. "It was the year we didn't have a tree, remember? I asked Daddy, 'Why don't we have a tree this year?' He said, 'We don't have a Christmas tree because we can't afford it.' We had to buy food, or something."

"We had to buy *food?*" Mom asked. "Really?"

"Yeah, he said that," Auntie Terry said. "There was no gift for me that year. I figured it was because I was older and didn't need one. Then, Daddy said, 'Reach up on the top of the window frame, maybe there's something there. Oh, Jennie, I went to feel above the window, and there was the wristwatch!" Auntie Terry clapped her hands, then pretended to read her wristwatch. "I felt very grown up and special. It was a round one with a black band. Oh, I was so happy to not have one of those dolls!"

"A doll with a mole?" Mom asked, laughing.

"Thank God!" Auntie Terry laughed. "I couldn't look at another doll with a mole."

"But *I* wanted a doll," Mom said. "I liked another doll you got, a baby doll."

"What did she look like?"

"She had a plastic face, but her body was made with cloth, a tiny checkered, gingham pattern. She had eyes that opened and closed. She was so cute! I remember thinking, 'Why don't I get a doll?' I didn't get a doll for Christmas until we moved to Tracy."

"Really?" Auntie Terry asked. "How old were you when you got a doll?"

"I must have been about eight," Mom said. "That's a long time to wait for a doll. The twins and I got our first doll the same day. If I was eight, then they were six." Mom sat back in her chair and smiled. "Oh, that was the best

Christmas ever!"

"Were you surprised?" Auntie Terry asked.

"Since you ask," Mom said, glowing with childlike excitement. "I remember seeing three shoe-sized boxes under the tree, labeled for Emily, Molly and Jennie. I took the girls aside. I said, 'Look at the shape of those boxes. Maybe we got a doll!' They said, 'No, Jennie, we never get a doll.' I said, 'Well, maybe!' We went to ask Mama, hoping she'd tell us what was inside. 'Mama, what's in the box?' She said, 'Oh, that's a pirinola.' Those old-fashioned tops, when you pump them, they spin? We said, 'No, Mama! Really, what is it?' We begged her, but Mama never told us. Christmas Eve finally came, the day we were allowed to open our presents at Midnight. But I couldn't wait until then, I just couldn't…"

Auntie Terry touched Mom's arm in disbelief. "You opened it?"

"Well…" Mom said. She bit her thumbnail and smiled. "When nobody was looking, I took one of the boxes into Mama's room…"

"Oh no, Jennie!" Auntie Terry said. She laughed, then pretended to disapprove. "How could you do that?"

"The boxes were so flimsily wrapped," Mom said. "They weren't wrapped tightly, with gold paper, like some were. I felt for a weak spot on the box. When I found it, I pushed my finger through, and moved it around… and I felt doll-hair!" Mom leaned forward in her chair and rubbed her arms. "Look, I just got chills," she said, showing her goosebumps to Auntie Terry. "Oh! I was so excited! It's a doll! It's a doll! I went to get the twins. I told them, 'I know it's a doll! I felt the hair!' They looked at me, in disbelief. I explained how I felt the hair through the box. I said, 'That's how I know!'"

"How excited were you when you unwrapped it?" I asked.

"It was more exciting to know I *had* a doll," Mom said, clutching both hands to her chest. "After I knew, my life changed! I'll remember that moment forever." Mom sat back, glowing. She looked at Aunt Terry. "Do you remember Sam Matthews?" she asked her. "He was in your class at Tracy High."

Auntie Terry considered the name, carefully. "No," she said. "I don't remember."

"Anyway," Mom said, waving her hand in the air. "Sam was the editor of the *Tracy Press*.[14] One year, at Christmas, he wrote a story about the Christmas

---

[14] The Tracy Press has been dedicated to covering the city of Tracy for more than 100 years. Subscriptions: https://www.ttownmedia.com/site/services/

he got his first bicycle. It was such an exciting story, I decided to write and tell him the story of *my* best Christmas, with the doll." She tapped Auntie Terry's elbow with her hand. "Guess what? He published my story about the dolls! In his next column, he wrote: "Following last week's column about my Christmas bike, I received an email from Jennie Ryan, thanking me for 'a walk down memory lane' and telling me about a Christmas she will always remember.'"

Auntie Terry clapped her hands. "Jennie! Your story was published? Good for you!"

"Well, it was a letter to Sam," Mom said. "But he printed it."

I felt so proud of Mom. An avid reader, she also writes (and edits) very well. I wasn't necessarily surprised she had the story published, but suddenly, I felt connected to her in a different way: we shared a joy, seeing an original story we wrote, being published.

Later, I searched Tracy Press archives for Mom's story, and found it, in the e-Edition of the Tracy Press, dated January 4, 2016.[15] There was the sweet story of Mom's first doll, that fateful Christmas in December of 1945.

I used to think of Tracy, my home town, like its local paper, *The Tracy Press*, as small-time. Now, I see how vital and important their local stories are, as well as the circulation of them. It perpetuates story, necessary for survival. Every time I go back to Tracy, I find the latest issue of *The Tracy Press* in my parents' family room, and read it. I love that newspaper, now, more than any other.

Without Relief's help, there would be no dolls, no watch, no stories of enchanted gifts under the tree or on a window frame. The watershed moment, for Grandpa, was at the Relief office, when he accepted help from a government that hadn't yet proven itself worthy of his trust. In that moment, Grandpa accepted the U.S. as his country, with its flawed and nearsighted government. Relief helped Grandpa rebuild his life; soon, he had no need of it. Sometimes, our greatest shame makes way for our biggest blessings.

One of my favorite poets, Natalie Diaz, once said: "We are alive because of story. It is one of our ancestors' most powerful technologies. And we are all storytellers."[16]

---

[15] https://www.ttownmedia.com/tracy_press/our_town/brighter-christmas-rolls-on/article_4bd6e1e2-b351-11e5895c-e336bf00cd29.html
[16] "Energy, an Interview with Natalie Diaz." *Poets and Writers*, Volume 48, Issue 2

We are alive because of story.

The remarkable staying power of story is connected to our survival. We live lives dependent on our history, and survive the vortex of life that keeps spinning, because of story. Our brains are hard-wired to finish stories. From hermits who distance themselves in remote areas, to the most visible billionaires, we understand the power of the narrative mindset. Every civilization has had ancients that bear lessons in story. It's why cave-dwellers chiseled on walls.

23. Changes

In 1945, people in the United States were breathing a collective sigh of relief—WWII was OVER! The U.S.A celebrated victory over Japan and Emperor Hirohito's unconditional surrender. Citizens who had been serving overseas were coming home. For the first time since the Great Depression, things were looking up. The U.S. and Mexican governments redefined the Bracero Program as the Mexican Farm Labor Program. The United States needed thousands of Mexican workers to work the manual labor jobs, specifically in transportation and agricultural fields. Mexican day-laborers were between a rock and a hard place—there was plenty of work, but not enough respect. Employers were exploiting undocumented laborers, paying them extremely low wages and working them long hours. The conditions of the Bracero program were ignored by some unscrupulous employers.[17] Even if Mexican-American laborers were returning veterans, or their children had fought for this country, they were still treated as lesser-than, or other-than Americans. Some employers rationalized this thinking, simply because farm laborers were born in Mexico.

In 1945, my grandfather, Ignacio Gonzalez, was still struggling to make ends meet in Malaga. He had been working a Fresno vineyard, but had been receiving extremely low wages. For Grandpa, *anything* was better than not

---

[17] The Bracero History Archive, a project of the Roy Rosenzweig Center for History and New Media, George Mason University, the Smithsonian National Museum of American History, Brown University, and The Institute of Oral History at the University of Texas at El Paso.

working. Grandpa needed to work. With a little help from Relief, his children had shoes and food, but even with government assistance, there still wasn't enough.

To boost the family income, Grandpa worked seasonal harvests, and took my uncles, Frank and Smiley, to different farms in Northern California. Together, they picked vegetables, cotton, fruits. One of these farms was in Tracy, owned by a Spanish family named Ruiz (no relation to Monico and Maria). Mr. Ruiz liked the man they called Nacho. He recognized his strong work ethic, as well as farming experience. Nacho could speak both English and Spanish. He knew how to drive a tractor. Nacho took care of the farm equipment like it was his. Since Grandpa couldn't drive back and forth from Malaga to Tracy each day, Mr. Ruiz offered him a small house on the property, for his family to stay.

Grandpa felt recognized and respected by Mr. Ruiz, a rarity for farm laborers in those days. He accepted the offer of the little house for his family. For years, the Gonzalez family split their time between Tracy and Malaga. Tracy for the harvest; Malaga for the winter.

Grandpa and Grandma both knew that life in Malaga wasn't great for their family. Grandpa made almost no money in the vineyards, the kids walked to school, and then there was the overlying tension, between Tía Maria and Grandpa, that wouldn't go away. As time progressed, Grandma's strong family ties started to wear thin. She had to admit her sister, Maria, had very little free time. Maria owned every house on the property, so she functioned as a landlady. She also ran a profitable boarding house and restaurant. Before long, Tía Maria and Tío Monico bought a larger house in the city of Fresno, and moved away from the Malaga compound.

Esther, Tía Maria's daughter, remembered her family's move from a child's perspective. "I'll never forget the day we moved into the D Street house in Fresno. I was only six years old, so the living room seemed very grand to me. It had two beautiful glass chandeliers, hanging from the ceiling. It had three bedrooms, but only one bathroom. In those days, people had one bathroom, but it was *inside*" she said, laughing.

"It was a beautiful home," Auntie Emmy said. Like her siblings, she was genuinely happy for Tío Monico and Tía Maria, and their family. "As soon as our family saw it, we knew they were moving *up*."

"We loved that house," Auntie Molly said. "It had a tree, with three different kinds of fruit on it." She smiled and shook her head. "Three different fruits on one tree."

"My parents bought the house from an Italian family, who were accomplished gardeners," Esther said. "The previous owners had grafted the tree together, and we got all kinds of fruit from it. The backyard also had a beautiful grape arbor, with ladyfingers and Thompson seedless grapes, hanging down."

Auntie Emmy smiled broadly. "Inside, there were two bedrooms that were connected by a big closet," she said. "We loved to go through that closet!"

"Remember their huge, standing radio?" Mom asked. "It was like a piece of furniture!"

She put her hand over her heart. "As soon as we saw that, we *knew* they were rich!"

"Yes!" Auntie Emmy said, laughing. "That radio was *proof* they were rich!"

"When they turned the music on, we could feel the vibrations coming up from the floor," Mom said, smiling. "We loved that! Our family had a little radio, that sat on a table."

Their enthusiasm, describing the opulence of Tía Maria's new Fresno house, made me laugh. They remembered things without malice or jealousy, but even as children, they could feel the tension it caused. For their father, the house was a reminder of his own shortcomings, the necessity of collecting Relief, and how their family split their time between two temporary homes.

"Going back and forth from Tracy to Malaga was hard on our family," Mom said. "Daddy knew the hardship it caused for Mama. We had to pack up our things, and make the journey over there, live there for a while, and then move back to Malaga. Finally, he decided we needed to stay in one place. That place was Tracy."

Almost as an answer to prayer, the boss, el patrón, the Spanish, landowning Mr. Ruiz offered Grandpa a permanent job at the farm in Tracy. The small laborer's house, where the Gonzalez family stayed during seasonal trips, had been given a facelift, and now had indoor plumbing. Grandpa loved the thought of living in one place, almost as much he loved the idea of getting away from his sister-in-law. He told Grandma and the kids to pack up their things again, which they were used to, but this time was in the middle of the school year. Nevertheless, they all knew Grandpa was in charge. If he told them to get ready to move, they obeyed.

To anyone outside the family, the distance between Malaga and Tracy seems measurable. It's one hundred twenty-seven miles, or two hundred and seven kilometers. In 1945, it took a little over four hours by train, without stops. Once the highway was built, it was faster by car.

For Tía Maria and Grandma, however, Tracy and Malaga were worlds apart. Neither of them could drive a car. Because of their dependence on their husbands to take them from one place to another, neither woman knew how much they'd see each other. The sisters were forced to make peace with separation again.

Part Eight: Enchiladas

"Let us gather in a flourishing way
with sunluz grains abriendo los cantos
que cargamos cada día
en el young pasto nuestro cuerpo
para regalar y dar feliz perlas pearls
of corn flowing árboles de vida en las cuatro esquinas
let us gather in a flourishing way

~Juan Felipe Herrera
"[Let Us Gather in a Flourishing Way]"

Chicken Enchiladas

1 whole chicken, neck and giblets removed
1 package tortillas (flour, wheat, or corn)
2 onions (preferably white or yellow)
8 dried red California chiles, or 1 cup California Chili powder (4 bags)
2 cans tomato paste
1 can sliced olives (if you want)
2 cups shredded cheese (we like cheddar or mozzarella)
A few garlic cloves, pressed into mince
coarse salt (Kosher),
peppercorns bay leaf, cumino, chili powder all to your taste

1. Boil chicken in big pot of water with 2 tablespoons salt, chili powder, pepper, cumino, bay leaf and pepper(corns) to your taste. Add 2 whole garlic cloves and 1 whole onion, (leave their skins on for color and flavor). Boil for 50 minutes. If you're using dry chili, remove seeds, then grind up in molcajete with peppercorns and salt. Add to pot. Any extra chili flakes can go into the sauce.
2. Cool boiled chicken, then remove (carefully) from broth. Skim the fat off the top of the water, and remove any yucky floating things. Strain broth into another pot. Discard boiled peppercorns, onion, garlic.
3. Sauce: Return broth to stove. Stir in chili and tomato paste. Add cumino, salt, pepper to your taste. (Add more chili, but if you like a hotter sauce) Let sauce simmer while shreds the chicken meat. You should have at least six cups of shredded chicken before you start stuffing. Chop up the other onion. Salt and pepper the shredded chicken, then stir in chopped onion and chopped olives.
4. Stuffing the enchiladas: Once you have your sauce, take a flour or corn tortilla, dip in warm sauce and turn. It should be pliable. Put on plate. Fill with chicken mixture and cheese. Add a little sauce to top. Roll up and put on greased pan, seam side down. Avoid flat cookie sheets—the sauce leaks. Repeat until tray is full. Bake at 350? for 20-30 minutes.

24. Tracy, California

"Now you can write about Tracy," Grandma says, smoothing out the front of her green cobbler apron. She's standing in the doorway of my office, a petite four-feet, ten inches tall. Grandma's arms, once plump and shiny, are now thin and covered by her pink cable knit sweater. Her blue-plaid dress finishes just below her knees. Her bowed-legs look just like mine. I love this similarity.

"I get it now, Grandma," I say. "You were right."

She smiles, and sits down in Mario's straight-backed Danish chair, glowing triumphantly. I can feel her satisfaction as I begin.

***

Geographically speaking, Tracy rests in the center of California, only forty-eight feet above sea level, in the southeast portion of San Joaquin County. The generous San Joaquin River provides a source of fresh water, and Tracy is where the Delta-Mendota Canal begins. This aqueduct was designed to provide Central California farmers a supply of water for agriculture and livestock, but today, water is a political question. Once a sea of farms and ranches, Tracy is now an ocean of residential neighborhoods. A true slice of Americana east of San Francisco, south of Sacramento, and north of Modesto, where *American Graffiti* was filmed, Tracy is a city that is easiest to find when referring to somewhere else.

Tracy is part of the San Joaquin Valley, with fresh water and fertile soil. If that soil could speak, it would bear witness to war, genocide, destruction, greed, and the treaties that people signed to make these all happen.

The first residents of Tracy were the Yokuts, a tribe of hunter-gatherers, whose sustenance came from wild game and acorns from the surrounding oak trees. They hunted deer, fished the San Joaquin River, but leached acorns as their primary form of protein. Now and then, they traded with the occasional white merchant who wandered through.

California was once home to over a hundred Tribal Nations, before the state was colonized by Spain, in the 18th Century. New Spain, as California was once called, set up Catholic Missions and Rancheros, with the help of the surrounding tribes. People who had lived as free tribes, were forced into slavery by the Spanish, or paid in food and shelter to work for them. Short of leaving their homeland, or death, these people had no viable options but to cooperate with the colonizers.

Mexico had long been enduring the same Spanish oppression. On September 16, 1810, Father Miguel Hidalgo y Costilla, a Catholic priest, issued el Grito de Dolores (the Cry of Sorrow), a call to arms, that began the Mexican War of Independence. Eleven years later, in 1821, Spain sent Viceroy Juan de O'Donojú to sign the Treaty of Córdoba, recognizing Mexico as an independent nation. All Spanish-American lands now belonged to Mexico—except for California's Missions and Rancheros, which remained under Spanish rule.

From 1846—1848, the United States fought with Mexico for the land between the Oklahoma Territory and the Pacific Ocean. The Mexican-American War raged, until the U.S. emerged as victors. On February 2, 1848, the Treaty of Guadalupe Hidalgo was signed, acquiring California, Nevada, most of New Mexico, Arizona, and Colorado, for the United States. Nobody signing the treaty had considered the native people, still living on sacred lands. Nobody signing the treaty had heard the news about gold being found in a California river, only days before.

On January 24, 1848, a man named James Marshall found gold nuggets in the American River, near a water-powered sawmill in Coloma, one hundred miles north-east of Tracy. The foreman overseeing construction, Marshall noticed gold flakes of metal in the tailrace water, and decided to explore the river. He pulled the gold nuggets from the northern fork, but went back to work. By the time he set out for Sacramento, to show them to the owner of the mill, a few of Marshall's work crew had found more. The person with the deed to the land was Marshall's boss, Captain John Sutter. A Swiss immigrant, Sutter had come to the United States with dreams of building his own agricultural empire, which involved the servitude and slavery of its people. In Sacramento, John Sutter's fortified ranch was surrounded by fields and orchards, managed by the Maidu and Miwok Indians. Marshall showed the nuggets to Sutter, who tested them, found them to be pure gold, and sent them off to Washington D.C., to stake a claim.

Sutter asked Marshall to keep his discovery secret. Sutter knew that news of gold would bring people from all over the world, and this would ruin his plans of an agricultural empire. Marshall agreed, but news had already spread, as fast as the flakes of gold through the river. Soon, California's Gold Rush was on. By 1849, prospectors from all over the world took over the area, just as Sutter said they would. These miners, dubbed the "forty-niners" for the year they came, brought in viruses, germs, and diseases, killing off a large part of the Miwok, Maidu, and Yokuts Nations. Many who did survive were murdered. It was genocide.

California was annexed to the United States in 1850. Only a few people struck it rich from gold, but many became rich selling shovels and pans. Levi Straus made a fortune on durable pants, made from tent canvas. The enterprise charging toward California was the railroad. Most failed miners, looking for a job, represented a new and diverse immigrant population that was desperate to work. The most harrowing, dangerous jobs, like lighting fuses of dynamite to clear a passage through the mountains, belonged to immigrants.

The Transcontinental Railroad was completed in 1869, and Tracy was an important outpost, at the junction of the Central Pacific Railroad's Altamont, San Pablo, and Tulare lines. Businesses, schools, and churches were quickly built to serve the workers. In 1878, the Central Pacific Railroad set up a post office, and had the audacity to name the city after an Ohio grain merchant and railroad director: Lathrop Josiah Tracy.

In the early 1900's, Tracy was a relatively small town, with two forms of industry that put it on the map: railroad and agriculture. The tracks separated its population. The area south of the railroad tracks, where the railroad originally established section houses, was home to the Chinese, Japanese, and Mexican laborers who worked for the railroad.[18] Two roundhouses, at the railyard near the center of town, serviced and repaired the steam locomotives that came through Tracy. Many of the people who serviced them were Mexican-American, often called "greasers" for the dirty jobs they were given.

---

18 Tracy Historical Museum. *Images of America: Tracy*. Arcadia Publishing, an Imprint of Tempus Publishing, 2004.

Farm laborers, who came to Tracy for the harvests, stayed in makeshift labor camps on the outskirts of town, often temporary buildings or tents. Restaurants and grocery stores, specifically for the Mexican workforce, cropped up, all along the south side of town.

When the United States entered WWI, and then WWII, Tracyites of every race and ethnicity served their country overseas and domestically. In 1942, a massive Defense Depot opened on Chrisman Road, east of the town center, which supported all branches of the armed services. To residents of Tracy, however, it was called "the Army Depot."

When the Gonzalez family made a permanent move to Tracy in 1945, it was still a sleepy little town, but what would happen in the next few years, would change Tracy forever, and consequently, change our family.

25. El Ranchito

Gonzalez familia on the Ruiz Ranchito, approx. 1944 (l to r) Jennie, Lucy, Smiley, Terry, Nacho (Grandpa), Frank. (front row) Emily, Molly and Joey Ruiz (the boss' grandson)

The Ruiz ranch was located on the outskirts outside of Tracy, near the intersection of South Bird Road and Durham Ferry Road, about eleven miles southeast of the town center. The Gonzalez's new home was part of the property, which they fondly called "the ranchito." Surrounding fields produced tomatoes, beans, and alfalfa, in season. Orchards of nut and fruit trees were within walking distance. The ranchito had a main house, where Mr. Ruiz (el patrón), his wife (la partróna) and their family lived. Outbuildings, including a garage with living quarters on top, a barn, chicken coops, and storage buildings dotted the landscape.

The Gonzalez family house was a converted storage shed, located near the irrigation canal. It had one bathroom, two bedrooms, a kitchen, and a living area. There wasn't much adornment around it, other than a simple fence and gate, but it was a remarkable improvement to their living conditions in Malaga.

The Ruiz family lived in a house fairly close to the Gonzalez's, in the residence area, but the Ruiz home was remarkably different. With a California ranch model, the yards that surrounded the home had beautiful gardens, with outdoor patio seating, and special furniture. Grandma remembered la patróna's house as filled with modern conveniences.

"They had a television," Grandma said. "They had a stereo record player, and their own telephone. They would let us use the phone, anytime."

Mom and her sisters remembered la patróna as a kind woman, who gave them treats, like sugared almonds or walnuts. Every Easter, the Gonzalez kids were invited to hunt Easter eggs in the Ruiz's grass, since their house had no lawn. The disparity between employers, Spanish landowners, and the laborers, didn't go unnoticed. The Ruiz's were active in the Spanish community of Tracy, and would often entertain guests.

"I thought Spaniards were part of a different social class," Auntie Molly said. "The Ruiz family was Spanish. They hosted other Spanish families for parties, but we were never invited. Their guests would arrive in nice cars, and since we lived next door, we could see this."

"Our house started out as a little shack in the back," Auntie Lucy said. "They lived in the front of the farm, in a really nice home. It was obvious we were their servants, since we lived in the *servant's quarters*." Auntie Lucy shook her head. "La patróna would ask my mother to make tortillas and beans, but they'd never invite her or Daddy to their parties. Mama didn't really mind, because she liked helping, but it bothered me. It didn't seem to bother anyone else...."

"It bothered us," Auntie Molly said. "Maybe we didn't talk about it as much, but it bothered us. The way I saw it, the Mexican people had to work really, really, really *hard* for everything we had, but we never had much to show for it. Didn't we always see Daddy working so hard?"

All the sisters agreed that their father was the hardest worker they had ever seen.

Auntie Molly stifled a laugh, then said: "One time, when she was in school, Lucy filled out a form, and for father's occupation, she put: 'SLAVE.'"

The sisters laughed.

"That's how hard we saw him work!" Auntie Emmy said.

"It's true!" Auntie Lucy said. "Both our parents were hard workers, but Daddy *loved* to. The hardest times in Malaga were the winters, when he didn't have work. *That* was the worst."

"Daddy drove himself harder than any boss could," Auntie Emmy said. "And he really liked how the patrón valued his opinion. One day, the boss and his son came over to our house. I could tell they were trying to get

Daddy's opinion on when the harvest would be ready."

"I remember that," Auntie Molly said. "El patrón asked Daddy, 'What do you think, Nacho? Maybe four o'clock tomorrow morning?' Daddy said it was better to start earlier, and explained his plan. So, the patrón said, 'Good! Let's do it that way.'"

"He liked being asked for his opinion," Auntie Emmy said. "He felt respected."

Grandpa did, indeed, receive more respect and appreciation from Mr. Ruiz than any other boss he had worked for in los Estados Unidos. For Grandpa, peace and purpose was found in driving a tractor, managing the farm, and taking care of the land. Even small jobs kept him busy—and a busy Nacho was a happier Nacho.

***

Auntie Terry, as the eldest daughter, was Grandma's right hand. In Malaga, one of Terry's jobs was water. Every morning, she had to wake up, go to the pump outside, fill the bucket, and bring it in. Like Grandma, the water-duty fell to her. The new house in Tracy, with its indoor sink and water on tap, was a huge blessing, especially to Auntie Terry.

"When we first moved there, I still got up early," Auntie Terry said. "I forgot we had a tap, so I would wake up and remember." She smiled, peacefully. "Oh, it was so nice!" She thought a while and turned to Mom. "Did I ever tell you, I used to think there was a mermaid in the river?"

"The river?" Mom asked, smiling.

"Okay, the irrigation canal," Auntie Terry said, nudging Mom. "One morning, after Daddy had already left to work, I was up early, and I happened to look out the window as I drank a glass of water. I saw something in the distance." She looked far off in the distance, squinting her eyes. "Far away, in the water, I saw a woman bathing. I didn't know who it was. I decided to keep it to myself." Mom and I tried not to laugh, as Auntie Terry added mysterious, fictional elements.

"I couldn't hold it inside me anymore," Auntie Terry said. "I told Frank, 'There's a woman, like a mermaid, who bathes in the river. She throws up her hair like this, and raises her arms like this,'" Auntie Terry demonstrated these motions, as graceful as a ballerina. "Frank said, 'Maybe it's a ghost.' That scared me. Every time I woke up early, there she was again."

"Who?" Mom asked.

"The mermaid, in the irrigation," Auntie Terry said, irritated that her sister wasn't following. "Anyway, one morning, I told Mama, 'I've been seeing someone bathing in the canal, but I don't know who it is. Can you help me?' My mother listened to my whole story. She asked me, 'What time are you seeing her?' I told her I saw her early in the morning, before I got dressed. Mama said, 'You have to stop spying. Don't be a spy!' I had not realized, until then, that the woman I'd been seeing was my mom, bathing in the canal."

"Remember, this ditch was for irrigation." Auntie Lucy said. "Mama bathed there. As kids, we used to swim in it! It was maybe four feet deep. There was no concrete bottom, just mud. It was a ditch!"

"We packed the mud down, and made slides," Auntie Emmy said. She pointed to Auntie Molly's arm. "Show her your scar, Molly." Auntie Molly lifted up her sleeve and revealed a faded pink scar, the size of a hairpin, on her forearm. "See that?" Auntie Emmy said, tracing it with her index finger. "Molly slid down a mudslide one day, and didn't see glass in the mud. She cut herself and got that scar."

"Poor Molly," Mom said. "The next thing we knew, she was bleeding."

"Back then, Mama didn't take us to the doctor," Auntie Emmy said. She mimicked Grandma, examining Auntie Molly's arm. "She'd clean it up, stop the bleeding, and that was it."

Esther remembered how much fun her cousins had swimming in the irrigation canal.

"In the summer, my cousins would ask if I wanted to go swimming in the canal," she said. "But I said no, only because I was afraid of the water."

"We were allowed to go swimming there," Mom said. "But only the part that was next to our house. Mama wouldn't let us swim anywhere else in the canal."

"They would go swimming, and it looked fun," Esther said. "But I wasn't used to the water, so I didn't want to go in."

"I was used to the water," Mom said. "But one time, I almost drowned."

"What!?" I said, turning toward her. I probably looked as shocked as I felt, because Mom laughed, and then covered her mouth.

"I told you this story before, didn't I?"

"No, you never told me this story before," I said, trying to calm down.

"The water was deeper over by the bridge, and moved faster," Mom said. "There were whirlpools churning as it went underneath."

"We used to call that place 'the depend,'" Auntie Molly said. "We didn't know Mama was telling us not to go in the *deep end*. We thought she called it

143

the depend."

"The deep end is where I fell in," Mom said. "Terry, Lucy and I were walking home from the store, which was across the street. We were balancing on the cement border of the bridge, which wasn't too high off the ground. I lost my balance and fell in. I knew how to swim, but I fell from the street, down into a whirlpool of water, and got sucked under, right away. The water was around my ears, sucking me down, and bringing me back up again. This happened about three times. All of a sudden, Smiley dove in, with all his clothes on, and saved me. He grabbed me, and pulled me to the side. By that time, I had been sucked under a few times, so I was shaking and panicking. You can imagine what that swirling water does to a little girl."

"Oh my gosh," I said, covering my mouth. I considered the terrible reality of her loss. Mom told me this story when she was in her eighties, and with it came the reminder of what a fragile blessing our lives are. Thought of my mother possibly drowning shook me.

"God's plan is perfect," Mom said. "Smiley was right there, and I was okay."

I was suddenly overwhelmed with the miraculous love I had for her, and for her life. I thought about Mom crossing Bird Road, a road where truck and cars speed through like a highway, then balancing over a rushing irrigation ditch. I realized, only then, how much more fragile life is for children of farm laborers.

26. Gender Roles

Before school, September 1945.
Back row: Lucy, Jennie, Terry. Front row: Molly and Emily

Every day Grandma woke up early, and prepared her family elaborate breakfasts. As Auntie Terry described it, the aromas and sounds of Grandma's kitchen filled my senses.

"Mama made fried potatoes, eggs, mush, and beans." Auntie Terry said. "Sometimes, we didn't have eggs, so Mama served wieners and beans. I helped her prepare the kitchen. She would start rolling out the tortillas, and then, she'd call, 'Time to get up! Get ready for school! Wash your face! Get dressed!' Every morning, Mama had her hair braided, and wrapped around her head like a crown. As she prepared breakfast, I had to get the little ones up quickly.

"We had a little restroom at the back of the house," Auntie Terry continued. "We'd take turns getting ready in there, and then come to the table and sit down. I made sure everybody was clean, while Mama got the plates all ready for breakfast."

"Poor Mama!" Auntie Lucy said. "She catered to everybody! She'd sit us down at the table, and every kid asked for something different. Emily and Molly wanted this; Jennie wanted that. I wanted my eggs just right—not runny, not too hard. Smiley? He was never happy with anything Mama gave him."

"There were days when there was no pleasing Smiley," Mom said. "He would look at the breakfast Mama served, and say, 'I don't want that!' Mama would ask him, 'Well, what do you want?' He'd say, 'I want hot chocolate.' She'd bring him hot chocolate. Then, he'd say, 'I don't want that.' She'd ask him, "What do you want?" He's start crying and say, 'I want a horse!'"

Everyone laughed, except for Auntie Lucy.

"Smiley hated me," she said, quietly. "He didn't respect me at all. I couldn't sit next to him at the breakfast table, because if I so much as accidentally touch his shoe with mine, he'd get up and smack me." Auntie Lucy's face, usually the picture of confidence, morphed into a five year-old's expression of puzzlement. "My mother told me, much later, that Smiley was the baby of the family for two years, and then I came along. He got no attention after that. So, he resented me from the time I was born."

School picture of Smiley Gonzalez, 1939

None of the sisters disputed this. Instead, they were resigned to the reality of Smiley and Lucy, both strong personalities, being on opposite sides of the table.

"Lucy had to put up with a lot from Smiley," Auntie Emmy said.

"And we couldn't skip breakfast," Auntie Molly said. "That was Mama's rule."

"But Smiley was terrible to her everywhere," Mom said. "And he'd be mean to any of us if he found out we were nice to her."

"Once we moved to the ranch, Smiley built a little clubhouse out of scrap wood," Auntie Lucy said. "It was cute, cute, cute! He'd invite everybody in, except me. He didn't allow me to be part of his club, or to see the inside of that place." Auntie Lucy thought about this for a moment and then leaned forward in her chair. "Do you know how much that hurt my feelings?"

I could actually could relate to Auntie Lucy's story. In my childhood, my sister Patty, was born thirteen months before me. I often received the same cruel treatment, maybe for the same reason. When I would report her behavior to Mom, she told me to ignore Patty, and not make a fuss. I would cry and tell Mom she favored Patty because she was older, and maybe her favorite. Mom would disagree with my emotional reaction.

"That's not true" she would say, calmly. "Mothers don't have favorite children. That's like asking me to choose my favorite finger."

One day, almost as a test, I asked Grandma if she had a favorite child.

"Jennie was the easiest child," she said, rolling out a tortilla for me. I was standing next to her, waiting to eat it. "Jennie did everything just right. She was cute. She had a pretty voice. She was always happy..." Then, she smiled and whispered, "but Smiley was my favorite."

I winced.

In my mind, Grandma was perfect, and perfect mothers didn't have favorite children. I couldn't imagine *Grandma*, the most loving person I knew, preferring one child over another, let alone *Uncle Smiley*. I felt disappointed, but tried not to show it. *Why Smiley?* According to an old generalization, traditional Mexican women favor their sons above daughters, simply because they were male. I wondered if this were true with Grandma. I didn't have the guts to ask.

She handed me a tortilla, and I ate it.

***

Life wasn't easy for my uncles, Frank and Smiley, who learned how to work hard at a young age. They lived a life working next to their father, often separated from their sisters. When they were united with their sisters, they often clowned around.

"My brothers were always teasing us," Auntie Terry said, smiling. "They were always trying to make us laugh, especially Frank. Smiley was more serious."

"Much more," Mom said, nodding.

"They had different chores," Mom said. "Most of the time, they worked with Daddy."

"Dad was always trying to impart a strong work ethic to Frank and Smiley," Auntie Terry said. "He taught them that men have more responsibilities." She laughed, and nodded at Mom. "Right? That's what Daddy said to them. Mama believed whatever our dad said, and trusted him with the boys."

In traditional Mexican-American households, what might have been acceptable for one gender, might not have been acceptable for the other. Because of this patriarchal structure, there were different chores and rules for males and females. The Gonzalez girls, under Grandma's care, were exposed to the powerful arts of housekeeping, storytelling, and cooking. The sons worked outside, even in the fields as soon as they were able.

"In the summers, Daddy would come home at lunch break," Auntie Terry said. "He didn't eat until eleven-thirty or twelve o'clock. He worked from two o'clock in the morning until it was done. He'd come home at lunch time, eat, and take a shower..."

Mom and Auntie Terry looked at each other and spontaneously laughed.

"We're laughing because our dad's shower was outside," Auntie Terry said, covering her mouth as she guffawed. "It was a tank, filled with water, over a shower stall. In the summer, the sun warmed the water in the tank, and Daddy would take a shower. Afterwards, he'd eat his lunch. Then, he took a nap on a hammock outside. Sometimes, he'd make us fan him in the hammock when it was really hot."

"What?" I asked, a little too loud. I looked at Mom. "You had to fan Grandpa when he was napping?"

"Oh, yes," Mom said, still laughing. "We took turns."

"Our dad would put each of his kids to fan him," Auntie Terry said, slowly waving an imaginary fan with her hand. "We had to do it like this. Daddy liked to feel the air moving. Everyone took a turn, except for Lucy." She looked at me and raised her eyebrows. "It wasn't her style."

"Smiley didn't want to, either," Mom said.

"Smiley hated doing it," Auntie Terry said. "But Smiley was there while we were fanning, and Daddy saw him. Smiley thought he could get away with it, but Daddy knew. When the weekend came, Daddy would make Smiley clean the yard. My dad would say, 'See those tiny little leaves between the gravel? You get to pick out each one.' Smiley would say, 'I can't see them.' Daddy said, 'If I can see them, so can you. Pick out each little one.'

"Well, that took forever. Smiley would get so mad. My Dad wanted to keep him busy, just because Smiley wanted to get out of fanning him."

"Maybe that's why Mama favored Smiley," Mom said. "She felt like Daddy was too hard on him."

"Mama had a way of dealing with Lucy's behavior," Auntie Terry said. "We would go inside, away from the heat, and Mama would say, 'See what happens when the boys don't listen, Luz? You have to listen to Daddy, too.' And then, she would shift to Lucy, and make her embroider."

"It was like torture for Lucy," Mom said, smiling. "We would have hoops and threads. We'd embroider dish towels, or pillow slips. Grandma thought it was a special skill, but Lucy didn't like doing it."

"It's not that I *didn't like* embroidering," Auntie Lucy said. "I *absolutely hated* it!" Auntie Lucy scooted forward, and spoke emphatically. "Embroidery was dumb and boring! My mother—bless her heart—would buy patterns, then apply them to pillow slips or dish towels. She would get her ironing board out and iron the transfer to the cloth." Auntie Lucy demonstrated, even making the sound of the steam iron. "We would put one hoop on the bottom and one hoop on the top, and pull the fabric tight, so it would be firm. We'd have to sit up straight and start." Auntie Lucy sits up straight and mimics the motion of embroidery, slowly and steadily, while making a stiff, refined face. "Oh my gosh! We were supposed to be so *delighted*! We were supposed to be *jumping with joy*! Why? All I could think was, 'This is so boring!'" Auntie Lucy sat back in her chair. "I thought, 'There has to be more to life than this!' Jennie, you never minded that, did you?"

"I didn't mind it," Mom said. "I wasn't *wild* about it, but I wasn't going to complain like you did, Lucy!"

Auntie Lucy laughed. "Of course not!" she said. "I was so hard to be around on embroidery days. My poor Mama! She wanted to make a lady out of me."

"Daddy had it good with Mama," Auntie Molly said. "She didn't *ever* argue with him. She did anything to please him. She was an *obedient* wife."

"Mama was more than obedient!" Auntie Emmy said, laughing. "She was *submissive*!"

The sisters laughed, and agreed that Grandma served Grandpa in the archetypal role of the Mexican-wife-who-doesn't-question-her-husband.

"We loved to go pick walnuts in the orchards," Auntie Terry said. "One day, the patróna came to Mama and said, 'The walnuts are ready. Bring the kids, and we'll go get some.' It was so much fun. Mama took us, without asking my dad. When Daddy got home, Jennie showed him her little hands, and said, 'Look, Daddy, my fingers turned black!' My Dad turned around to my mom, and asked..."

"Where have you been?" Mom said, finishing the sentence.

Silence.

Mom and Auntie Terry withdrew from their adult selves, and became little girls, looking up at Grandpa, like he was right there.

Auntie Terry continued, quietly. "Jennie told Daddy we went to the orchard to pick walnuts, and..." she looked at me. "You know how the walnut husks turn your hands black?"

I nodded. "I picked walnuts in Tracy, a couple of times, over the summer."

"That's right, I remember," Mom said, and smiled. She was Mom again, and I was relieved.

Auntie Terry continued. "Daddy said to Mama, 'So, you did this behind my back, huh?' Mama got real quiet. Daddy didn't yell or get mad—but we never went to pick walnuts again."

"Not without permission," Mom said.

"Oh my gosh," Auntie Molly said. "Mama *always* obeyed Daddy. She never asked why or why not. She did exactly what he said, even about little things."

***

Summer and Autumn were the harvest seasons, and Grandpa worked hard, physically, every day. His schedule was almost a graveyard shift, in bed by 7:30 p.m. to get up at 2:30 in the morning. During the winter months, as the work slowed, so did Grandpa's income.

"Our family didn't go out often," Auntie Terry said. "Not even to church on Sundays. We would say, 'Daddy, are you going to take us out this weekend?' He would continue reading his newspaper. 'Why can't we go to church? Don't you like church, Daddy?' Our dad gave no answer. The only time Daddy would go out was to go shopping for supplies. It was the highlight of our week."

"Dad's the one who shopped," Mom said. "He would go into town for provisiones. That's what he'd say. My mother would write a little list of the things she needed. I recently found one of these lists, it's about this big..." Mom turned to Auntie Terry and outlined a shape about the size of an index card. "It says ajotes," Mom turned to me. "That means green beans, and manteca, which is... do you know what that is?"

I raised my eyebrows at her. I knew manteca meant lard. I almost resented Mom for translating simple things for me, but in truth, I still needed help with Spanish. Mom knew this.

"If Dad took us shopping, sometimes he'd take us to the movies," Auntie Lucy said. "Daddy would drop us off at the Grand Theater, to see a Saturday show. Then, he would leave and go somewhere. We assumed he went shopping, but we never knew what he did. It wasn't until much later when we found out later that he was gambling. He played cards for money."

Auntie Mildred, the woman who later married Uncle Smiley, remembered Smiley telling her about this.

"Grandpa would leave the older kids at the movies," Auntie Mildred said. "He would sit the kids down to see a movie, and leave. Smiley said they would see the movie once, and then again. Sometimes, Smiley said, they would be there watching the same movie three times, before Grandpa would show up to get them. He'd been off gambling, to make extra money for the family. Getting left in that theater scared Smiley. It made him very upset."

Auntie Dorothy, the woman who married my Uncle Frank, also heard about the times Grandpa went gambling, and how it affected Grandma.

"Ignacio, your grandpa, would gamble on the Southside of Tracy," Auntie Dorothy said. "I knew all about this, because at the time, I was dating Frank. Sometimes Grandma would send Frank out to look for him. 'Mijo, you have to go find your dad,' and Frank would go out and look. Sometimes, he couldn't find him. Sometimes, he was in a place Frank couldn't go inside. Frank was underage, and he couldn't go in. Grandpa's gambling problem caused a lot of problems between him and Frank. It *really* affected Frank and Smiley as men. Even as adults, they didn't like gambling."

"But that's how Dad got our spare money," Auntie Lucy said. "Sometimes he lucked-out and made enough money to buy extras. Of course, I didn't know any of this back then. I just knew, when Daddy dropped us off at the theater, we'd have to see the movie more than once."

Grandpa's gambling activities were always kept secret, as if they never happened. He justified gambling by saying he was earning extra money. In reality, Grandma worried, and his children could sense the odd dysfunction when it happened in their family.

"But overall, we had a beautiful life growing up," Auntie Terry said. "Daddy did his best. Mama was very loving and took care of us. And those days on the Ruiz farm were beautiful."

"We all have different memories," Mom said. "I loved growing up on the ranch, with the orchards around us. We had a beautiful view, with the beautiful outline of Mount Oso. But Lucy? She absolutely hated it. She'd look at those mountains, and say, 'I know that somewhere, on the other side of those mountains, there's a better life for me.'"

Auntie Lucy laughed. "I couldn't *wait* to leave the ranch," she said. "I'd say,

'Somewhere, over those mountains, is another life. There has to be a better life than this." Auntie Lucy, like all of her siblings, had the unusual restrictions of childhood, growing up in a beautiful but remote setting. As children, their dilemma was how to join their homelife with the life they lived at school.

Part Nine: Mexican Rice

"Things to remember:
you are a one-way ticket.
Say goodbye, not hasta luego."

~Leonora Simonovis
"In the Airport" from *Study of the Raft*

Mexican Rice

1 cup uncooked rice about ¼ cup lard (or oil)
1 onion, chopped fine (preferably white or yellow)
1 can (7.75 oz.) El Pato tomato sauce, Mexican hot style (yellow can)
2 cloves garlic, minced
2 cups water
2 tbs Knorr chicken bullion (or Knorr cubes) They have a chicken on them.
½ cup frozen vegetables (peas, corn, or peppers, if you want)
 coarse salt peppercorns
dash of cumino and chili powder –to your taste

Cook rice in a little bit of fat, on medium heat, until it looks toasted. Maybe this takes five minutes, maybe more. Put toasted rice in a bowl. Fry up chopped onion and garlic in a little bit of fat, until they smell good and onions are clear. Add the water, (it will sizzle) and stir in bullion and rice. Heat until boiling, and then turn down to low to simmer. Stir in 2tsp salt and a little pepper and cumino. If you want to add other chiles, you can, but the Cook over low heat for about 25 minutes, or until the rice is fluffy and tender. Add frozen vegetables in the last 5 minutes. When serving, fluff rice up with fork, and work in frozen vegetables (if you use them).

From Grandma: *I never had this kind of rice until I came here, to the United States. They call it Spanish Rice or Mexican rice, but the Spanish eat their rice with saffron, and the Mexicans eat white rice with fresh vegetables—when they eat rice.*

27. School Days

New Jerusalem School, in Tracy, where the Gonzalez kids spent their elementary years, was so different from Malaga School that it seemed otherworldly. The Ruiz ranchito just happened to be located across the street from their bus stop, so Mom and her six siblings crossed the street to catch it. To hear Mom tell it, you'd think they had their own limousine service.

"The school bus would come and pick us up in front of the store across the street," Mom said. She took out a piece of paper and drew a cross. On one side, the bus stop was at the corner store, and the Ruiz ranch was on the other side of the street. "We didn't have to walk far at all, thank God! The store was here, on the corner, with a residence upstairs, for the people who ran it. The shop-owner's kids were even luckier than us. They just had to walk out the door to the bus. At one time there was a trailer park on the other side of the store, so kids who lived there would get the bus, too."

New Jerusalem School was a country school, both geographically and culturally, with most of its student population coming from nearby farms and ranches. Some students were children of landowners. Others, like the Gonzalez family, had parents who were farm laborers. There were no rules about who could ride the bus, or where they could sit. The bus was a great equalizer.

"All kinds of kids rode that bus," Auntie Lucy said. "But most of them came from wealthy families who owned farms. I still remember, vividly, one boy. He was a spoiled brat. I won't tell you his name, but I will tell you he was an only child. He boarded the bus before we did, so we had to hear his teasing every day when we boarded. He'd say, 'Oh boy, Al! I can feel those tires going down! Here come the Gonzalez kids!' He would shout this, pretending to talk to the bus driver, whose name was Al, but all the kids heard him. He was teasing us, because there were so many of us Gonzalez kids." Auntie Lucy paused, an angry expression on her face. "I would *glare* at him, with that Lucy Gonzalez *glare*. He was an only child, spoiled-rotten, I could just tell."

Mom started New Jerusalem School in the second grade, so Auntie Lucy was in fourth grade, Auntie Terry and Uncle Smiley, in the sixth grade, and Uncle Frank in the eighth. My twin aunties, Emmy and Molly, started in first grade, rather than kindergarten.

All of their names were changed. When they entered New Jerusalem School, Francisco was renamed Frank. Teresa, rather English-sounding, only had the pronunciation of her name changed, from "Ter-ay-sa" to "Ter-**ee**-sa." Luz became Lucy. Mom was immediately renamed, "Jennie," from Juanita. Amelia and Amalia became Emily and Molly.

"In those days, there was this sense of being *thrust* into American society," Mom said. "The teachers would say, 'Oh, you're American now! Your name is Juana? We'll call you Jennie.' They said it, like they were doing me a favor," Mom said, shaking her head. "They didn't even ask our parent's permission, they just started calling us our new names."

The teachers did ask Grandma's permission when they wanted to rename Ismael, my Uncle Smiley. His new name, so different from the Spanish, had to be signed-off by his parents. "The teacher told Mama 'Ismael' was too hard for the children to pronounce," Mom said. "I don't know how *true* that was. Maybe it was too hard for her to pronounce, but that's what she said. His teacher asked my mother, 'Is it okay if we call him Smiley? Because he's always smiling. We thought that would be a cute name for him.' Mama said, 'Sure, whatever. Do what you think is right.'" Mom smiled, but lifted her eyebrows in a way that told me she wasn't a fan of the logic. "So, that's what he was called at school."

"But was he always smiling, really?" I asked.

"No," Auntie Emmy and Molly answered at the same time.

"Out of all of us, he was the one who probably smiled the *least*," Auntie Molly said.

"My parents didn't call him Smiley at home," Mom said. "They never called my brother, Frank, anything but Francisco. At home our names stayed the same."

Renaming, a common practice during the early and mid-twentieth century, wasn't always a written policy, just standard procedure for Americanization. When children from Mexican immigrant families enrolled in school, most children had Spanish first names. Anglicizing their names, or renaming, set a precedent for their new identities, as English-speaking students, like everyone else in the classroom. They were immediately fast-tracked to looking, speaking, and even playing like the typical American student. It was intentional, not "just something we do." It was recharacterization, not unlike cutting the hair off the heads of incoming Indian students at State schools.

Instruction, at the elementary level, included textbooks with caricatures of other cultures that were explicitly racialized, and xenophobic. Little Jose from Tijuana wore a large sombrero, with ratty edges; he had no shoes on his feet. Most children in the textbooks were American, and looked like most students in the classroom. They had light skin, and spoke English—the only language they would ever need. The message was clear: leave Spanish at home. Unlike the Gonzalez kids, some students didn't get the message. These students had to be told not to speak Spanish on campus, and disciplined if they didn't comply. Children usually complied, because of their peers. Peer pressure becomes the solidifying factor for most children.

My Mexican-American grandparents, who complied with all of it, came to this country to make a home. Like most immigrants, they were respectful of church and state authority, and to them, teachers represented the school. Teachers would help their children fit in to American society. Mexican-immigrant parents often cooperated because they wanted the best for their child, and consequently, their family. It brought them one step closer to "becoming American," something they wanted.

"Didn't it bother you?" I asked. "Did your name change embarrass you?"

"Not really," Mom said. "That's just how things were then. Today, most teachers celebrate diversity! They encourage kids to share their ancestry. Kids are encouraged to *hold on* to their culture. Back then? Not at all." Mom thought about this for a while, and then offered an opinion. "You would think they would have called me Joanna, if they were trying to select a name that sounded like mine. Doesn't Joanna sound more like Juana than Jennie?"

Mom asked me this question, but didn't expect an answer, from me or from herself. She's always had that rare, good-natured personality, able to overlook thoughtlessness or casual insults. Despite the name change, Mom has made peace with the name she's used most of her life. It's on every one of her official documents, and fits with her husband's name: Jack. To everyone they know, Dad and Mom are Jack and Jennie Ryan.

***

"Every day we went to school," Auntie Terry said. "I have pleasant and happy memories of school, until I got to eighth grade."

"Terry struggled in school," Mom said. "She was sick a lot, and missed too many days."

"I did," Auntie Terry said. "But I always knew I wasn't as smart as my sisters, who never struggled in school. Reading came easy for them, they had good handwriting, and they learned math easily. I understood my lessons up until fifth grade. Then, things started getting harder. The teachers were always encouraging me to continue, anyway. They said, 'Just keep studying. You'll make it to high school.'"

"And you did!" Mom said, patting Auntie Terry's back. They smiled at each other.

"I did," Auntie Terry said. "When you're in school, you need someone who understands what you're going through. My teacher said to me, 'I used to study you, and I saw you were very quiet. You don't share your feelings with anyone.' She was right. I had a friend, who sat behind me in class. He always ate lunch at his desk, so I could smell sweet fig bars." Auntie Terry paused, closed her eyes, and inhaled through her nose. "Oh, they smelled so good! He always offered me one, but I politely said no. He knew I was struggling in school, but he would always encourage me. One day, he handed me a note. It said, 'Don't give up! You'll go to high school, just like me!' So, he was the first to encourage me like that. I appreciated that encouragement."

"Teresa was the eldest daughter," Auntie Lucy said. "When you're the eldest daughter in a Hispanic family, *so* much is expected of you. Terry helped Mama in the kitchen, helped all her siblings, and never balked at anything our parents asked of her. She never complained, never got angry. 'Oh, you have homework? After you help with...'" Auntie Lucy shook her head. "There was always something for Terry to be doing. Homework? She didn't have *time* for homework! It wasn't because she wasn't trying in school."

Mom agreed. "We also have to remember how we moved a lot when Terry was growing up," she said. "I was in the second grade when we moved, permanently, to Tracy, but Terry was seven years older than I was. She had to keep up with her work, but because she changed schools so many times, it was harder."

"In the eighth grade, I took my final exams," Auntie Terry said. "When the results came back, the teacher called me to her desk. I thought for sure I hadn't passed, but when I got to her desk, she smiled at me. She said, 'Thank you for being a good student, and for trying your hardest. You passed by one point.'" Auntie Terry put her hand over her heart and leaned back in her chair. "I said, 'Oh, thank God!'"

"It was a happy day for her," Auntie Lucy said. "It was also a happy day for Mama. It was like Mama was graduating eighth grade *with* Terry!"

"Yes," Auntie Terry said. "I finally made it to high school, but I had to keep going, and try to graduate. I had to think about my future."

***

In post-WWII United States, the economy, culture, and even popular music was changing rapidly. The Gonzalez family felt music influencing every aspect of their lives.

"We started singing because of Dad," Auntie Terry said. "He wanted us to become a family of singers who performed. When we had big family gatherings, he'd call us together. The excellent one was Jennie," she said, nudging Mom. "She could hold that high note, which Dad loved. He would say, 'Come on, honey, show them what you can do!'"

"Always when we had company," Mom said. "Most of the time, we were embarrassed."

She illustrated this, looking around with childlike shyness, arms in front of her.

"We were on the spot," Auntie Terry said. "Now, we're all supposed to sing!"

"My dad would bring out his guitar," Mom said. She settled an air guitar in front of her and lifted her chin, confidently. "Then, he'd call us: 'Cha-chas!'" She and Auntie Terry laughed. "It was like he was saying, 'Bring out my performing monkeys! Do your tricks. Get up on the table and do your little somersaults!'" We laughed at Mom's impression of her father, which was impressive, as she matched his confident tone and facial expressions. "So, I remember singing in front of people, but we wouldn't look at them. We'd just look at each other."

"He wanted us to sing *Mexican songs* for our company," Auntie Lucy said.

"That way, he could say, 'See what I've taught them? These are my daughters, and they can sing *traditional* Mexican music!'"

"Daddy would be strumming on the guitar," Auntie Molly said. "And later he taught Frank and Smiley. He loved singing Spanish songs."

"He taught Jennie and I how to harmonize with each other," Auntie Lucy said.

"Jennie could hold that high note," Auntie Terry said, lifting her hand above her head. "Which is important in Mexican music, and Daddy loved that."

"So, Daddy would show her off," Auntie Emmy said.

"Jennie was his little star," Auntie Molly said.

"Music was really important to Daddy," Auntie Emmy said. "But Molly and I? We could not carry a tune!"

"We couldn't," Auntie Molly said, laughing. "Dad tried to teach us, and he wasn't mean about it, but he'd say, 'Try again,' or 'Try this…' and eventually, I think he just realized that we just couldn't carry a tune."

"It was the only time we ever saw Daddy give up," Auntie Emmy said. "But he already had Terry, Lucy, and Jennie singing. Smiley and Frank were playing the guitar. All of them were very musically inclined. It was like he had his own band again!"

"Daddy played songs, like 'El Rancho Grande,'" Auntie Lucy said.

"And La Barca de Oro," Mom said. "Remember that?"

Auntie Terry took this as an invitation to start singing it. Mom joined in. Auntie Lucy harmonized. Auntie Emmy and Auntie Molly mimicked the reaction of the audience, going for their wallets and purses.

"Our Aunts and Uncles would give Jennie money when she held the high note," Auntie Emmy said. "Well, Tia Maria would."

***

Most of the time Mom told us about her school days, she was talking about Tracy High, the alma mater she loved. We, her five children, went to the same school, twenty-some-odd years later. By the time I got there, Mom's favorite teacher, Emma Baumgartner, now had a building named after her—the theater. It was where the public speaking rooms were and, being a nerdy speech team member, where I spent most of my time.

"Mrs. Baumgartner was such a good teacher," Mom said. "She made sure we were prepared for the world with perfect English!" Mom is eerily proficient in English grammar. It served her well as a secretary, and mother to five kids. She became a wonderful proofreader.

Mom's yearbooks from Tracy High are filled with black-and-white glossy pages of her and my aunties in the sports section. In some pictures they wore varsity letter sweaters. Mom played volleyball, softball, and basketball. She and her sisters served as officers in Block T, a club for female athletes.

"You must have been very popular," I said. It was hard to imagine my clothes-folding lunch-packing, dinner-making mother in high school, let alone a coordinated, athlete. "No," Mom said, sighing. "I wasn't what you'd call popular."

Page from 1955 El Portal, Tracy High Yearbook. Mom is in the front row with her sisters, Molly and Emily, and also on the ladder of officers, third from the top.

I found out much later what Mom meant. The Gonzalez family lived on the ranch, in a remote location. Traveling to town involved strategy. Grandma didn't drive, so the family had to rely on their father to drive them to town.

"Before we got to high school, I thought life on the ranch was fun,"

Auntie Molly said. "Once we got into high school, it felt very lonesome. Our friends were always going to places, dances, participating in high school functions. We couldn't do any of that."

"I never wanted to live on a ranch when I grew up," Auntie Emmy said, smiling sadly.

"Our dad didn't think it was necessary for us to do anything besides go to school," Auntie Lucy said. "If he said no, to anything, we couldn't even try to change his mind." Auntie Lucy sighed and shook her head. "I've always been very social, *and* very musical. In high school, I was in the band, but not the marching band. The marching band played at football games. They wore uniforms and sat in a special section at games. *But* the football team had away games, and the team traveled by bus, with the marching band. Daddy didn't like that. He wouldn't let me travel on the school bus, even though there were several adult chaperones. He said no, and that was it.

"One day, I went to the marching band advisor. He was our music teacher, and he knew me. I asked him, 'How can I be in the marching band, if I can't travel to the out-of-town games? My Dad won't let me travel on the bus. Is there an instrument that I can play, where I can be part of the marching band at home games, only?' He understood my dilemma and actually found an instrument for me to play: alto clarinet. I was able to be part of the marching band at home games. I was so happy! If there were out-of-town games, I couldn't go, but I didn't complain, because now I could play at home games." She laughed, sardonically. "Can you imagine? My dad didn't trust the leaders?" She sighed, leaned back in her seat. "I guess Daddy was worried what would happen to me if I rode the bus. My mother later told me that Daddy was like this because he was such a cad as a single man. He thought all boys on the bus had intentions, which is why he protected us so much. He was afraid of what those men could do."

Grandpa knew what the men could do, because he was a young man once. As strict as he was with his sons, he was much more with his daughters.

For my uncles, Frank and Smiley, independence came in the form of driving. Then, in the form of love. The Gonzalez family was about to have their insulated world invaded by two sisters, whose family would be forever entwined with theirs, and now ours.

28. Addition and Subtraction

Grandpa worked as a foreman, or permanent liaison at the ranch, helping el patrón with the hiring of seasonal workers, men who traveled with the harvests. These trabajadores often traveled with their families, and their kids attended local schools, as migrant enrollees. The Gonzalez siblings often met the kids of migrant farmers at school. Two of their new friends were sisters—Dorothy and Mildred—who would later marry my uncles, Frank and Smiley.

"My brother, Frank, was a fashionable guy," Auntie Terry said. "He would dress up in nice pants, with a fresh white shirt. He'd look at me and ask, 'Terry, how do I look?' I would say, 'You look good, Frank.' Then, he'd pull down a piece of his hair and make a curl on his forehead. He'd say, 'How about now, Terry?' I would laugh and say, 'Oh, Frank, now you look terrific!' He liked that. That's what he wanted to hear." She laughed.

Uncle Frank, posing here with his cousin, shows off his signature curl. Approx. 1952

"When I was in high school, Frank told me about a girl he really liked," Auntie Terry said. "'She's in your Spanish class. She's Mexican. Her name is

Dorothy Pain.' I said, 'Okay, Frank, I'll look out for her.' So, I looked around, and saw Dorothy for the first time." Auntie Terry turned to me and touched my arm. "Now, mija, I'm not saying Frank was ugly, but I just thought, 'Oh, no. She's *way* too pretty for him. I don't think she'll be his girlfriend.' That was my first reaction, because Frank was my brother."

"I had the same reaction," Mom said, smiling. "The day I met Dorothy, my brother Frank introduced her to us. I just stared at her, thinking, 'What a beautiful, beautiful girl!' And *she* loves my ugly brother?"

Dorothy Pain would be the first outsider to penetrate the fortified walls of the tight Gonzalez familia. Dorothy, the same age as Uncle Smiley, was the second eldest daughter of a single mother. In her family, she functioned a lot like Auntie Terry did. The whole family noticed her beauty, and also a rare humility that came from helping her mother raise her brothers and sisters. Uncle Frank, like his family, found this combination enchanting.

Dorothy Pain, approx. 1951

"We all thought Dorothy was the most beautiful girl," Mom said. "I loved it when Frank started bringing her over to our house. She was easy to hang around with, and she had a lot of brothers and sisters, so she knew what growing up in a big family was like. We all got along. Pretty soon, her family started coming with her. Dorothy had a little sister, Mildred, who was my age."

Dorothy would later marry my Uncle Frank. Her sister, Mildred, would later marry Uncle Smiley. Their mother, Nellie, would be called "Grandma Nellie," by everyone in our family.

Dorothy Pain Gonzalez, still gorgeous in her eighties, vividly remembered her first visit to the ranch, where she met the entire Gonzalez family.

"I met everybody when Frank took me to the ranchito," Auntie Dorothy said. "I was excited, because I was finally going to meet his family. They were all so sweet, so nice to me. The twins were so small. I just loved them, even though I couldn't tell them apart." Auntie Dorothy laughed at this memory, her first time seeing identical twins. "I not only fell in love with Frank, but I fell really in love with his whole family. They asked me all kinds of questions, and welcomed me in. That was my first memory of them."

Hanging at the ranch (l to r) Dorothy, Esther, Jennie, and Lucy

It didn't take long for Dorothy to get the green-light to bring her whole family to the ranchito for bar-b-ques. Grandpa and Grandma welcomed Dorothy's mother, Nellie, a Mexican-American single mother of seven children, at the time. Dorothy's elder sister, Priscilla—everyone called her Prissy—was only a year older. Four years after Dorothy, Grandma Nellie had Mildred, who was Jennie's age. Three years after Mildred, Nellie had a son, Ray, and then three other boys, in rapid succession: Johnny, Bobby, and Gilbert. Grandma Nellie's baby, Dolores, nicknamed Loli, was born later, and in 1955, Nellie gave birth to her last baby: Judy.

Grandma instantly connected with Nellie, Dorothy's mom. Grandpa loved how Nellie's children, a cache of seven rambunctious kids, responded to his strong father-figure presence.

Like Auntie Dorothy, Auntie Mildred remembered visiting the Gonzalez family on weekends. She remembered the ease of life on the ranch. When she was there, she didn't want to be anywhere else.

"I met the Gonzalez family when Dorothy started dating Frank," Auntie

Mildred said. "We'd go over to their house for bar-b-ques, and I got to be friends with Jennie and the twins. We hit it off right away, especially me and Jennie, because we're the same age. Back in those days, they had pomegranate trees. Grandma would go get one of those big pomegranates, break one open, take out the seeds, and make bowls of the seeds for us. We would walk around eating those seeds, just talking. We were so happy just doing that and nothing else."

Softball and bubblegum on the ranchito (l to r) Jennie, Millie (Mildred) and Lucy

The two families melded together with uncommon ease. Grandma soon considered Nellie to be more sister than friend. They both loved cooking, family, and gossip. They could entertain themselves in the kitchen all day long, telling stories about their childhoods, wayward neighbors, even wayward neighbors from childhood. Grandma Nellie appreciated Grandpa with the kind of admiration he valued. She saw him as a man who stayed with his family, and took care of them. She loved the way he influenced her sons, who were often left without a strong father figure.

"We were living in a work camp in Vernalis at the time," Auntie Dorothy said. "I used to take the same school bus as the Gonzalez girls. Terry and I used to sit together, and we'd plan the outfits we were wearing the next day. We'd say, 'What are you wearing tomorrow?' and our conversations went from there. Terry and I became very close."

Frank fell in love with Dorothy, which led to both families spending lots of time together, and the convergence of two families.

No one was expecting another war.

***

In 1950, war broke out between North and South Korea, each side being backed by larger superpowers. Communism, the new enemy of the United States, had to be stopped. To secure the freedoms and liberties of free trade, and to stop the spread of communism, the United States entered the war. My uncles, Frank and Smiley, enlisted in the armed services: Frank in the Navy, and Smiley in the Marines. Far away, in Boston, Massachusetts, Jack Ryan, my father, enlisted in the U.S. Army. Before long, these sons left their families, and were far from home.

The radio was often the only connection to the boys. Grandma and Nana listened to the news of fighting, the war overseas, holding their breath. The radio was a lifeline.

In between news reports, it pumped in a steady stream of popular music, changing with the 1950's.

"Prissy learned all the new dances," Auntie Dorothy said. "She'd learn the steps, and then she'd teach us. We'd all dance together at home, listening to the radio, on our days off. Anytime a good song would come on, we would get up and dance!"

"Priscilla was a good teacher," Auntie Mildred said. "She taught us; we taught the Gonzalez kids. We learned how to mambo, cha-cha, and swing dance, like the jitterbug." Auntie Mildred leaned forward, and smiled. "Then, BAM! Rock and Roll happened!" She clapped her hands together, as if a meteor hit the earth. In a way, that's exactly what happened.

"Ray Grijalva and I used to bebop together," Mom said. "Every time 'Rock Around the Clock' by Bill Haley and the Comets, came on, Ray would come over to me. He'd say, 'Come on, Jennie!' and we'd dance the bebop together to that song."

"Ray was a good dancer," Auntie Mildred said. "Dancing was so much fun!"

"This music on the radio influenced us," Auntie Lucy said. "Jennie and I would listen to the radio as we washed dishes. We'd figure out the harmony to songs, like the Everly Brothers' song, "Dream." That was one of our favorites. We went to Daddy, and showed him how we could sing it. He very grudgingly accompanied us on the guitar." Auntie Lucy strummed an imaginary guitar with a solemn face. "Daddy didn't really like the new songs. I think, to him, the new music represented a change of culture. Daddy wanted to keep his music in us, because he wanted to keep his culture in us."

"Daddy didn't like change," Auntie Terry said. "It was the Korean War, and his sons were away. We had family in Oxnard, so we went there for a wedding, and I saw Uncle Phil there. Daddy liked Uncle Phil. He thought he was a good young man, hard-working and serious, but he wasn't ready for us to fall in love."

"Terry was the first daughter to get married," Mom said. "She left home in 1951."

"For our dad, it was painful," Auntie Lucy said. "His sons were gone, but he knew they'd be back. He didn't like the thought of Terry finishing high school, getting married, and moving away. No. His daughter, leaving home for good? That hurt. He'd get his guitar, and he'd play, a sad, sad song." She laughed, almost in spite of herself. "To daddy, this change was terrible. He'd spent all that time teaching Terry and I to sing together, and the thought of Terry leaving home? Jennie and I singing new songs, *in English*? It was like a *death* for him."

"And for me, too," Auntie Terry said. "My days of playing the guitar were finished," "You played guitar?" I asked, surprised.

"I only played a couple of chords," Auntie Terry said. "I stopped when I got married." She reached across the table and touched my hand. "Don't look at me like that, mija. I can tell this is upsetting for you," she said, laughing. "I was really *happy* to get married."

I tried to smile. "Were you sad to stop playing guitar?" I asked.

Auntie Terry shrugged, and turned to Mom. "Remember how Daddy saved his money, and threw me that big wedding? Frank came home from the Navy?"

Auntie Terry started talking about her beautiful wedding, but I could only think about her loss of the guitar. My own guitar, Vanessa, was always there, like my books and journals. When I needed to escape, or process something, she was there, letting me inhabit the best part of myself. I couldn't imagine a world that required Auntie Terry to stop playing, just because she was getting married.

29. Separation

In 1951, life continued on at breakneck speed for the Gonzalez family. The world around them changed dramatically. Children were growing, daughters were getting married, wars were being fought.

I asked Esther how the changing world affected their families—especially seeing each other.

"We stayed close," Esther said. "I always liked to go down to the ranch. They had their own little house there, with a canal and a bridge, in the back." She stopped to reminisce. "I really liked visiting my Tía Juana. She was such a good cook! Every time we'd go, I'd say, 'I hope she has beans,' because they were always so good. I always enjoyed going out to the ranch." Esther smiled. "Our cousins thought we wouldn't enjoy ourselves, because we were city folks by then, but we did."

"Yeah, they visited often," Mom said. "We went to their place, too. I admit, we had a long stretch of time between the visits."

"Mom and Tía Juana were always so happy to see each other," Esther said. "You could feel it, how happy they were to be together again! Whenever we'd go there, Mom would bring maybe a hundred pounds of flour, fifty pounds of lard—we used lard to make tortillas in those days—and all kinds of Mexican sweet bread, some canned food. Mom brought all kinds of things, just to give to my Tía Juana. We would stay there for two or three days, so Mom contributed to the food supply, because we'd all eat. And…my uncle didn't like that." Esther sighed.

"My Dad still didn't like her bringing things," Mom said, raising her eyebrows.

"There was a consensus of opinion that Uncle Nacho was very strict,"

Esther said. "He liked to keep my Aunt Juana under his thumb, but my mom? She wouldn't have any of that. So, Mom and Tío Nacho were never kissy-kissy with each other. While we were there, they both tried to get along, for mi Tía's sake."

"And, oh! It was such an emotional scene when they said goodbye," Mom said, raising her hands. "You wouldn't believe the tears! Mama and Tía Maria would start crying, and hugging and kissing. Then, they would stop, and get ready to go, and then someone else would start crying, and it happened all over again. There was a lot of emotion between those sisters."

"They really loved each other," Esther said.

"They got on with our lives, because they had to," Mom said. "The periods between visits were longer, as years passed. Mama had seven kids, and Tía Maria still had her boarding house, and a restaurant, and then she had Nancy."

"Wait...Nancy?" I asked. "Did Tía Maria have another baby?"

"Well..." Mom said. "Not really."

***

"Nancy was born on August 2, 1942," Esther said. "She was the first child of Ezequièl, Mom's first son, and his wife, Dolores, or Lola. Nancy was born two-and-a-half months before she would have reached full-term. As soon as the medical staff at the hospital saw her, they told Lola the baby would die within hours. She weighed only a little more than a pound, and wasn't breathing well.

"The doctors convinced Lola the baby wouldn't make it," Esther said. "She was too small, and too weak. At that time, they didn't have the equipment or technology they do now, and doctors were a lot different back then." Lola panicked at the sight of her baby, and left her at the hospital to die.

"My mother heard about this," Esther said. "Well, she wasn't going to let the baby die. She stopped what she was doing and went to the hospital to get her. The doctors tried to discourage her from trying, because they said the baby was dying. There wasn't even a bottle small enough to feed her, the preemie bottles were too big. Mom asked if she and my older sisters could feed the baby with an eye dropper. The medical staff kept saying no, no no, but finally, they let Mom try. Nancy started to drink milk from the eye dropper, right away. Everyone was so surprised.

"The hospital kept Nancy for about a month, until she gained a little weight. Either Mom or one of my sisters went there every day, to check up on Nancy, to feed her. Finally, they let Mom bring her home, even though Nancy was still really small. Mom made a bed out of a big shoebox, and lined it with flannel to make it warm. She put in a half-quart bottle, filled with warm water, wrapped in a towel, and kept it next to the baby to keep her warm. She didn't have an incubator at home, but she did the best she could. Anyway, Nancy survived. Now that little baby is all grown up and she lives near San Diego."

I was shocked. I had stopped taking notes, and wondered why I had never heard this story. I was also shocked that Nancy didn't die, which I found to be miraculous.

Thanks to Esther, I was able to call Nancy, and talk to her.

"I don't know much about the circumstances," Nancy said. Her voice was like Esther's, with a light, musical pitch. "Esther remembers more than I do, because she's five years older than me, but I was a baby. I'm used to people telling me how I used to be so small. People see me now, and they say, '*You're* Nancy? You were so tiny, and we all thought you were going to die!'"

Nancy had been living in San Diego County with her husband of forty-eight years. I wondered how she felt about her birth mother, or her father. How she's lived with the story.

"Lola, or Dolores, was the woman who gave birth to me," Nancy said. "She wasn't raised by her mother, either. Dolores grew up and married my dad, Ezequièl. Right away, they had me. So, Lola left me at the hospital because I was supposed to die. No one knew what to do with me, not the doctors or nurses, and Lola didn't know what to do. The woman who saved me is the one who raised me, the woman I called Mom," Nancy said. I could tell she was smiling.

"Maria's my real mom. After she brought me home from the hospital, she kept me with her all the time.

"Two years later, Lola had my sister, Ruby," Nancy said. "About a year after that, Ezequièl died. I was only about three years old when this happened. Ruby was only one when he died, so I didn't really know my dad.

"Lola used to come and visit me once a year, on my birthday," Nancy said. "But I would run and hide from her, because I was afraid that she'd try to take me away from my family—from my real mom. Lola would always bring a gift, like a pretty little dress, but I didn't want to see it. I hid the whole time she was there, and I didn't come out until she was gone." Nancy paused to laugh. "I didn't want to take anything from her, or call her 'Mom.' Maria was Mom and Monico was Dad." Nancy said, emphatically.

"Lola moved to Wilmington, took a job at the fish cannery there, and Ruby went with her. I was glad she went away. I was always afraid she'd want to come and take me away."

Nancy was generous with her story, and seemed peaceful with it. As she finished, I could tell she was trying to help me understand.

"I was my father's first child," she said. "Maria loved her son, and she wanted to get me, just to see if she could help me *live*. Lola believed the doctors who said I was going to die, but Mom thought I might *live*. She did everything to help me live." She was quiet for a bit. "Putting those water bottles next to me? Just to keep me warm? That was Mom."

Nancy saw her survival as a testament to Maria's tenacity. It proved to Nancy that she was worth it. Esther agreed with Nancy's synopsis.

"Mom kept all those little things she used for Nancy," Esther said. "Now and then, she'd bring them out to show her. The little dresses, the eyedropper she fed Nancy with, the box Nancy slept in. She wanted to show Nancy how small she used to be, and what a miracle it was that she survived. Nancy grew up to be especially grateful that Mom kept her and raised her."

Esther paused for a moment and sighed. "Everybody used say, 'Oh, of course Maria did it! She's got money!' They didn't know Mom at all. Mom's riches were her family. She gave most of her money away, or she used it to help other people. Mom was the main support of our whole family."

The story of Maria taking Nancy, even when the doctors advised against it, even when she already had so many children, shows how big her heart was. Maria often forgot to show her children physical affection, and as Esther said before, didn't sit down and talk with them.

Maria's love language seemed to be serving others, or being generous with what she had. In our American culture, Maria's actions may seem exceptional, but according to Maria, it was natural. That's what family does.

30. Becoming "American"

My grandparents had dreamed about applying for citizenship in the United States for years, but as undocumented aliens, they couldn't do it. In 1952, the U.S. Congress passed the Immigration and Nationality Act (INA), also known as the McCarran Walter Act of 1952. For most people, this legislation slipped by unnoticed, but for people seeking to apply for citizenship in the United States, it was significant.

Senator Pat McCarran (D-Nevada) proposed the immigration bill because the country was in an alert stance. After WWII, communism became the new enemy for the United States. The INA's design was to safeguard against Communism, Jewish interests (actual wording), and "undesirables that could pose a threat to national security."[19]

The INA combined aspects of past immigration laws, but relaxed immigration policies for countries in the Americas. For the first time in years, Mexico was exempt from quota ceilings—there were no limits to the number of Mexican immigrants applying for citizenship per year—and current residents could apply, even if they were undocumented. Only one condition applied: they had to be in good standing.

The INA was the green light my grandparents had been waiting for.

Grandpa's boss, Mr. Ruiz, el patrón, knew that Ignacio and Juana were "immigrants in good standing." He helped Grandpa apply for citizenship, vouching for his character and work history. Grandpa enrolled in citizenship classes at Tracy night school. With help and validation from the patrón, Mr.

---

19 Marinari, Maddalena. "Divided and Conquered: Immigration Reform Advocates and the Passage of the 1952 Immigration and Nationality Act." *Journal of American Ethnic History*, vol. 35, no. 3, Spring 2016, pp. 9–40

Ruiz, the formal immigration process was started.

"Grandpa understood the benefits of citizenship," Grandma said. "He wanted to go back to Mexico to see our families. Really, we didn't even know who was alive or not. I knew my Daddy was dead.

"My daddy died around the time I was having the twins, but I didn't find out until a year later." Grandma said. "I was on the phone with Maria, and I asked her, 'What's the matter with Dad? I know something is wrong. He doesn't write me letters anymore.' Then Maria said, 'Well, I didn't want to tell you, but he died.' I said, 'When? Why didn't you tell me?' She said, 'We didn't want to tell you, because you were having the twins, and you were *real* sick back then.' They all knew, but they didn't let me know."

Esteban Avila, the only connection Grandma had to her family in Michoacán, had passed away. All Grandma had left of her father were the few letters he had written to her.

"My dad couldn't read or write," Grandma said. "He used to walk to a place where somebody would read and write letters for him. He was about eighty-years-old when he died, and that was it. That was the end of Daddy."

Grandma's attachment to her home country had grown weaker with each passing year, but now it was almost severed. Grandpa was different. He wanted to go back home, and knew that his family was still alive. He missed his mother, Gomezinda. Citizenship would mean he could travel back and forth to Mexico again. Grandma agreed that Grandpa should go first, taking citizenship classes in 1952.

Grandpa attended weekly classes, and did homework, for a whole year, before he was recommended for a naturalization interview. Grandma told the story of how Grandpa came home from his interview, obviously worried.

"Grandpa told me, 'They ask a lot of questions,'" Grandma said, sighing. "'I don't know if they're going to recommend me.' That was all he said. He went back to class the following week, and one of his teachers handed him the letter of recommendation."

Grandpa's letter of recommendation meant he could apply for citizenship at the San Joaquin County Offices in Stockton, which he did the following week. With a rubber stamp, and the swipe of a pen, it was done. Grandpa was given a date for his swearing-in ceremony.

It wasn't real until Grandpa held the certificate in his hand. His picture, wearing a suit and tie, shows how handsome he remained. On the date of his swearing-in ceremony, he signed the certificate of Naturalization, and gave them the picture. He received the original official document in the mail, six weeks later.

Ignacio Gonzalez, born July 31, 1900. Male, medium complexion, brown hair, brown eyes. Height: five feet, eight inches tall. Married. Former nationality: Mexican. Citizenship issued: 16th of February, 1954.

After thirty-four years of living and working in the country, Grandpa was now a U.S. Citizen. He was officially able to enjoy all the benefits our country had to offer, including land ownership. Grandpa loved being a U.S. Citizen. He even considered paying income tax a joy. As we looked through official documents, Mom handed me a worn, folded paper in a business envelope.

"Here's a copy of Grandpa's tax return," she said, smiling softly. "He loved paying his income taxes."

I was shocked by Grandpa's gross pay. *How did he ever manage to keep his family alive on this income?*

***

Grandma didn't start her citizenship classes until 1960. It was after her children were grown, and by that time, she could read and write English with greater skill.

"I went to night school for a whole year," she said. "I learned their way. I had to remember all the Presidents of the United States. They ask you a lot of questions, and I used to answer them. Once they think you are ready, you have to take a paper test, where they ask you all the questions you learned for a year. I was so nervous!" Grandma inhaled, dramatically. It sounded like she was remembering how hard the written test was. With only two years of formal schooling, Grandma was determined to do anything to pass the test.

"I thought, 'Oh my gosh, if I don't remember, what should I do?' But I passed!"

"I went to the interview," Grandma said. "I remember how Grandpa's interview had so many questions, and I was nervous. The judge looked at me, and asked me only one question: 'Have you ever committed adultery?'"

Grandma laughed at this. "Oh my gosh! I got a big kick out of that! A whole year of school, and the only question they ask me is 'Have you ever committed adultery?' They asked a lot of questions to Grandpa. The judge thought I was funny, because I was so nervous. I told him, 'No, not yet.' Everybody laughed and laughed, out loud."

Juana Gonzalez, born October 31, 1906. Female. Medium complexion, brown hair, brown eyes. Height: four feet, ten inches tall. Distinctive marks: scar on forehead. Married. Former nationality: Mexican. Citizenship Issued: August 11th 1961.

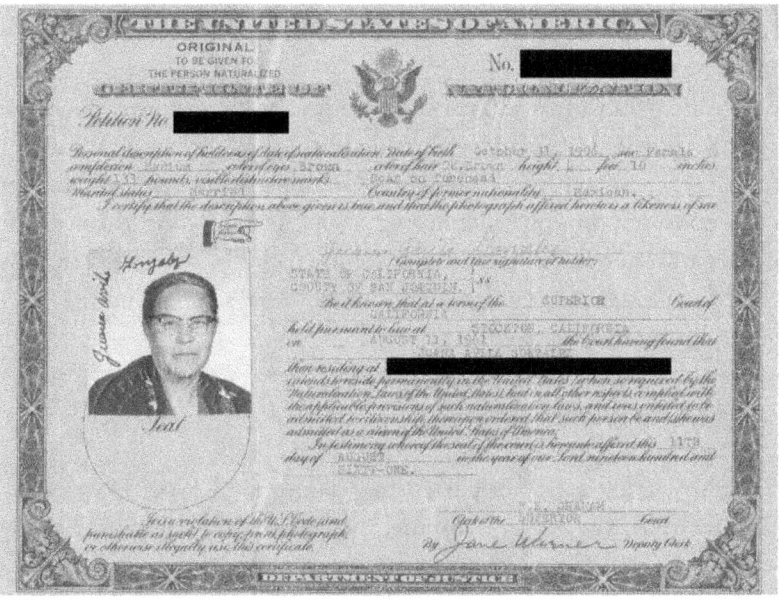

Grandma's hair is still dark brown in her picture on the Naturalization certificate. Her long braid is wrapped around her head in her signature crown.

I can't help but smile when I look at this picture. Did the judge really ask her this question about adultery?

"It's true," Mom said, much later. "Mr. Ruiz was right there, and he said everybody laughed."

I'll bet.

***

I was a teenager when Mom told me we were going to Grandpa and Grandma's to meet Francisco, her half-brother, Grandpa's "other son" from Mexico. Francisco had come to Tracy to visit Grandpa and Grandma, and brought his wife, Lipa.

I gulped.

What?

"Who is Francisco?" I asked Mom.

"Grandpa's other son, from Mexico," she said.

"And what should we call him?"

"For now, you can call him Francisco."

"Isn't he our uncle?" I asked. Mom didn't answer.

Recently, Mom told me a fuller story.

"We were just kids on the ranch when Mama told us that we had a half-brother who lived in Mexico," Mom said. "Our dad was sending money to his mother, for the support of his child, and she needed to tell us what for. Apparently, our dad didn't know about Francisco's mother's pregnancy before he came to the United States, and by the time my parents had their first child, my oldest brother, Francisco, he found out he had another son, with the same name, in Mexico. His mother sent our parents pictures over the years, and Mama told us about him, I think in the hopes that we'd meet our half-brother someday. We had this concept of a half-brother, but we never knew him as a person. My brother Frank was a little jealous, because this half-brother of ours had the same name he did."

"I think the thing that bothered Frank was that his dad had another son," Auntie Dorothy said. "Yes, it bothered him that his name was Francisco, too, but most of all he was bothered by his father's behavior. He said, 'How come Dad didn't come clean with Mama and tell her that he had another child? He had the nerve to give him my name.' So, when Francisco came to Tracy, Frank said, 'I don't want to meet him.' Some days went by, and Frank changed his mind and he did. Afterwards, he learned to like him. He started thinking differently about his Dad, and the fact that the other Francisco was born. He said, 'These things happen.' He saw how his own mother loved and accepted Francisco, and tried to make him and his wife feel welcome." Auntie Dorothy smiled. "Grandma always said, 'It wasn't Francisco's fault how he came into the world.'"

Uncle Smiley, Grandpa, and the "other" Francisco

"We got to meet him the same day you did, in Tracy," Mom said. "By then, we all had our own families. We went to the gathering at Mom and Dad's, and there was our half-brother, Francisco! He had a wife, Felipa, or Lipa, as she was called. We were all nervous and excited about meeting Francisco, but as soon as I saw him, I could see how much he resembled our dad. Francisco was very sweet, cordial, but not overly-familiar. He spent a little time with each of us, one-on-one, and we could ask whatever questions we had on our minds. It was kind of a relief, seeing that this half-brother of ours was a real human being! Up until then, we had known him in photographs. By the time we met, Francisco had two adult children with families of their own."

The day we all met Francisco was at a gathering at Grandpa and Grandma's, much like the hundreds of gatherings we had before. Patty and I talked and hung out, like we normally did, walking around the yard. After dinner, Grandpa played the guitar, and Mom sang with him. Francisco and Lipa watched them, in hypnotized fascination. I, in turn, watched Francisco and his wife. When Francisco looked up, he smiled at me, and I noticed a silver tooth. I smiled back. Was he really older than Uncle Frank?

Our family never had a formal meeting, processing who Francisco and Lipa were, or explaining what happened. This made me a little angry. *Was anyone going to explain this to us? When did Grandpa have another son?* To me, the thought of Grandpa messing up, or having another family, apart from ours, wasn't as bad as our family avoiding the discussion about it.

"My father died in 1985," Mom said. "My mother died in 1992. They owned their home on Lorraine Road, and the one-acre lot, on which that house was built. They had made provisions for their estate to be divided among all the children—share-and-share-alike, is what they call it, legally—which included Francisco, our half-brother. My siblings and I were happy our parents did this. Life in rural Mexico is very poor, and it seemed like a happy ending to this story."

"Grandma agreed to leave the same amount of money for Francisco, as the rest of the kids," Auntie Dorothy said. She shook her head, in awe and admiration. "Wow! Wasn't that the nicest thing to do? Afterward, the family took a check to Francisco and Lipa in Mexico, where they lived. This was a huge blessing. Apparently, their living conditions were very, very poor."

Grandma told me about the day she said goodbye to Francisco and Lipa. As she gave them food to take with them, Lipa hugged Grandma, and said, "I'm going to go home and make Francisco give me a real floor, just like this one." Grandma shook her head. "In Mexico, everybody has dirt floors. Everybody. Unless you're rich."

Grandma always took special pride in her sparkling-clean, robin-egg blue, speckled, linoleum flooring, especially now. She felt empathy for Lipa, who couldn't stop admiring it. Grandma could still remember the feel of dirt floors beneath her bare feet. She remembered the day when she and her sister scratched in the dirt to rescue some bits of corn, trampled by horses, so their mother could make them a few corn tortillas.

Lipa's comment about Grandma's flooring reminded her of how far she had come.

Part Ten: Meatloaf

"Since the girls are potential mothers and homemakers, they will control, in a large measure, the destinies of their future families."

~Pearl Idella Ellis
Americanization Through Homemaking, 1929

"But Mary kept all these things, and pondered them in her heart."

~Luke 2:19

Jennie's Cheesy Meatloaf

1½ lbs. ground beef
1½ cups bread crumbs
2/3 cup American or cheddar cheese
½ cup onion, chopped fine (preferably white or yellow)
2 tablespoons green pepper (bell pepper)
2 slightly beaten eggs
1 can (8 oz.) tomato sauce
1 tsp. salt
1 small bay leaf, crushed
Dash of thyme, garlic salt, or chili powder (to your taste).

Combine beef, crumbs, cheese, green pepper, and seasonings in a big bowl. Add the eggs to tomato sauce, and blend into meat mixture. Form into a loaf and bake in shallow baking pan. Bake for about an hour in moderate oven (350 degrees). Serve with mustard and ketchup. Mushrooms can be heated in butter and then put on top.

To freeze: Bake meatloaves in loaf pans or foil-ware trays, and cook in moderate oven the same way. Cool thoroughly. Wrap in foil, then freeze. To serve: defrost in refrigerator, overnight. Make sure loaves are defrosted when you unwrap. Cook in moderate oven (350) for the same time, or until heated throughout.

31. The Way Things Are

Back in my office, Grandma seems unsure about sharing private details are usually kept buried.

"People will say bad things about us," she says.

"Are you talking about the stories about Grandpa's gambling, or about Francisco?"

"Yes," Grandma says, crossing her arms. Her lips are shut, tightly, in a rigid half-smile.

"But these stories are important," I say. "They shine a light in unexpected places." Grandma doesn't look at me, and I start nervous-talking, trying to explain what I mean. "These stories tell about our family in different ways. They're not bad."

Grandma is still silent.

"And you welcomed Francisco and Lipa, right?" I ask, leaning forward. "I remember that part. You didn't judge Grandpa for having a son with another woman."

"No," she says, quietly considering her pantuflas. "That's just the way things were. It wasn't Francisco's fault. I didn't want to be like my daddy, who was mean to me just because his mother said I wasn't his." She looks up. "I had his toes! How can he say I wasn't his child?"

The memory of Esteban's rejection stays with Grandma, even though she lives in my version of heaven, with her perfect, heavenly Father.

"But some people will read those stories and say, 'Greasy Mexicans!'" Grandma's face wrinkles into a severe frown. She puffs out her chest and continues: "'They come to this country, have too many kids, speak bad English, gamble, they have babies out of wedlock....'" She stops herself, leans back, and sighs. "People will say Grandpa should have stayed in Mexico."

I start to tell Grandma this won't happen. I want to assure her that people will read this and see Grandpa as a hard-working man, who did the best he could. They'll recognize themselves in him—a flawed human being with layers. Instead, I shut my mouth. Part of me knows Grandma is right. Some people will say those things about him, and it will hurt.

"Let's not worry about those people, Grandma," I say. She shakes her head.

"Grandpa left Mexico before he knew that woman was pregnant," she says. "Maybe Francisco's mother didn't even know she was going to have a baby." After thinking, a small smile lights up her face. "But Francisco was born and he looked just like Ignacio. All the boys look like him."

"Family stories are messy," I say. "No one is perfect."

Grandma nods. She's thinking deeply, and two lines form between her eyebrows. I have those lines, too.

I look down at my hands. When I look up, Grandma's gone, and I'm alone in my office.

***

I understand why writers of memoir want to withhold difficult stories—I've done that in some places, but only where a story isn't mine to tell.

I recognize how my family has a way of not talking about things. As much as we share, we withhold. Our aversion to painful subjects or bad memories shows up in our shared DNA. What you hold in your hand is our collective story, one that every contributor has consented to share with the world. These are the stories we've allowed to live.

It's impossible to distill a person, or their families, into one chapter of a book, but this section is just that. Compressed, like meatloaf, the next section contains the voices of each Gonzalez sister. As they left the nest, they became mothers to families, the ones who steered their children's future. I don't have interviews with my uncles, Frank and Smiley. They died many years before this book was an idea. Their wives, Dorothy and Mildred, are here, and their voices will show how the women carry the memories.

The Gonzalez Siblings 1955
Back row: Frank, Lucy, Terry, Smiley. Front row: Molly, Jennie, Emily

The goals of assimilation continued, reinforced by popular media. Television, the medium replacing radio, depicted American housewives as shiny, white models, like Harriet Nelson and June Cleaver. Some viewers could hear Lucy Ricardo, and even a wisecracking Alice Kramden, addressing social issues with sardonic humor, but for the most part, a woman's role was to stay at home and care for family. Soon, the commercial advertising machine began to focus on the nuclear family. They depicted housewives, dressed beautifully, wearing pearls and lipstick, as thin, smiling, satisfied robots. They scrubbed toilets, made dinner, bathed the children, and hosted dinner parties. Everywhere they looked, the Gonzalez women were given these messages. Almost against the odds, the sisters lived in peaceful coexistence with the American culture. They continued in close relationship with each other and were happy.

Did they know the secrets to happiness?

32. Seven Questions—Dorothy

Francisco Gonzalez, my Uncle Frank, was born on May 11, 1929, in Lone Pine, California. He was the eldest child, born to Ignacio and Juana Gonzalez in the early days of their marriage. His birth order, as well as his gender, guaranteed he would grow up next to his father. His childhood was almost nonexistent. He was forced to grow up as soon as he could walk. Outside of school, Frank often spent his afternoons working with Grandpa, and when Grandpa was away, he was expected to serve as chief protector of Grandma and his siblings. It's safe to say that Uncle Frank had the shortest childhood of all the Gonzalez kids. Uncle Frank was funny. He had an engaging personality, and people liked how bright and friendly he was.

Dating: Dorothy and Frank approx. 1950

It seems fitting that Uncle Frank fell in love with Auntie Dorothy, who was one of her family's eldest children. The pressures and responsibilities of being an elder sibling in a large family were daunting. Together, they understood this. They escaped the demands of their lives, and fell into a romance. Auntie Dorothy still describes my Uncle Frank as the person who made her, and others, laugh out loud.

"He had the best sense of humor," Auntie Dorothy said. "I think that's what really drew me to him. There was never a dull moment with him! He was just like his name—Frank."

Despite both of them being pretty damn good looking, Uncle Frank and Auntie Dorothy had pet names for each other: Feo and Fea (Ugly guy and Ugly girl). These pet names lasted their whole marriage, and were even spoken with special tenderness. Together, they had three children: Rocky, Debbie, and Craig—who are all now married, with adult children. Frank and Dorothy raised their children in a beautiful but modest home in Fremont, California. Most of this interview took place there, in April of 2018. Despite Auntie Dorothy being in her eighties, and recovering from recent knee surgery, her house was spotless. She even served me a nice meal when I arrived.

1. How do you view your childhood? What was growing up like for you?

"I have a lot of bad memories about my childhood," Auntie Dorothy said. "It's kind of sad, in a way. Prissy and I never met our dad. He was from New Mexico and we only had one picture of him.

"One of my first memories is when we were living in Brawley, California with my grandpa. I remember him taking me and Prissy for a walk, and then he had a heart-attack and died. That's the last thing I remember about my grandpa.

"Most of my childhood memories are of my mom, your Grandma Nellie, being married to Lupe, my step-father, the father of five of her children. I was about five or six when they got married. Mom had three kids then—Prissy, Dorothy and Mildred.

"I remember a lot of Lupe's anger and abuse. I went through a lot, watching all of that. I ended up feeling very protective of my mom. I grew up seeing Mom running from her abuser, and then, going right back to him.

"One day when he came home—he must have been drunk—he was mad for whatever reason, and started throwing all of Mom's dishes into the backyard. We could hear crashing and smashing. I knew the beautiful blue and white dishes—my mom loved the Blue Willow pattern—were all destroyed. As I think about this now, I'm embarrassed. I'm surprised our neighbors never called the police. That night, as Lupe was breaking dishes, my mom gathered all the kids. Prissy and I helped her. We got the little ones out of bed, put them in one little buggy, and we all ran away. Some of us didn't even have shoes on. Mom was afraid Lupe was angry enough to kill us. We ran through dark alleys, and we ended up at one of mom's cousin's house. We stayed for a while, but Lupe found us, and Mom went back to him. All of us went with her.

"Mom had a brother—I call him our savior—named Tom. Our Uncle Tom came and got us when things got really bad. We would pack up our things and go to Tracy with him. We'd be there for a while, and here comes Lupe again! Of course, he told Mom that he would change, he won't do it again, he loves her. You know, the same story women in abusive relationships hear.

"So, we were like gypsies, going back and forth, back and forth. Those were most of my childhood memories. I was one of Mom's older children. My younger siblings don't remember a lot of that. Even now, when we talk about it, they say they were just too young to remember.

"Mom was always struggling, financially. As a single parent with a lot of kids, there wasn't much of anything, so if it weren't for my Uncle Tom, Mom wouldn't have had anyone helping her. Prissy and I really did a lot for her. We washed dishes, did the cooking, the washing and ironing. I would wash clothes and Prissy would iron. I still have pictures of our clothesline full of little jeans. Our four little brothers needed us, so Prissy and I practically raised them. We bathed them, fed them, made sure they were clean, and did our best to take care of them. It was more my responsibility, since Mom and Prissy were always going out to work.

"I think the saddest part of my childhood is that I wanted a dad, but I didn't have one," she said. Auntie Dorothy looked down at her hands. "I wanted to say, 'Daddy,' to him, like the other kids did. I could never could call my step-father 'Daddy' because I hated him. So, I didn't have much of a happy childhood."

2. Do you have any good childhood memories?

"I loved school," Auntie Dorothy said. Her face lit up as she said this. "I did well, considering I never went to middle school. We were always moving from place to place, so I didn't get to finish *any* school year. By the time I was in high school, I was pretty far behind. By then, Mom was living without Lupe, which was good. I started high school at Ceres High, but I didn't know if I could finish. Prissy had already quit school in the sixth grade, and never really wanted to go back and graduate, but I was the opposite.

"I was *really* far behind in math," Auntie Dorothy said, rolling her eyes and shaking her head. "I explained my life to my teachers. Most were really supportive. By the time I got to Tracy High, after I had worked and worked, I actually made the honor roll!" Auntie Dorothy beamed. "Oh, I loved school! My favorite was typing class and Spanish class, where I met your Aunt Teresa. I learned a lot in that class. The Spanish I spoke as I was growing up wasn't what the teachers called 'the right Spanish.'" Auntie Dorothy punctuated this with air quotes.

"Years later, when I started working for the school district, I realized how much I learned from reading," Auntie Dorothy said. "I'm even a self-taught reader, if you can believe that. I'm really not that smart, but most of my education came from reading. I regret that I didn't get to go to college. I wish my mom could have sent me but, how could she? We had no money."

As she spoke, I wanted to interrupt Auntie Dorothy to tell her she *is* smart. Instead, I just listened. At first glance, Auntie Dorothy is the most confident person. I would have never guessed she endured this childhood, the one she was telling me about for the first time.

3. How did you meet your spouse?

"One day, at Tracy High, I was talking to a cousin of mine, Johnny," Auntie Dorothy said. "Frank was with him, and Johnny introduced us. So, Johnny started everything!" Auntie Dorothy smiled. Her eyes sparkled like a teenager's.

"The first time Frank saw me, I was wearing my mom's leopard coat," Auntie Dorothy said, laughing. "When Frank saw me wearing that leopard coat, he thought our family had money. Then, that day, my mom picked me up in my Uncle Tom's brand-new Buick. Frank thought it was *our* car!" This struck Auntie Dorothy as hilarious, and she laughed hard.

"Anyway, that's how we started. Frank asked me out, and I said yes. I couldn't go out with him unless my sister went with me, so we had a double date with Prissy and Johnny. We went to the movies in Stockton. On our third date, Frank asked me if I wanted to be his girl—if I wanted to go steady with him." Auntie Dorothy said this with so much tenderness, I felt like I was trespassing on her memory.

"Then, Frank found out how poor we were," she said, laughing again. "On one of our first dates, I wore a little sundress which had a matching jacket. I had sandals that tied around the ankle. They went so well with that dress! The day of our date, wouldn't you know it? The shoe flap came off! I tried to fix it with bandaging tape, and then I polished the tape to match the shoe.

I was hoping it would hold together for just that night. When we got to the theater, Frank parked the car pretty far away. We had to walk a long way, and by the time we got there, I could feel something flapping. Once we got into the theater, I tried to press the flap down, hoping the tape wouldn't come off. The movie ended, and we started walking back to the car. I heard my shoes flapping: *Flip-flip-flap-flop*. I said to Frank, 'You want to skip to the car?' So, we did!"

Auntie Dorothy and I laughed together. "It's a funny story now, when I look back on it, but then? I was so embarrassed! I couldn't afford good shoes."

Even through Auntie Dorothy's laughter, I saw how her childhood poverty still disappointed or bothered her. Being poor affected her education goals and her social life. In my childhood, Auntie Dorothy was always cheerful, always dressed fashionably. She never bragged. She was a kind, generous, and beautiful woman. She told me these stories from her beautiful home in Northern California, and she knows she's come a long way.

Sailor Frank Gonzalez and Dorothy, 1951

"The last time Mom went back to Lupe, after so many years without him, was in my last semester of high school. She started packing up our things, and getting ready to go back to Los Angeles to be with him. I begged her, 'Please, Mom, let me stay with my aunt and uncle. I want to finish high school.' Mom said, 'Okay, you can stay. But, the *day after* graduation, you have to come live with us.' I agreed.

"I finally made it to my high school graduation! But guess what? My own family wasn't there. They weren't there for me. Guess who was? Frank. Your Grandpa and Grandma were there. My Uncle and Aunt, and my favorite cousin, Charlie. I was so happy to graduate from high school! And yet, part of me was really sad. The one I needed most was my mother, and she wasn't there. My siblings weren't there. I was supposed to go to Los Angeles the next day, but I didn't. I had my diploma. I was eighteen. What could my mom do?"

4. When did you decide to get married?

"Frank and I had been dating for a while, when we got engaged," Auntie Dorothy told me. "We wanted to get married, but we couldn't afford to. At that time, Frank was in the Navy Reserves, and he would regularly go off to Stockton for training meetings. The Korean Conflict had already started. Both of us knew that Frank could be called up for active-duty at any time.

"One day, in 1951, Frank went to Stockton, for training. From there, they sent him to Honolulu, Hawaii. He was in the reserves one day, and called up for active duty the next. We decided to get married when he came back. By this time, we'd been dating four years. We hadn't saved enough money for a church wedding. We decided we would exchange bands in a simple ceremony at the county offices. At that time, the Catholic Church required at least a three-weeks-notice if you wanted to get married, anyway. No one had that.

"Grandpa and Grandma could see how important a church wedding was to us, so Grandpa went to my Uncle Tom, Mom's brother, and asked for my hand in marriage for his son."

Auntie Dorothy dabbed at her eyes. "That's the traditional way, you know. Grandpa and Uncle Tom agreed to give us a wedding—a real church wedding!" Auntie Dorothy glowed with happiness. "We got married in St. Bernard's Church in Tracy, on Eaton Avenue, December 2, 1951. We were the second couple to get married in the new church building."

Frank and Dorothy Gonzalez, Married Dec. 2, 1951

5. What was the greatest challenge in your marriage?

"That's such a big question!" Auntie Dorothy said, exhaling. She seemed prepared to answer it, despite its weight. "The biggest struggle was when Frank was drinking. Those were the worst years." I didn't expect Auntie Dorothy to be this candid, but we all knew about Uncle Frank's alcoholism. Uncle Frank, played Santa for every Christmas Eve at Grandpa and Grandma's house. He flirted with Auntie Dorothy, gave her a passionate kiss when she gave Santa a box of Korbel. He played the guitar and sang. As a child, I didn't notice his drinking, but as a young adult, I noticed the awkward drunkenness. Our family never talked about it, not until he got better. Uncle Frank did, and spent his final years in recovery.

"When he was drinking, Frank never treated me bad," Auntie Dorothy said. "But he wasn't there for me. I would have his dinner ready, when he came home from work, and we'd eat in the dining room, then watch TV, or sit outside. All of a sudden, Frank would be passed out. He'd wake up, get himself another drink, and then he was out again. That was the worst part. I felt like a widow when I wasn't a widow.

"When I think about it, I have to admit I put up with it," Auntie Dorothy said. "I never thought about leaving him, because I didn't want to put my kids what I went through. I grew up without a father, and I didn't want that life for my kids. I vowed to stick it out till the very end. I knew I picked a good person to marry. Frank was a good husband and father, but the downfall was his drinking. There were times when he would come to kiss me, and I would think, 'I don't want to smell that liquor breath.' It's in his pores, in our bedsheets, in our towels, everything he used smelled like liquor.

"One day, when your Aunt Lucy, my mother, and Grandma were over here, Frank called me from work. He said, 'Fea, I made up my mind, and I'm finally going to take care of my problem. They're waiting for me at the hospital.' I couldn't believe my ears. I started crying. My mom and Grandma thought something bad happened, but I told them, and they started crying, too. Lucy told me to pack a bag for him, because he wouldn't be coming home today. She said, 'Come on, I'll go with you.' She went with me and was a big help to me at that time. We drove to the hospital, signed the papers, and then they admitted him. We said goodbye, and I felt really sad to leave him, but it was for the best.

"One day, when I was talking to him on the phone, he said, 'Fea, can you do me a favor and bring me a carton of cigarettes?' I said, 'No, Feo, I will not. You can't go from one addiction to another. I won't be a part of that.' He said, 'It's not for me, but for my friend who taught me how to use the washing machine.'" Auntie Dorothy started laughing. "I said, 'He taught you which buttons to push?' Frank had never done his own laundry, and he didn't know anything about the washing machine. His friend saw that, and he showed him how to load it, put in the soap, and keep an eye on the time. Then he showed him the same thing for the dryer. All of those things had always been done for Frank, all those years. It was time for him to grow up.

"After that, Frank didn't drink again, at all. I thought, 'I don't know if he's really going to stop,' but he stayed sober. I had doubts, especially when I was at work, and Frank was here by himself. He never drank again.

"People saw Frank differently once he got sober. Sometimes, he'd say, 'I'm not fun anymore.' Someone would invite us over, and he would say, 'No, I really don't feel like going out right now.' I knew he didn't want to be around the liquor. But I liked him so much more. Can you believe it? Fifteen years he was sober. He gave me fifteen good years, before he died. It felt *soooo gooood* to be able to kiss without having that smell. I got my husband back!"

Auntie Dorothy was rewarded with the simplest thing: seeing Uncle Frank as the man she fell in love with. His demeanor changed. He was sincere and peaceful.

"I still remember the day that Frank was dying," Auntie Dorothy said, in a solemn voice. "All of us were around him, me and our children. We were just looking at him, all of us peaceful. Then, Rocky asked, 'Dad, is there anything you want to tell us?' Frank was so peaceful. He looked at me, and said: 'Fea, I love you so much. In fact, I adore you.'"

50th Wedding Anniversary, 2001

6. What advice would you give the next generation?

"I would say, 'Don't give up.' It's hard when you look around, and everyone seems to be doing better than you. With us, we had a really hard time getting ahead.

When Frank came home from the service, he didn't want to go back to doing ranch work. He wanted to start a new thing for himself. Smiley called him one day, and told Frank there was an opening at the bakery, where he was working. We drove there, and we stayed with Smiley and Mildred, and later rented the apartment next door to them. Frank worked for the bakery, and when he lost that job, we had nothing. Frank went to the unemployment office, to see if he could find something. I said, 'Maybe I could do that, too.' So, we went together, and both of us found jobs. I ended up working at Macy's for six months. Mildred kept Rocky for me during the day.

Frank found a job in the pharmaceutical business, and he worked in that field for most of his life. From there, we moved to Oakland. Frank took another job with better pay. We found a little place, and lived there for ten and a half years. Then, we came here, and I've been in this house for fifty-three years.

"It took a long time for us to find stability, but we didn't give up. I wanted our marriage to work. Your mom, Jennie, always said, 'Never go to bed mad at your spouse, and never go to sleep without saying I love you.' I tried to do that every day. Sometimes, I'd go to bed so mad at him, I didn't even want him to touch me!" She stopped to laugh. "Even feeling like that, I would still do it." She gritted her teeth and growled: "Goodnight. I love you. Marriage has bad moments, but, hopefully, more happy moments. That's the thing! If the good outweighs the bad, you'll be okay. In the end, Frank and I loved and respected each other."

7. Grandma's last words were 'Keep the family together.' Do you think we've done this?

"I've tried to do that," Auntie Dorothy said. "It really *is* nice to be part of a family that loves each other. We're all different, but we're respectful. We grew up happy, but we were never spoiled with all kinds of things. What we had we took care of. Family is the same way. When family takes care of each other, then people want to stay together."

Auntie Dorothy's answer makes me reconsider Grandma's charge. Was she talking about individual families keeping their nuclear families together? That seemed a lot easier, but still challenging. It's our greatest task as leaders of the family. Auntie Dorothy's family has stayed together, and they still meet in her house, the same warm and inviting place she raised her own children.

33. Seven Questions—Terry

Teresa Gonzalez, my Auntie Terry, was born on April 30, 1930, in Lone Pine, California, the first daughter of Ignacio and Juana Gonzalez. She came almost one year after Uncle Frank. Her birth order and gender guaranteed her a close relationship with her mother, who always had her by her side. Auntie Terry is described by her siblings as remarkably patient and angelic, just what Grandma needed her to be. Her childhood was challenging, since she faced a lot of illness, but overall, Auntie Terry has happy memories. "I think we had a beautiful life with our parents. I enjoyed it. Those are the good memories we can think back on." Auntie Terry often spent her days working with Grandma. During the rare occasions Grandma was away, she acted as mother. It's safe to say that Auntie Terry was a second mother to the Gonzalez kids.

Auntie Terry (middle, white dress), walking in downtown Tracy with her cousins, approx. 1950

It seems fitting that Auntie Terry fell in love with Uncle Phil, Fidel

Villaseñor, my matador uncle. He was handsome, tall, always stood up straight, but said almost nothing. He wanted a wife who had been raised with all the right Mexican traditions. Auntie Terry was exactly that. Uncle Phil, a young man, glorious being to behold, was stunned by Teresa's angelic beauty.

"We had an instant connection," Auntie Terry said, snapping her fingers. "From that day, he knew I would be his wife. *That* kind of a connection."

Uncle Phil and Auntie Terry had three children: Anna, Fidel Jr. (Butchie), and James (Jimmy). They've lived in the same house for as long as I can remember, in an Oxnard neighborhood the locals call *la colonia*. Despite drastic changes all around them, Auntie Terry still holds fast to tradition. She continues to provide a loving, solid home for her family.

***

1. How do you view your childhood? What was growing up like for you?

"I had a beautiful life, growing up," Auntie Terry said. "I was very proud of my Dad, who came here from Mexico. He went through a lot, in the United States. He came to Los Angeles with no English, but managed to make it on his own. So, that made me proud of him. He met and married my mom, who fell madly in love with him. Our family grew. We were really proud of my dad and my mom. Daddy was very strong and strict, and Mama went along with my dad. To me it was a privilege to be a Gonzalez, and the oldest girl. Growing up on the ranch was really nice for me because we used to go swimming. After we came out from swimming, Mama would say, 'Lie down on the cement and I'll bring you some cookies.' That was a big treat for us. We all were comfortable. I have really happy memories growing up on the ranch."

2. What's your favorite childhood memory?

"I liked a lot of things," Auntie Terry said. She leaned forward in her chair and smiled. "We did so many things. There were so many chores. My favorite memory is...the ironing."

I waited for her to laugh. When she didn't, I did.

"You liked the ironing?" I asked. "That was your favorite *memory*?"

Auntie Terry nodded, a serene look on her face.

"Yes, that's it. I loved the ironing. Know why? I had peace." Auntie Terry drew an imaginary box around her hips. "I had my own private space, and I was in charge. No one bothered me. It was so quiet. Mom would bring a big bucket for me, with all the clothes to be ironed, and I started. I didn't have to go anywhere. I learned from my mother and followed in the ways she taught me. Mama used to say, 'When you do your laundry, be very, very careful! Especially when you wash shirts.' Mama showed me how to fold them, you know how the crease goes, right? My mother was a perfectionist, and I wanted to be just like her. I enjoyed it! And I'm still doing it that way. I still fold the shirts like that."

The peaceful tone her voice, and the blissed-out look on her face made it seem like Auntie Terry discovered a secret porthole to joy. Still, I wasn't sure she understood my question.

"I guess I should explain what I mean," I said. "I was hoping to find out a time when you had a happy memory, like a...."

Mom, sitting next to Auntie Terry, interrupted me. With one hand on Auntie Terry's arm, she reached over and touched mine. "Janet, Terry *loved* to do chores," she said, smiling. "Let ironing be her favorite childhood memory."

I raised my eyebrows at Mom, then looked back at Auntie Terry. "Okay, Auntie," I said. "*Ironing* will be your favorite memory."

"Yes," she said, smiling broadly. "I enjoyed cooking, too, but ironing? Oh, that was my favorite! It was just my space," she said. She looked up at the sky and smiled. "On ironing day, I ate my breakfast, and then I was put to do the ironing. That was my favorite chore in the whole world. I took breaks when I wanted to. Mom loved my work. I got all the shirts done just right."

Mom and I looked at each other and smiled.

Damn.

3. How did you meet your spouse?

"Our cousins were cousins with Phil," Auntie Terry said. "We knew each other for a long time, and we came from traditional families. Phil and I would sometimes see each other when we were growing up, but we never had a reason to talk or play. He knew me when I was going to school. He liked the way I dressed, with my oxfords and loafers, my socks folded down in the way we used to wear them. I would have on my Block T sweater.

"When I was twenty years old, I came to Oxnard for the wedding of my cousin. I was in the wedding, so the wedding party met beforehand. Fidel, your Uncle Phil, was also in the wedding. He had already told someone else that I was his ideal girl to marry. My dad heard about this, and he knew Phil was someone very special. Daddy knew he was a hardworking man, a very serious man. I saw Phil before the wedding, and fell in love with him, right away. He says he fell in love with me, too. We didn't know where it would go, but there was strong chemistry.

"Our family went with the wedding party to a hospital in Ventura, to see a cousin who was sick with tuberculosis. She wanted to see the wedding party, and we went to see her because we didn't know whether she would live or die. She ended up being a survivor. She survived the tuberculosis. We all gathered at the hospital, and other girls were calling Phil, 'Hi, Phil!' 'Hi Phil! Remember me?' All the girls were trying to get his attention. I walked past all of that to go into the room, but Phil stopped me. He took my hand, gripped it tightly, and looked into my eyes. He said, 'Be careful!' So, there was a connection, but no other words spoken until we went to the wedding dance.

"As soon as we got to the dance, my dad told me, 'Don't dance with another boy, only Phil.' Daddy knew Phil wanted to marry me. My dad was controlling, and he liked Phil's family. Daddy knew Phil was a serious man, who didn't joke around or flirt with girls. What I didn't know was that Phil's mother sent the same message to her son. She said, 'Don't dance with no other girl except with Teresa.' So, what did I do? I was asked to dance with someone else and I said yes. I went out to dance with that other person. Then I thought, 'Oh, no! I forgot the advice my father gave me.'

"The next dance, Phil came over to me, very serious. We danced together, and he looked at me and said, 'Weren't we supposed to dance together? Didn't your dad tell you to dance only with me? Didn't my mom say for me to only dance with you?' He said this quietly, but he let me know he meant business."

I smiled. Uncle Phil always seemed stoic and serious to me, so her description was no surprise. Did she feel manipulated? Scolded?

"Oh, no, mija," Auntie Terry said, with a soft smile. "I felt protected and cared for. Uncle Phil wanted us to honor our parents. He wasn't jealous at all."

I was relieved. Uncle Phil seemed gentle, a silent uncle who would watch over us, as children. He was patient and kind, would bar-b-que with Grandpa, hang out with the other men, but he'd stop everything to help us get a ball out of the tree. At night, he would turn on the hanging string lights, over the patio, so we could see better.

On one occasion, at a family gathering, Uncle Phil had a dish of his favorite salsa in front of him. Uncle Frank asked if he could try it, and Uncle Phil consented. "Think about it before you try this salsa." Uncle Frank took the dare and tasted some.

"It was too hot for Frank," Dad told Mom, as we drove away. "I've never seen a grown man cry like that."

4. When did you decide to get married?

"After my cousin's wedding," Auntie Terry said. "Phil asked, 'How would you like to be engaged today? Will you marry me?' I didn't know how to answer. He could tell I needed time to think. I said, 'Let me think about it.'

When we arrived at home, I told my dad what happened. He tried to see how I really felt.

'Do you care for this young man?' Daddy asked me.

I said, 'Yes. He's a very fine young man, Daddy. I like him.' At first, Daddy wondered why I didn't answer Phil right away. I explained to my dad what I said. 'I told Phil I had to think about it.'

"Daddy understood that I needed time, so he and Phil backed off and let me think about it all by myself. It took a while for me to figure out this was more than just emotions. Phil was handsome and strong, but he was also a family man and a good leader. In a few months, I knew my attraction to him was more than physical. I could plan a future with him.

"So, I wrote a letter to Phil, accepting his proposal. We began making plans to be married and plan our future. I wanted to work, but in those days, Daddy didn't want me to leave the house to go to work. 'A young lady doesn't leave the house. Only when you get married.' So, I did as my dad said, all those years. I helped my mom.

"Now I needed money for the wedding. I went to my dad, and asked if I could apply for my dream job: a nurse's helper. Daddy said, 'No, not that. I'll find you another job.' Well, he found me a job alright—out in the field!" Auntie Terry suddenly broke into laughter. She clapped her hands, as if Grandpa had played a good trick on her. "He put me to drive the tractor in the nighttime, bailing hay. From two o'clock in the morning to eleven o'clock or noon. Now, mija, I had been doing this since I was fourteen, so it wasn't too much for me... but I always wanted to be a nurse's helper. There was no way Daddy was going to let that happen.

"When it came time to get married, Daddy took me aside. He said, 'Mija, every day you worked in the field, you earned twenty-five dollars. All that money will go to your wedding.' When I got married, Daddy threw me the biggest wedding I had ever seen. There were flowers, food, everything! I had a brand-new dress and veil. No expenses were spared.

Fidel and Teresa, married October 28, 1951. Bridesmaids were Dorothy and Lucy

"It was a perfect day. Guess what else? My brother, Frank got home from the Navy just in time to see his sister get married, and his girlfriend be in the wedding. Oh, mija! The men wore fancy tuxedos. The girls had matching dresses and shoes. Flowers were everywhere! It was such a beautiful day, because I never expected such a big wedding. I could hardly believe it. All those worries I had, about not having enough money? Daddy made it up to me. He cared so much for us, his children. He was very generous, and he had wonderful taste. Everything was perfect. It was just right."

4. Does your family still speak Spanish?

"I speak Spanish all the time," Auntie Terry said, her face glowing. "Spanish and English, all the time, depending on who I'm talking to. I heard Phil talking to some of his family, after we got married. He said, 'I had to teach Terry how to speak Spanish.' I said, 'No, you didn't! I knew how to speak Spanish, because we spoke it at home, just not at school.' Then, Phil said, 'I mean the *real* Spanish.' I think his family thought I spoke Spanish with an English accent, and when I speak English, people say I have a Mexican accent." She laughed, and shook her head. "I can't win! You know? I couldn't believe Phil, 'I had to teach her.' Yeah, right! I knew how to speak Spanish, just like I knew how to speak English. When I grew up, in my dad's house, we spoke Spanish *first*. It was *our* language in my dad's house, all the time. If I tried to speak to my parents in English, and my dad heard me, he would say, 'No, no, no! What did I say? En Español, mija!'"

This made Auntie Terry laugh, but not with joy. Her Spanish didn't sound "Mexican enough" for her new in-laws. She wasn't polished enough in grammar.

As a young girl, Auntie Terry was forced to stop speaking Spanish in school, where she learned English, a language she used at school, but not at home. After marriage, she had to re-learn the Mexican-Spanish in a way that pleased her husband's family. For her, this was a laughable irony.

5. What advice would you give the next generation?

"Mija, I would tell them to be true to what they believe," she said. "When I was eight years old, just a little girl, I first sought out my God, Jehovah." Auntie Terry smiled broadly. A Jehovah's Witness, she was officially baptized in the mid 1980's. This decision surprised her parents and siblings, since Terry had always been a devout Catholic. For more than forty years, Auntie Terry has remained steadfast to her religion, even when people question her logic. She seemed eager to talk about this.

"At first, my family didn't understand," Auntie Terry said. "They didn't think it was a good idea for me to leave the Catholic church, but they all supported me. We never had really hard disagreements. When they asked, I just said, 'Look in the Bible, where all the rules are.'

"One day, my dad came over to my house. My kids were still in school when this happened. He started reading the Watchtower on the table, and said, 'Now I know why you read these books. The information is from the

Bible.' He said that! He could tell I was really serious about reading them.

"I wanted to join the Witnesses because they helped me when I needed help, and they told me all about the Bible," she said. "It felt so different from the Catholic Church. When I went to the priest, he told me I couldn't go to no other church, but I knew I had to leave. I wanted to study the Bible. I was drawn to the Witnesses, who kept coming over. It's important to me, and that makes me happy. In the 1980's, I went to ministry school, and decided to get baptized. I was so happy!

"I think the hardest part of this is how my husband didn't come with me. He acknowledged my choice to be a Witness, but he never came. He was either working or too busy. When he got older, he didn't come with me because he couldn't hear. He didn't read the books, or even listen to the people talking. I think that's the saddest thing for me."

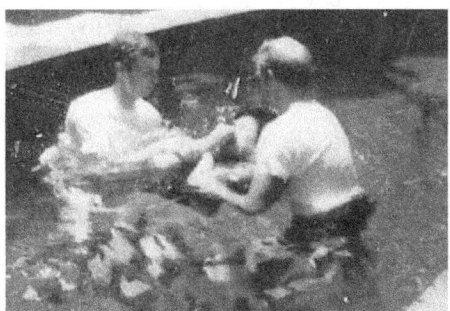

Auntie Terry's baptism, 1986

Uncle Phil, who has recently been incapacitated, now stays in his bed. He's dependent on Auntie Terry and their grandson, Gilbert, for care. On most days, Uncle Phil watches TV and occasionally joins in on a family gathering or a phone conversation.

"The way I see it?" Auntie Terry said. "God heard my prayer about becoming a nurse's helper! Now I get to care for my husband. I got to be a nurse's helper after all. Phil loves being beside me, in our bed. Every time I turn over, there he is."

7. Grandma's last words were 'Keep the family together.' Do you think we've done this?

"Oh, yes!" Auntie Terry said, without hesitation. "I like to remember the early years of marriage, but I think our lives go on through our children and grandchildren. This is the special thing about family. The way I see it, we had a good mom and dad, who got married and had us, so we did the same.

"I'll never forget when Anna was born. Everybody was so excited! She was the first child born to the next generation of our family. Anna's birth was very special. We have children, then grandchildren, and now the great-grandchildren! It makes me very happy, to have our family growing.

"I asked Anna, 'Who is going to have a baby? We need a baby because everybody is grown up.'" She laughed, and said, "Nobody is ready. No babies for a while. Being the matriarch of the family is a joy. What does the Bible say? 'Be fruitful and multiply.'" Auntie Terry leaned back and folded her hands on her lap. "I'm still at it," she said. "I'm *still* at it."

Uncle Phil and Auntie Terry, May 2020

34. Seven Questions—Mildred

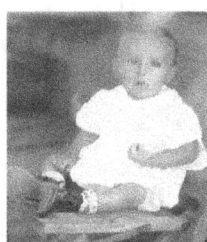

Ismael Gonzalez, Lone Pine, 1931

Ismael Gonzalez, my Uncle Smiley, was born on September 4, 1931, in Lone Pine, California, the second son and third child of Grandpa and Grandma. As the third baby, Uncle Smiley became the third ball in the air that Grandma had to juggle. The addition of a third baby would strengthen and challenge Grandma as a mother, as the addition does for all mothers. Ismael's birth order and gender almost guaranteed that he would be in close competition with his brother, Frank, only two years older, with Ismael feeling slightly overlooked. According to Grandma, he was born beautiful, with a strong resemblance to Grandpa, which endeared him to her even more. Uncle Smiley became the next best thing to Grandpa, and Grandma seemed to favor him. Even as a toddler, Ismael was incredibly strong-willed. Growing up, his siblings remember their brother being moody and temperamental—until the Marines redefined him.

After he enlisted in the U.S. Marines, Uncle Smiley went to Korea and was involved in heavy battle. He was awarded the Purple Heart for acts of bravery. He returned to California, grateful for his life. He would no longer be the person he was before the war, the man his family knew. He was kinder, especially to his sister, Lucy. The Marines changed Uncle Smiley's life in many ways, including the spelling of his name.

"Smiley was born Ismael Gonzalez, with a 'z'," Auntie Mildred told me.

"But the Marines made a clerical error when Smiley enlisted. They spelled Gonzalez with an "s" at the end. At first, he didn't notice, even though it was on his identification, his dog-tags, everything. But when he was awarded the Purple Heart, he noticed the spelling of his name was wrong. *Gonzale**s***, not *Gonzale**z***. When Smiley got out of the service, he realized everything in his name had been spelled that way. To get a GI Bill, a driver's license, an I.D., a job, he had to stick with that spelling. Back then, there wasn't an easy way to correct it. So, he decided to keep it."

Walking in Stockton, 1954

When Uncle Smiley fell in love with Auntie Mildred, he had met his match. Mildred's strong will proved to be the perfect complement to his own. They met when Grandma Nellie's family became part of the Gonzalez circle. Frank was dating Dorothy, and Mildred came along for the ride.

"Dorothy is four years older than I am," Auntie Mildred said. "When she started dating Frank, we used to be invited for gatherings at Grandma and Grandpa's house. Jennie and I became very close. Very, very close. I knew Smiley, but he was older than me. It took a while for us to see each other as anything more than friends. Once we did, we knew it was meant to be."

Uncle Smiley and Auntie Mildred had five daughters in quick succession: Jeannie, Stephanie (Stevie), Lorrie, Doreen, and Kathleen (Kathy). They lived in San Jose for years, before moving to their beloved Oregon. After I had children, Uncle Smiley became sick with diabetes, and eventually had to have both of his legs amputated. Auntie Mildred nursed him through it all, until he died.

I interviewed Auntie Mildred at her beautiful house in Yamhill, Oregon, the same one she shared with Uncle Smiley in his last days. I was impressed with the smart use of space. One room held her awards: ribbons, plaques, and trophies from state and county fairs, won over the years for home goods and canned preserves.

"This year, I put up two hundred and fifty pints of salsa. I also made jam—strawberry, raspberry, blueberry, peach, peach-pineapple, and peach-bourbon. One of the bedroom closets is a pantry, to hold all my canning things."

As we walked down the hall, Auntie Mildred seemed a little embarrassed about the dings and scratches on the walls, made by Uncle Smiley's wheelchair.

"I don't have the heart to paint over these," Auntie Mildred said, running her fingers along a black smudge. "It's silly, but it's a part of him. I'm not ready to erase these yet."

The sweetness of this made me smile.

***

1. How do you view your childhood? What was growing up like for you?

"I know, because my sisters told me, that our mom raised us in a harsh environment," Auntie Mildred said. "I don't really remember all the violence that Dorothy and Prissy do. I was the third daughter, and I'm four years younger than Dorothy, so I didn't see a lot of what she saw. When we moved to Tracy in the 1940's, we started hanging out with the Gonzalez family, because Dorothy started dating Frank. We'd go over to their house for bar-b-ques.

Mildred as a young girl

"Back then, there were sheep on the ranch," Auntie Mildred said, laughing. "Jennie and I, and the twins would try to ride them." She imitated the way they tried to straddle sheep, like horses. "Sometimes the sheep would get bruised, and the men couldn't figure out how they got like that." Auntie Mildred was laughing so hard that her Cocker Spaniel, Sweetie, looked up at her.

"The Gonzalez ranch was really the only place our family went," she said. "We didn't have money, so we never really went anywhere. Later, we moved to Vernalis, when Dorothy was still in high school. I had just graduated from seventh grade. One day in 1951, Mom gathered us together and told us we were moving to L.A., to be with Lupe again. Dorothy stayed behind in Tracy, because she was about to graduate. We moved to L.A., and Prissy and I helped with the boys. At that time, I didn't see any abuse with Mama, but she left Lupe, again. We moved to Ceres. My mom was always working, Dorothy was gone, and then Prissy got married. I was the only daughter left at home, so it was my job to take care of the boys.

"I wanted to get a job in town, just to be part of things. I begged my mother, 'Mama, please let me work.' She said, 'Okay, if you can find a job, you can work.' I walked from Ceres, where we lived, *all the way* into Modesto, five miles from home. I hit all the fast-food places. I asked if they were hiring, but no one would hire me. I walked all the way back home. I got home, so tired, so defeated. My mom said, '¿Ves? ¿Ves? (See? See?) *This* is your job! Your job is staying home and taking care of these kids.' She could tell I was sad, so she said, 'If you help me, I'll buy your school clothes.' I agreed, because what else could I do?

"Before school started, Mom took me shopping. I bought two outfits. I learned how to interchange them. The following year, I got to pick out two more outfits. I would just interchange my clothes all the time. That's the way we did it back then. We learned how to change up our outfits with separates. No one that I knew had a lot of clothes."

2. What's your favorite childhood memory?

"I have so many!" Auntie Mildred said, smiling. "I have one memory of a time when an aunt came to visit us from New Mexico. She had an RV, and parked it in our yard. She invited me inside, and I went in. It was so nice in there! She said, 'Let's have a tea party.' She brought out little cups, a tea pot, and we had a little tea party, just me and her. She wouldn't let Ray, or any of the other boys come in. It was just me and her. I remember that making me feel special.

"When you're in a big family, something *just for you* is very special."

3. How did you meet your spouse?

"I went to Ceres High School until the middle of my junior year," Auntie Mildred said. When we moved back to Tracy, I had to start a new school, in the middle of my junior year. I didn't really know anybody. I knew my cousin, Rosemarie, and Jennie, your mom. I hung out with Jennie at school. Smiley had come home from the service, from Korea, and he lived with them again. He was working alongside Grandpa, on the ranchito.

"Not long after we moved to Tracy, I went to Open House at Tracy High, with your mom and Grandma. Grandpa dropped us off, and left to go do something. Jennie and I were walking, and we turned around and saw Grandma walking all by herself. I said to Jennie, 'Look, your mom is walking, all by herself. Let's walk with her.' So, Jennie and I walked with Grandma, all through the open house. I felt right at home with the Gonzalez family.

"I was sixteen years old, and I had a locket necklace that my godmother gave me. I had a crush on Smiley, so I put a picture of him on one side, and my picture on the other side. I didn't think I was going to marry him, or anything, I was just a young girl with a crush. When my family went over to the Gonzalez house, I'd hang out with Jennie and the twins, and Smiley saw me as a kid, or just his sister's friend. We never talked or connected.

"One day, Jennie told me something Smiley said about me. Apparently, he thought my skirt was too tight, and he told Jennie I should be more modest. Oh, that made me so mad! The next time I went over to the ranch, he said hello to me, and I said, 'How dare you! Talking about my clothes being too tight? Am I supposed to come over here wrapped up in a blanket?' He was so surprised I was talking like that to him. 'A pencil skirt is designed to be a form-fitting style. I'm not being immodest.'" Auntie Millie laughed, remembering Smiley's reaction. "When I finished saying what I needed to say to him, I went to go spend time with Jennie.

"The next few times I went to the ranch, Smiley wasn't there. We stopped running into each other, and part of me thought that was purposeful. One day, I came over, and Smiley was there, getting ready to go out on a date. When he saw me, he said, 'Can I talk to you?' He waved his hand toward the bathroom, off the hallway, because that was the only place we could talk privately. I said, 'I'm not going to go in the bathroom with you.' He said, 'I promise, I'll leave the door open.' So, I followed him in. He apologized, saying how sorry he was for making a rude remark about my clothes. He was sincere, and embarrassed, so I forgave him. Then, he said, 'Can we seal this with a kiss?' He gave me a little kiss, and then left. He went out on a date with his girlfriend." She laughed, remembering Uncle Smiley's audacity. "He knew I had a crush on him, and he asks if he can kiss me? What nerve!"

"Not long after that, my cousin Rosemarie and I were invited to the wedding of a friend. It was in the Methodist Church on Carlton Street. We wanted to go, but we had to walk. As we were walking home, we took off our high heels and carried them. It was a long walk home, and a pretty nice day, so we walked barefoot. We heard a car pull up beside us, and a voice call out: 'You girls want a ride?' We turned around, and it was Smiley. Rosemarie looked at me, surprised. We both had a crush on him, but we were shy. Still, a ride was a ride, and we climbed into the back seat. Smiley's girlfriend was in the front seat with him, practically in his lap. When we got into the car, she slid *all* the way over to the passenger side." Auntie Mildred laughed and slapped her knee. "She was so mad at Smiley for picking us up! She didn't say one word to us. Smiley said, 'How are you girls doing?' We said, 'Fine.' We didn't want to say too much, because we could tell his girlfriend didn't like him talking to us.

"Pretty soon after the car ride, the Junior-Senior ball came up. I wanted to go, but I didn't know anyone. I asked your mom if she thought Smiley could take me. Your mom said, 'Why not ask him?' Smiley had already graduated from high school, so when I asked him, he seemed surprised. I told him the high school allowed outside dates for students, so he said, 'I'll take you. Promise that if somebody in high school asks you, you'll say yes to them.' So, I promised, even though I wasn't going to do that.

"After a few days, Smiley called me. He said, 'Can we start practicing the dances?' I said, 'Sure! Come on over, so we can practice.' He came over, and Prissy taught us all the new dances. Smiley and I had fun practicing together.

"Anyway, he took me to the dance, and that was it. May 14, 1954 was the dance. After the dance, Smiley didn't call me, and I didn't see him. After about two weeks, he called, and after that, he called me *every day*."

Mildred and Smiley before prom, 1954

4. When did you decide to get married?

"I knew I wanted to marry Smiley," Auntie Mildred said. "He represented stability to me. As I grew up, we were uprooted a lot, going from one temporary place to live after another. We went to one temporary school after another. I wanted our move to Tracy to be our final move. As I got closer to the end of high school, I really wanted to stay. Smiley and I were dating by then. One day, my mom said we were moving again, this time to Gustine. I begged her to let me stay. I said, 'I only have one more year in high school and then I'm finished. Please let me stay.' She said, 'No, you're not of age yet, and I need you to come with me.' I said, 'Can I stay with

Prissy?' Prissy was married to John by then, and they lived in Tracy. Mama finally agreed. "Mama moved to Gustine with my brothers and my littlest sister, Loli. Soon, Mama started writing anxious letters—writing, writing, writing. She told me she really needed my help with the kids. Her last letter said, 'I'm coming to pick you up,' because she needed my help with the kids. According to her, that was my job, to help with mothering them.

"One day, Smiley saw the letters. He said, 'You're not going.' I said, 'I don't want to, but what can I do?' He said, 'I think we should get married.' As excited as I was to hear this, I knew I needed my mom's permission, and she wasn't going to give it. She wanted me to move back with her." Auntie Mildred leaned forward, and whispered, like we were high-school friends. "So, we *did it*," she said. "We had sex. I knew, if I got pregnant, we'd *have* to get married.

"Almost immediately, I missed my menstrual cycle," Auntie Mildred said. "To tell you the truth, I was so excited. Smiley knew we'd need proof for our families, so we decided to get a doctor's note. I made an appointment with a doctor in Modesto, who Mama had me see when I had bad migraines. Smiley didn't want anyone to know where we were going, but the day of the appointment, I told Jennie. She was my best friend, and Smiley's sister, so I knew I could trust her. Her face turned *white*. I could tell she was worried. I asked her to cover for me, in my classes, and she said she would.

"The doctor confirmed I was pregnant, and we were excited. Still, we knew it would be hard for us, and hard for our families. When we came back to Tracy, the first one I told was your mom, Jennie. She was shocked. When I got home, I told Prissy. She was devastated—so heartbroken, she could hardly *talk*. Smiley told Grandma and Grandpa, and they were extremely upset.

Grandpa told Smiley not to marry me. He said, 'How can you marry her? Don't you know she's crazy? She's always sick, with those headaches.' He was talking about my migraines, which were terrible. Everyone knew about them. Smiley said, 'I don't care, I'm going to marry her.'

"Oh, that was a hard time!" Auntie Mildred said, shifting in her seat. "Frank and Dorothy were living with Grandpa and Grandma at that time. They drove us down to Gustine, where Mom was living with Julian, Judy's father. Mama thought I was coming home to stay, and she was glad to see me. When we all sat down, I told her I was pregnant. She became livid! She kept saying, 'How could you? How could you?' I told her, 'We had to. You wouldn't give me permission to get married, and this was the only way.' It turned out, *Mama* was pregnant with *Judy*. That's why they wanted me to move to Gustine.

"Smiley asked my uncle's permission to marry me. My uncle was devastated. Everyone was angry and so disappointed. We drove back to Tracy, and Mom came with us. Smiley and I couldn't get married in a church. No priest would marry us.

"On October 14, 1954, we went to Stockton, the county offices, to get a marriage license. We had a Civil Ceremony Service, and Mom and Grandma were with us. Afterward, we stopped at Woolworths, to pick up a few items we needed. On our way to our little motel, I ordered a cup of chicken soup, because that was all I could eat. I was nauseated from my pregnancy. That was my wedding dinner!

"So, my wedding day wasn't everything I dreamed of. No one was happy for us, and no one celebrated. Did anyone say, 'Let me at least fix you something to eat,' or 'I'll bring you some food'? Nothing like that. Everyone left us alone. At first, it didn't matter to us all that much, because we were in love. I was happy to be able to marry Smiley. After a while, the pain of family rejection set in.

"Our oldest daughter, Jeannie, was born, in June of 1955. Everyone loved her! Your mom graduated on the same day, so Jennie came to the hospital with her cap and gown, to see her. Grandma helped take care of her. She stayed with me for a full two weeks after the baby was born. She was the best mother-in-law ever! Even Grandpa came around. He loved Jeannie, and accepted me. Finally.

"Our five daughters went all out to give us a nice 25th Wedding Anniversary party, because we never had a real wedding. They arranged for a banquet room in Tracy, a dinner, a big band and dancing. *That* was our real celebration."

25th Wedding Anniversary announcement in the Tracy Press, September 19, 1980

Uncle Smiley and Auntie Mildred's 25th Anniversary Party was a formal gathering with a catered dinner and 15-piece orchestra, like Benny Goodman or Cab Calloway's big band. After dinner, the band played swing music from the 1940's. Uncle Smiley and Auntie Mildred took to the dance floor, and jitterbugged to "In the Mood." When it was over, they hugged laughed and the whole room applauded. They were wonderful dancers, and in my mind's eye, this is how I remember them.

5. What was the greatest challenge you had to face in marriage?

"As a wife, I had to learn how to speak up for myself," Auntie Mildred said. "I had to learn to speak up for myself the *right way*. I didn't want to fight with Smiley, but I didn't want to let him take advantage of me, either.

"In the early years of marriage, I did everything Smiley wanted. I tried to make a loving home, be a good wife, and work hard as a mother. At the same time, I didn't know how to be my own person. It took me ten years before I could speak up for myself. When I did, it wasn't easy. I had to let Smiley know, 'This is who I am. Don't take advantage of me.' Love can go a long way, but not without respect. Both people have to respect one another. I had to learn to speak up, so we didn't get into situations where everything was Him, Him, Him, Him. It was exhausting, and I couldn't pretend it was okay. I needed something for me, too.

"Things changed when I took a job with Raytheon," she said, sitting up straight in her chair. "I worked at Raytheon for eighteen years before we moved to Oregon. I started off as a microscope operator in diodes. Pretty soon, I moved up to QT inspector. By the time I retired, I worked in the engineering department. They gave me a big send-off in the cafeteria. Pretty good, for someone who doesn't even have a high-school diploma!"

After retiring, the Gonzales family moved to the Portland area. In Oregon, all of my cousins found joy. Weddings and babies came. Then, Uncle Smiley's health started deteriorating. Auntie Mildred recounted the final years of Uncle Smiley with tenderness, sometimes with tears in her eyes.

"The last years of our marriage were tough," she said. "Uncle Smiley had a lot of health concerns. He actually died on us three times, but he came back each time. The doctors had to perform so many procedures, so many times, once he lost his legs. He went through a lot."

"Just like all marriages, we had our ups and downs," Auntie Millie said. "There's no such a thing as a perfect marriage. There's no time in your marriage that's perfect. Sometimes, you're down each other's throat!" Auntie Mildred laughs, and winks at me. "But that doesn't mean you don't love one another. Marriage is hard work, but somehow, me and Smiley made it last."

Auntie Mildred was quiet for a while. She looked out the sliding glass door, and into the green meadow, dotted with spring daffodils. "We really did love each other," she said. "Smiley was the love of my life, and I was his. We tried to show this love every day, until he died. Just to be with him, to see the way he responded to me, was wonderful. Even at the end, even when it got really hard, I was still happy to be with him. It meant so much to be with him, at the end. I loved him so much."

6. What advice would you give the next generation?

"If you're entering a relationship and it's getting serious, be sure to let them know who you really are," Auntie Mildred said. "All of us can perform for each other when we're dating, but it's important to show your true self to the other person. That's what intimacy is. Don't let anybody try change you into the person they want you to be. That is just dangerous.

"Also, if you have a child, that's *your* child. You can always find a man, but you can't find another child. You really don't need somebody abusive in your life, or somebody that damages your kids. Ask yourself important questions all the time: What do I want for my life?

Do I want my kids to grow up and see me battered? What do I want their life to be like? Would they rather be raised by a single mother who loves them? You're better off raising your kids without a bad influence, that's for sure. If I'd give this advice to my own kids, I'd give it to anybody else."

7. Grandma's last words were 'Keep the family together.' Do you think we've done this?

"I can only answer from my side," Auntie Mildred said. "In a way, I feel like our family *bond* has fallen apart, because I never really hear from them unless I call them. We haven't kept in contact like we used to. I knew when we moved to Oregon, it would be a physical separation for sure, but I always thought we'd communicate better."

I was surprised by Auntie Mildred's candid answer. She's outspoken in pointing out our family's lapses in communication, but I agree with her. When Grandpa and Grandma were alive, their children and spouses blended together well, and we were all in and out of each other's lives, despite being separated by distance.

Why had we become so separated? What happened to the incredible family bond we had when Grandpa and Grandma were alive?

Grandpa and Grandma's 50th wedding anniversary party at the Tracy Inn. Surrounded by their seven children and their spouses

35. Seven Questions—Lucy

Lucy at the ranchito, approx. 1953

Auntie Lucy was born on September 9, 1933, in Malaga, California, the fourth child, and second daughter of Ignacio and Juana Gonzalez. In the middle of the Great Depression, a labor strike in Lone Pine forced a very pregnant Juana Gonzalez to board a train, bound for Fresno, with three little children clinging to her. Grandma arrived to find her beloved sister, Maria, waiting for her. The baby, born in Tia Maria's house, was promptly named Luz Maria—the light of Mary. Auntie Lucy was a burst of light during a long period of darkness. Lucy's birth order and gender normally would have guaranteed her to be overlooked during a turbulent time, but because of Tia Maria, Auntie Lucy's Godmother, Luz received plenty of attention and care.

"Maria loved Lucy," Grandma said. "Anything I needed for the baby, she'd buy."

By the time Grandpa returned to his family, he found two queens: Tia Maria and her Goddaughter, Luz Maria.

According to her sisters, Auntie Lucy was born with a strong personality.

Surrounded by traditional Mexican-American expectations of what a female should be, Lucy eschewed tradition.

"At home on the ranch, I would go out to the fence," she said. "I would face the hills to the south, and say, 'One of these days, I will go over those hills and live a different life.'" She laughed at this, and leaned forward. "And I did. Here I am." She waved her hand over her tastefully decorated condo, in Pomona, about thirty miles east of Los Angeles.

Auntie Lucy had one son: my cousin, Don. She married my Uncle Percy, who had children from his previous marriage, including one son, Tracy, who lived with them. Tracy and Donnie, as we knew them, were close in age. Together, they were a family.

When I interviewed Auntie Lucy, her caretaker, Blanca, accompanied us for lunch She made sure Auntie Lucy was eating, and reminded her of details my aunt couldn't remember.

"I am losing my memory," Auntie Lucy said, under her breath. At eighty-five years old, Aunt Lucy, still vogue and gorgeous, had been struggling with recent memory loss. Blanca helped oversee Aunt Lu's daily routines and medication. Despite short-term memory issues, Auntie Lucy remembered her childhood as well as any of her sisters, sometimes, better.

1. How do you view your childhood? What was growing up like for you?

"There wasn't much to do on the ranch," Auntie Lucy said. "It was boring. There was nothing to do, and Daddy was always working. We never had a real vacation because we couldn't afford it. We'd go back to school in September and the other kids would say, 'On summer vacation, we went camping, or we went somewhere.' I figured out, very early in my life, that we were different from other kids at school. They all had fun on summer vacation, and we couldn't do anything like that, because we were poor. We didn't have any money for nice things. "When we were kids, we swam in an irrigation ditch, which was about four feet deep.

When it was hot, we'd go swimming in it. That was our excitement. We lived in that little house. Did you ever see that house?"

I shook my head, no.

"It was a shack, a converted shack, and started out as nothing more than four walls and a door. Daddy made improvements to it, and eventually, we had indoor plumbing. The bosses lived in a really nice home. Their friends came over in fancy cars. It was so obvious to me that we were their servants.

1980: Grandma and Auntie Terry look at their old house on the ranchito, which had been turned into a storage unit. Grandma had been living in the house on Lorraine Road for nearly twenty years, and wanted to see the old house again. It has since been torn

"As I got older, I tried to control this environment. I liked the house to be spotless. My poor sisters would say, 'Let's clean up, because the *beast* is coming!'" She laughed at this, but with regret. "I had a lot of hang-ups back then, a lot of unresolved anger. I was ashamed of where I came from. I wasn't happy, joyous and free, as they say in the program, and as a result, I was difficult. I wanted more than what my family had to offer. I was cranky; they'll all tell you!"

I smiled, but didn't say anything. Lucy's siblings *do* remember her as bossy and cranky.

"I got to high school, and my brothers returned from Korea. When the war was over, Smiley came home, and he was a *different person*." Auntie Lucy leaned back and lifter her hands to the sky. "I didn't believe the change! Before he went to Korea, he hated me. Over there, he almost got killed, so when he came home, he couldn't do enough for me. He took me shopping, and bought me clothes. This was his way of compensating for the way he had been to me before. Can you believe it? He actually admitted he was terrible to me, and he asked for my forgiveness. Of course, I forgave him.

"In high school, things got easier for me," Auntie Lucy said. "Because I love music, there were so many ways for music to lift my spirits. I loved singing—our dad taught us how to harmonize—and I played in the band. I even played in the marching band. I loved dancing. Now and then, I'd even get to go to a formal dance, with Charlie Garcia. He was the only one that my folks trusted to take me to a formal dance. I had a blast dancing.

Auntie Lucy and Uncle Smiley, friends after Korea

2. How did you find your wings, or gain your independence?

"Our parents gave us great roots," Auntie Lucy said. "They created a strong family. I don't think they gave us wings. I found my independence after high school, when I started working. I got a job with the State of California, working at a state prison, and started to see different sects of life.

"I lived in my parents' house until I was twenty-five, still having to follow their rules. The thing that bothered me the most was how I could only date one man at a time. A guy asked me out, I dated him, and dated him, and dated him, until I either got *tired* of him or *he* got tired of *me*. And then *chhhk!* cross him off the list. Then, time for another one. 'Next!'

"One day, I thought, 'You know, I make a nice income, I'm over twenty-one-years-old, and I don't want to stay here anymore.' I decided to apply for a transfer to a job in Sacramento. I found a little studio apartment, very close to my new job, that I could rent. After all the details were taken care of, I told my mother. I said, 'Mama, at the end of this month, I won't be living here anymore. I've found another place to live, close to my new job…' Poor Mama! I couldn't even finish. She went *hysterical*." Auntie Lucy put both hands to her mouth and closed her eyes. When she opened her eyes, she shook her head.

"I broke her heart," she said. "I didn't want to. I wasn't trying to. There was an unwritten rule back then: 'All nice Hispanic girls live at home until they get married.' Live at home, meet somebody, and then *marry* him!" Auntie Lucy emphasized the last part, then laughed. "It's all so nice and proper, but not for me. I was ready to move out and live by myself. Mama could not accept it. It broke her heart. I didn't realize how much it would hurt her, but it did." Auntie Lucy sat back in her chair, and looked down at her hands. She shook her head. "I broke her heart, even when I didn't mean to."

It still bothered Auntie Lucy, the woman who is supposed to be so independent, such a free-thinker. In the end, she loved her parents and never intended to disappoint them. She never wanted to break her mother's heart. I related to this so much, I had tears in my eyes.

3. How did you meet your spouse?

"I've had two husbands," Auntie Lucy said, playfully winking at me. She knew I knew this, but for posterity, she summarized. "Howard, Don's father, was my first husband. My second husband, Percy Crow, already had children when we married. Tracy was only a year older than Don, so Tracy lived with us. He and Don grew up together. Both of my marriages ended in divorce.

"When I was getting ready to marry Howard, I should have realized simple things. Howard had been married several times before me. I should have realized that our marriage wasn't going to work. Some kind of alarm should have gone off in my head: 'Don't marry him, for God's sake!' No bell went off, no alarm." Auntie Lucy lifted her hand up, and made a slicing motion in the air. "I was in love, and that was it. Howard wasn't a demonstrative man. He was English. Cold. Never could relax. He didn't know how to be himself. In my opinion, there was something wrong with Howard, a disconnect with emotion. I wanted him to be a warm and loving person, but he didn't know how.

"I don't regret marrying him, because I had Donnie. My son, Don, was the result." Auntie Lucy said this with her usual confidence, dismissing a stormy marriage, and focusing on the silver-lining: her son, Don.

"I married Percy Crow, who was actually a good husband!" Auntie Lucy said, sitting up straight. "Percy was a professional man. He loved his work. Everybody liked him. He was a warm and loving person. He was a really nice man, kind to friends and family, and also kind to strangers. He affirmed me. We had a good marriage, a beautiful house in Claremont, I loved his son, Tracy, who was like a second son to me. I loved Percy's older daughters. Both men gave me a family. For that I'm grateful."

4. What was the greatest challenge you had to face in marriage?

"The greatest challenge in my marriage to Percy was..." Auntie Lucy paused to consider her words. "Percy's only problem was that he had a roving eye. He loved women."

I nearly fell off my chair. Uncle Percy, a large man, was not very handsome. I always thought my Auntie Lucy, glamorous, passionate, and successful, was out of his league. Hearing this shocked me.

"Are you serious?" I asked. "Uncle Percy?"

"Bless his heart," she said, laughing into her hand. She seemed amused by my reaction. "He had big appetites. Even when he was *dying*. Even in his last days, when he had terminal cancer, and they told him he didn't have long, he was still like that.

"I heard Percy wasn't doing too well. I went to go see him with my friend, Margie. I thought, *Yes, I'm his ex-wife, but by God, I'm going to bid him farewell.* He loved that I came to see him, dressed up in nice clothes.

"So, I walked in and sat with him—I hope you don't get embarrassed by this story—he was lying in his bed, and I was sitting next to him. We were chatting, and I was listening to him, kind of stroking his leg." Auntie Lucy demonstrated the stroking on her own leg, like she was petting a cat. "What does Percy do? He grabs my hand and puts it on his crotch!"

We laughed about this, and I shook my head. My Uncle Percy died in his seventies, terminally ill. It sounded out-of-character. Auntie Lucy assured me it wasn't.

"Can you believe that?" Auntie Lucy asked. "I pulled my hand away so fast! I mean, he's *dying* and he does *that*? My friend, Margie, couldn't believe it. She had to leave the room. On the way home, Maggie said, 'To the very end, he wants to be a sexy man!'

"So, that was the last time I ever saw Percy." Auntie Lucy She laughed, and shook her head. "Can you believe that?" I loved that story, maybe because it made her laugh so hard.

5. What advice would you give the next generation?

"Advice?" Auntie Lucy asked, as if she wanted to make sure she heard me correctly. "I don't know if I would offer advice. Maybe I would tell them to *own* their spirituality, religion, beliefs, or whatever you want to call it. Let it be your *own*, and live by it.

"It was ingrained in us from the time we were born that there was a God, who we were really supposed to believe in, and there was a devil. We learned that if you didn't behave, it meant you were going to go to hell. So, I was raised to love God, but also taught to *fear* God. I'd hear, 'You better be careful, don't do that or God's going to punish you!' I'd always think, 'Wait a minute! I always thought that God was a *warm and loving and gracious* God, how can He be a *punisher*?' Those were the two Gods I was raised with.

"Today, I believe in the God of my understanding, the God of my life. I still go to Mass, and I'm fortunate to have Catholic friends who pick me up and take me. My faith is very, very strong now, but I had to unlearn some wrong teachings that were deeply ingrained in me."

Auntie Lucy takes a moment to think about this.

"My faith is strong," she said. "I loved volunteering as a bereavement minister, assisting at funerals for church. I truly enjoyed that. I reminded myself of Mama. Remember how much she liked going to funerals?"

As she got older, Grandma loved funerals. They were better than weddings for her. She counted flower arrangements, wept with the families, and remembered things, out loud, about the dearly departed. She adored funerals.

"Mama and Grandma Nellie used to talk about the funerals they attended," Auntie Lucy said. "Mama would say, 'Mi comadre, I've been to *five* funerals this month.' Grandma Nellie, not to be outdone, would say, 'I've been to *six* funerals.' It was so amusing, their competition to see who went to more funerals. Then, I became a bereavement minister. Now, I talk like that.

"Anyway, my relationship with God—the God of my understanding— helps guide me and direct me in important things. Recently, I made the decision to stop driving a car. I had a car accident, which I interpreted as a sign. I'm not as sharp as I used to be. I can say, 'I better not do that anymore, because I'm getting older,'" she said, smiling. "I felt like it was a wake-up call. I said to myself, 'Lu, maybe God is telling you that you should give up driving. You're not as sharp or as aware as you used to be.' So, that's why I don't drive. That's how it is; that's okay."

6. Grandma's last words were 'Keep the family together.' Do you think we've done this?

"Yes," Auntie Lucy said, without hesitating. "We've kept the family together because nobody is back-stabbing anybody else. None of us do that. It would never even occur to us! We never criticize each other." She thought about this for a while, then said, "You know who I miss? Nellie's family. I don't really have an opportunity to see them, or talk to them. I used to go to their places, and stay there, but I can't do that anymore. I miss all of them."

Lucy "Lu" Crow, 2019

7. When you look back on your life, do you think you got enough love?

Auntie Lucy seemed thrown off, but also appreciative, when I asked this question.

"What an interesting question," she said, leaning back and smiling. "But the answer is...yes." She leaned forward again and clarified. "If you're asking if I had enough *romance*? The answer is yes. Uncle Percy really was the *love of my life*. I got a lot of love from him. I've had all kinds of love from family. I have Don, my son, who I love so much. He makes me feel loved. Tracy, my step-son, has always treated me like a mother. Percy's daughters are very loving. Now I have my grandchildren, and as you know, grandchildren are the best! I have *so many* friends, who give me loads of love. Now I have Blanca," she looked over at her caregiver, a beautiful woman named Blanca, who smiled at her. She was Auntie Lucy's right hand, after she showed early signs of dementia and memory loss. "Blanca is my honey!"

Auntie Lucy looked up at the ceiling, and smiled. "I think I might know what you're asking," she said. "It took a long time for me to accept how hard it was for my parents to understand me. Daddy was strict with his daughters, and didn't want us looking to the left or the right. Teresa, the eldest, was an absolute saint. She never balked, never complained, never got angry. Compared to her, I was mouthy. I used to do a lot of bitching and whining. Then, along comes Jennie, who was so sweet." Auntie Lucy paused, like she'd remembered something. "I'd take my frustrations out on Jennie, even though it had nothing to do with her. I had to vent, and she got to hear it. Poor Jennie! By the time the twins were growing up, my parents had *relaxed*. They stopped having these rules that were impossible to follow. They had gained some perspective. They could see what they'd done right and what they'd done wrong. By the time the twins were in high school, Daddy let them ride the bus with the band as majorettes." She smiled, sadly. "Don't get me wrong, I was happy for them, and proud of them. I never was jealous of anyone in my family. I didn't ask, 'How come they get to do that and I didn't?' But I did wish my parents could understand me. I wished they could see me as more than just a rebellious daughter. I wanted them to recognize me, to see I needed more from life than the ranch.

"Fast forward, many years later. Daddy had died. Mama was living by herself. She was getting older, and when she got sick, I moved into her house to take care of her. Near the end, she went into the hospital, to intensive care. All of us, her children, were gathered around her. When the doctors came in to check on her, Frank and I went outside to smoke.

"My sister, Juanita, walked up to me, as I was smoking. She said, 'Lu, Mama wants to talk to you.' I got up, and started walking fast. My mind raced, all the way back to the room..." Auntie Lucy paused, put hand to her mouth, and looked down at the floor. I thought she was crying. Then, I realized she was laughing. "I thought, 'I wonder what Mama wants to say to me?'" Auntie Lucy tried to finish the story without stopping, but she had to take breaks just to laugh. "I thought, 'Maybe she wants to thank me for all the attention I gave her at the end. Maybe she's going to apologize for misjudging me. What will her last words to me be?' I walked in her room, and Mama stretched her hand out to me. I drew nearer to her, and said, 'What is it, Mama?' There she was, so small, struggling to breathe. She said, 'Hi mija.' She lifted her oxygen mask up, just so I could hear her..." Auntie Lucy doubled over, laughing hard.

"What did she say?" I asked.

"'Put me in my blue dress,'" Auntie Lucy said, into her hand. I could tell she was trying to tell me the rest of the story, which was hard to do. "Mama said, 'Remember that blue dress that's hanging in the closet in my spare bedroom? Not the plain one in my bedroom closet...' Oh, honey! I had to be serious, but I wanted to laugh so bad!

"Here I was, thinking my mom was going to have some deep, last words for me. I was getting ready for that, but all she wanted to talk about was that *blue dress*?" Auntie Lucy took a while to compose herself. When she did, her face was glowing. "Oh! That's one of my favorite stories now. It shows how I expected something from Mama, some kind of resolve. *She* didn't expect it from me, *I* expected it from her. We expect people to be different, and then *we'll* be alright? People are going to be who they are. We can't expect them to be different."

Auntie Lucy leaned back and sighed. Her face was flushed, and she seemed exhausted from laughing. She never looked more beautiful.

36. Seven Questions—Jennie

Juana, or Juanita Gonzalez, my mother, was born on March 8, 1937, in Malaga, California, the fifth child, and the third daughter of Ignacio and Juana Gonzalez. It was during the never-ending Great Depression, and the fallout of dust storms on the U.S. prairie soil brought Midwest farmworkers to California, in droves. They arrived in overloaded vehicles and buses, expecting to work in the fields. Many Mexican braceros were displaced, as a result. The *New York Times* reported "two million of the two and a half million Mexicans in the United States were out of work." [20]

Mexican families, who had been working as farm laborers, were regularly rounded up, and "repatriated" to Mexico. It was a desperate time for most Mexican-Americans who were undocumented.

These factors, surrounding Mom's birth, combined with her birth order, socioeconomic status, and the tumultuous time into which she was born, should have sabotaged her chances of happiness. Instead, Mom was born with an easy temperament. "Jennie was my easiest child," Grandma always told me. "She did everything I ask her to do. She was real cute, real nice, she used to read books all the time, she had a real good voice..."

Mom was content and grateful, from a young age. To this day, she has good memories of childhood. "We were poor," Mom said, matter-of-factly.

---

[20] "For Aid to Mexican Idle; Cardenas Hears U. S. Has Many on Its Relief Rolls" *New York Times*, 18 February 1937

"But we had a lot of love, and that makes a big difference. Mama told me I was a cute baby, and I started singing at a young age."

Mom had to wear glasses from a young age. In the first picture we have of her—standing in a field, getting ready to start her first day of second grade—she wears them.

Behind their simple frames, Mom's eyes look straight into the camera, despite a bright morning sun. Holding hands with Emily on her left and Molly on her right, Mom wears a cotton dress that's slightly too small for her. Her hair and face shine, and she's beautiful. She still begins each day like this: calmly optimistic, ready to tackle the day ahead.

Molly, Jennie, Emily on the first day of Jennie's fourth grade, the twins' third grade

By the time Mom got to high-school, her eyes had corrected themselves, and glasses were no longer necessary. Her figure developed, and she lost her shyness. In 1958, while she was in her early twenties, Mom was named the Tomato Queen of Tracy, California, a serene beauty who championed the biggest cash crop that Tracy gave the world. Mom posed for a newspaper photograph on an elephant, in downtown Tracy in 1958, a couple of years before she met my father.

Mom as Tracy's tomato Queen, 1958

Mom met and married my father, John Gerard Ryan, my dad, who most people call Jack, or Deacon Ryan, if you're at St. Bernard's. An Irish-American from Boston, Dad grew up an only child with older parents; his father died when he was very young. Because Dad and Mom had challenging childhoods, they both have an unusual mixture of empathy and grit. They were married in St. Bernard's Church on October 8, 1960, the same church our family attended when I was growing up.

Mom and Dad walk down the aisle of St. Bernard's Catholic Church, October 8, 1960

Shortly after their wedding, my parents had a baby, Patricia (Patty). Four more children came, in rapid succession: Janet (me), Steven, Sharon (Shari) and Colleen. We lived in the house where they still live, in Tracy. Dad and Mom had strong feelings about their children having a solid foundation, with no geographical moves. This didn't keep us from travel. As we grew up, Dad and Mom took us camping, including a bold Bicentennial cross-country trip, where Dad drove the family station wagon, towing a pop-up camper, all the way to Boston, in 1976.

Once they retired, Dad and Mom traveled extensively. One of Mom's favorite stories is about the time she and Dad visited Ireland.

"As a young girl, my sister, Lu, and I would harmonize the song 'Galway Bay,'" she said. "We would sing that song as we washed dinner dishes together. When Dad and I were in Ireland, we checked into our room, which was actually overlooking Galway Bay. I looked out the window, into the beautiful water, glittering in the sun, and started crying. Dad came over and said, 'What's the matter?' I just looked at him, and said, 'Who would have ever thought I would be here?' It would have been a dream come true, if I ever let myself dream anything like that, but traveling to Ireland was an impossibility, so.... that moment was very touching."

Mom cried as she told this story. Dad put his hand on her shoulder.

Mom's real life has exceeded her dreams. Ruled by logic and born with a realistic mindset, Mom never expected too much. The miraculous twist is that she's experienced more from life than she ever thought possible. This, combined with gratitude, makes her happier than most people I know.

***

1. How do you view your childhood? What was growing up like for you?

"We had a very loving family," Mom said. "I know I've said that a lot, but it's important to repeat. We grew up with a lot of love. There's a certain amount of confidence that comes from growing up in a loving home.

"We were taught to respect and obey the authorities in place, and we chose to do that. My parents respected this country. I know there's a lot of mixed feelings about how immigrants were treated, but my parents taught us to obey rules and laws that were in place here, no matter what. I never heard my parents complain about the government. They weren't the 'fight the establishment' type. Especially my father. He was the kind of man who held his head high and put his best foot forward.

"When we were very young, we didn't go very many places with my dad, but as we got older, he would take us into town with him. He'd say, 'When you go out with me, I want all of you to be absolutely clean, because I don't want anyone calling you a dirty Mexican.' I never questioned what he meant by this. Do you think I ever asked, 'Why would someone call us that?' or 'Have you ever heard someone call you that before?' I know it must have happened at some point. Some Anglo probably called him a name, or said something to him. It goes without saying that prejudice is prejudice and some people are just going to call you what they want to call you, but my father wanted to be sure that that didn't happen to us. So, we were presentable whenever we went out. That meant being very, very clean. He had the same standards for us as he did with himself.

"It used to bother my mother that my dad would shop in men's clothing boutiques, rather than a chain store. She'd say, 'Why do you shop there? You're not a rich man, why don't you go and get it at that chain store over here? But Daddy didn't mind paying good money for quality clothes. Appearance mattered to him. Daddy was a strong force in our lives. I think I'm more like him than I am my mother."

Mom used to say this a lot. She felt her temperament was more like Grandpa's than Grandma's. I didn't know what she meant, exactly. To me, Grandpa and Grandma were two sides of one coin, a couple that was more than two people—they were an idea, a concept, a foundation stone. To me, they were one.

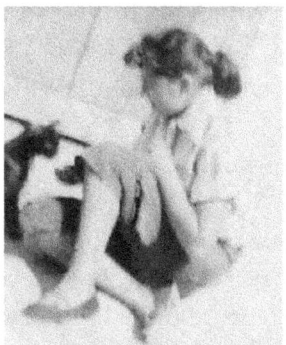

Juanita plays with a cat on the ranchito

2. Why do you think your memories of childhood are so happy?

"I think temperament enters into the picture," Mom said. "I'm pretty evenly tempered. I have good, solid memories of growing up. My sister, Lucy, on the other hand, doesn't have the best memories of growing up. She's a different kind of person, a 'tell-me-the-truth or else,' kind of person, and her temperament is totally different from mine. I think that counts when it comes to forming memories." Mom turned toward me.

"*Your* temperament is different from mine," Mom said to me. "With you, no one ever had to guess what you were feeling. To this day, we know how you're feeling because it shows, all over you. You have extreme highs and extreme lows. As a child, when you got excited about life, you were *way* up high and nobody could touch you. None of our kids were like you. When you were sad, you were very, very sad. Your lows were so extreme that no one could pull you up out of it. We gave up trying to make you happy when you're like that. That's the way you were made: things are either great or awful.

"Think about me, now," she said, looking at me. "I process things very differently. If something seems bad at first, it might turn around to be good. Something great could turn into a big headache.

I remember once, I had my heart broken by a guy I really liked. He broke my heart, without meaning to, but it *really* hurt. A song would come on the radio, and I would cry. Eventually, I got over him. And then, guess what? I met Dad!" Mom's face was radiant. "I found out what *real* love is. Not just emotion, but *love*. Sacrificial love. Faithful love. Your dad, the love of my life, to this day, is my knight in shining armor. So, you see? My heart really wasn't broken by that other guy, it just had a virus," she said, and laughed. "Maybe my pride was hurt."

"My memories of our time on the ranch, with all its beauty, are the ones I *choose* to remember. I used to go outside, look around, and say to myself, 'I really love it here.' I didn't sulk around, thinking about all my friends in town. I made the best of it, because my temperament is different. Maybe that's why I have good memories."

3. How did you meet your spouse?

Dad and Mom were together at their dining room table, as they answered this question. It was 2018, and both were in their eighties.

"We met at a Young Christian Workers meeting," Mom said.

"YCW was a Catholic youth group," Dad said. "It was run by a priest from St. Bernard's, John Ralph Duggan. I was a good, Catholic boy, and I was also single. Plus, Father Duggan asked me. He was a red-headed Irishman from Chicago, so we were cut from the same cloth."

"I was very struck by Jack, the first time I saw him," Mom said. "We met at the Guadalupe Center in South Side Tracy. I remember approaching the building, and I saw Jack and another young man standing at the entrance to the hall. I walked up the four or five steps into the hall, and two guys were out there talking. It was dark, but the hall lights were illuminating the entrance. I couldn't really see Jack in clear light, but I was very struck by him." Mom looked at Dad and smiled. "There was just something about him. He looked down as I was coming up the stairs, and he lifted his chin and said, 'Hi.' Mom's arms dropped to her sides, and she opened her mouth in hypnotic surprise. "You talk about, 'You had me at Hello!' That was something! I walked into the hall, almost shaking. I just had this *wonderful* attraction to an attractive, sexy person. Later on, Jack and the other guy walked in. Then, we had our meeting."

Dad smiled. "At this point, Mom usually says 'He wasn't particularly good-looking.'"

"I only say that because it explains chemical attraction," Mom said, smiling. She looked back at me. "When Dad came into the meeting, I could see he wasn't particularly good-looking.

Attraction isn't always about classic features. I was still *very* attracted to him, but *why*? Why was I so attracted to this person?"

"I can't tell you how many times I've heard that part," Dad said. "Talk about working on your humility!" He looked at Mom and they laughed. "My reaction to her was just the opposite," Dad said. "When I saw her in the light, I literally couldn't believe this person was single. I looked at her, a vision of loveliness, in a simple blue dress. I was thinking, 'There's no way this young woman could be unattached. In my day, someone like her wasn't single for long. I was kind of a shy guy back then, and part of the shy-guy-syndrome is fear of rejection. It took me a while to get the nerve up to ask her out."

I smiled. I would have never described my father as shy. He was outgoing, with a lot of friends. He sang in the choir, was a Catholic deacon, had speaking engagements, led marriage groups, was a leader at his workplace.

"One night, after the meeting, we went to have coffee as a group," Dad said. "I drove everybody to the Star Café. After we finished, I drove everybody back to their cars. Everybody got out of my car, including Jennie."

"It wasn't until the fourth or fifth meeting," Mom said. "So, we had known each other for a while. I kept wanting him to ask me out, but he hadn't. As I was getting out of his car that night, I thought, 'Oh, well. Not this time either!' I started walking to my car, and then I heard him call,

'Jennie?' I stopped dead in my tracks. I turned around and saw him in his car, still running, but he signaled me over. I walked back over to him, *really* hoping he'd ask me out."

"She was wearing the color blue again," Dad said. "A blue sweater, which made her look very nice. I decided to *really* turn on the charm. I said, 'We've been planning a social get together as a group, so how about you and me having a social get-together of our own?'"

We laughed, and Dad held up his thumbs, in mock suaveness.

"I didn't want to look overly-eager," Mom said. "I tried to take my time answering. I said, "Yeah. You know what? That's not a bad idea. Let's do that." In reality, my heart was racing and my knees were wobbling. I held on to the car door, just to keep standing. I kind of fell apart when he asked me. It was about five weeks from the time I met him until that day."

"I came from a big city, so I wanted to take her someplace nice," Dad said. "Anyone coming from a big city on the East Coast loves San Francisco. I'd go to San Francisco any chance I'd get. That's where we went for our first date."

"Dad had a Bostonian accent," Mom said. "When he asked me out, he said, 'I was thinking of going to have *suppah* in the city!'"

"In those days, San Francisco had a lot of nice clubs," Dad said. "I've always liked Dixieland music, and there was a place called 'The Red Garter' where the band played banjoes and wore red garters on their sleeves, and you'd get peanuts and beer. There were shells on the floor."

"They actually *encouraged* you to throw peanut shells on the floor!" Mom said, laughing. "I had a hard time doing that."

"Then there was 'The Hungry Eye,'" Dad said.

"Where we saw Phyllis Diller and the Smothers Brothers," Mom said.

"Most of our dates were to San Francisco," Dad said. "We'd have dinner and a show. Our first date, the one we went on right after I asked her out, was at a big club on Columbus Avenue.

It was the biggest club in San Francisco, like a big movie set of the 1930's, with a giant stage…"

"You're not thinking of Bimbo's, are you?" Mom asked.

"Bimbo's!" Dad said, snapping his fingers.

"That wasn't our first date," Mom said. "Wait here."

Mom went to her room, and returned with one of her scrapbooks. She opened to a page, where a pressed, dried corsage decorated a black-and-white photograph of them. They looked like kids, smiling shyly, all dressed up. They sat behind a linen-covered table.

"See, Jack? Our first date was October 24, 1959." Mom had the page adequately marked: 'First Date.' In the corner of the picture, the restaurant's name was stamped: Sinaloa.

I smiled. "Your first date was to Sinaloa?" I asked. "Chev worked there! He used to sing and emcee in a tuxedo." Chev, Mario's father, later became a Broadway actor. Before moving to New York City, Chev made his living as an entertainer In San Francisco. Sinaloa was his first paid gig.

"It had to be earlier than this, right?" Mom asked.

"Yes," I said. "Your picture is dated 1959, and Chev had already moved to New York."

"Look at us, Jack!" Mom said, her index finger tracing their picture. "What a couple of young punks we were. I dated it, see? October 24, 1959. That was our first date."

"And the rest, as they say, is history," Dad said. They smiled at each other, satisfied.

4. When did you decide to get married?

"It was July 9th when Dad actually proposed marriage," Mom said. "Our first date was October 24, and the following October 8th we got married."

"Things are different now," Dad said. "People don't seem to have the same concept of marriage and commitment. Marriage, now, involves a decision, but it's not a very deep one."

"We were good, church-going people, you know?" Mom said. "We would never have sex before getting married! For a man, he can only go so long before he has to decide if it's serious.

Nowadays, people become sexually active and *then* they talk about marriage."

Dad nodded. "Both of us had families who knew we were getting to that serious stage," he said. "Most of my family was still on the East Coast, but they knew I had been seeing someone. The Irish in Boston were ethnocentric. It was like they all got off the boat, settled in the same area, and stayed close together. There were unspoken rules that Irish guys married Irish girls. That's what you were supposed to do."

Dad's synopsis of ethnocentricity reflects both culture and tradition of the time. It was 1959, and marriages between a whites and non-whites were referred to as "interracial." California had only removed legal sanctions for interracial marriage twelve years prior. Nevertheless, even when the government had no power to forbid marriage, their families could. Dad and Mom were aware that some members of their family still held a prejudiced mindset.

"Two of my cousins in Boston had just married Italian girls," Dad said. "The old-school guys in my family almost disowned them. The way they saw things, the Italians had their own language, they lived on the north end of Boston, where you went to eat good Italian food, but not to meet Italian girls. That's how old-school guys thought. I moved to California, and those rules seemed very far away and archaic, until I fell in love with your mother. When I did, I wondered how my family would react.

"In the summer of 1960, I went back to Boston, for a wedding and family gathering," Dad said. "I was hanging out afterward, with my Aunt Kate Ryan, who was a real free-spirit. In those days, women and men would separate during a party. Aunt Kate would always stay with the men." Dad smiled, as if he'd been transported to his hometown, hanging with his family. "I remember Aunt Kate, leaning against the piano and singing. She could drink and smoke just as much as the guys. I loved my Aunt Kate, and felt a strong kinship with her. I decided to talk to her about getting serious with Jennie. I told her, 'I'm thinking of marrying this girl I've been seeing in California,'" Dad paused, struggling with what he said next. "I told her, 'But she's Mexican.' I braced myself for some strong words. Remember, my cousins had just married the Italian girls, and the family had nearly disowned them. Aunt Kate could tell I was serious. She asked me, 'Do you love her?' I said, 'I think I do.' Then, she said, 'Well, if you love her, then you should marry her, because that's all that matters.' This was tremendous affirmation for me. I knew that some people in the family wouldn't get it, but the people who were most important to me would. I already had my mother's approval. Nana was open-minded, and this wasn't even a question with her."

"So, Dad asked me to marry him," Mom said, breathing deeply. They looked at each other and smiled. "You have to remember, Janet, the times were so different. I didn't say, 'Oh, yes! Absolutely!' I remember thinking, 'Oh, well. *That* question just got asked. It's out there.' My response to Dad was, 'Are you sure that's what you want?' He said 'Yes, I wouldn't be asking you to marry me if I wasn't sure.' I was naturally fearful of our future. 'Do I really want to get involved in marriage with him?' I know he had the same thoughts. After all, I was thinking about marrying someone who was not Mexican. How would that sit with my family?"

"We had different cultural backgrounds," Dad said. "The big thing we had in common, of course, was our Catholic faith. I knew this was important to her parents."

Dad and Mom pose in their wedding "getaway car" - October 1960

Grandpa once told me about the conversation he had with a priest at St. Bernard's. They were talking about Dad's marriage proposal to Mom, and the priest asked for Grandpa's opinion.

"He asked me, 'Do you think this marriage will work?'" Grandpa said. "I told him, 'Yes, I think so. He's Catholic. She's Catholic. That's why it will work.' Then the priest say to me, 'I think you're right.'" Grandpa nudged me, and laughed. He loved hearing—from a Catholic Priest, representing the Catholic Church—that he was right.

Catholicism became a bonder in my parents' marriage. Recently, they celebrated their Diamond Anniversary, sixty years of marriage, in October of 2020.

5. What advice would you give the next generation?

"I would encourage them to get a fresh perspective of marriage," Mom said. "I see Jack as my Prince Charming—he always has been, and he always will be—which is one of the important things for me to keep romance alive. People stop seeing each other that way, and their relationship gets old. They stop treating each other like someone new, so their relationship gets stale. They become discontent. I still see him as my Prince Charming." Mom said. She took Dad's hand and squeezed it. He lifted her hand to his lips and kissed it. This romantic sweetness was common as I was growing up, and used to make us leave the room. Now, it's not so bad.

"One of the best things we learned, doing marriage preparation classes, is

'Love is a decision,'" Dad said. "*That* concept clarified a lot of things for me, because of what I'd lived through and experienced. Life is a lot of deaths and resurrections. Love is a decision. We decide every day, and throughout the day, to love." He smiled at me. "I don't have to tell you, do I?"

Dad's words are true. He doesn't have to tell me, or any of my siblings, because my parents lived this way as we grew up. I knew my parents had a rare relationship. I saw them disagree, but never insult one another. They were romantic, but still realists. They lived for God, solidifying their team by strengthening their faith. Their relationship would become the measure of what I wanted for my marriage. Mario and I incorporate the same principles they have taught us, even though we're not Catholic.

"Even happy people can make bad mistakes," Mom said. "People can say bad things, or do something bad, to deliberately hurt the other. The way I see it, you have to decide to get up the next morning and start over. I don't want to *continue* hurting them. I've got to work together with him. We used to say, 'Don't ever go to bed angry with each other,' but we've done that. Many, many times, we've gone to bed angry with each other."

Ryan family, approx. 1978. Front row: Shari, Jennie (Mom) and Jack (Dad). Back row: Colleen, Janet, Patty, Steve

"Especially when we had kids in the house," Dad said.

"When we had kids in the house, he thought I was taking the side of the kid, instead of his side," Mom said. "When you don't agree, you can say it's the kids making you fight, but it's not. What's making you fight is thinking you're right and the other one is wrong. You end up hurting each other.

"Every day, you have a chance to start over again," Mom said. "I think that's where the decision is made. You wake up, and say, 'Today I will decide to love him again. I will make the decision to have peace between us.' This really *is* a decision. Yes, love is a feeling, too, but the love that lasts is a decision. We learned that in Marriage Encounter, and when we taught that concept in our marriage preparation classes. These were some of the things that we could share with the people who were just starting out, and had a long way to go in marriage."

6. Why are the memories of women so important in building a family record?

"Women pay attention to the little details," Mom said. "Men can overlook the details because they want to tell just the main points of the story. Sometimes, it's the details that bring life to all those little memories in the family."

"I think women have a memory bank that's just fantastic," Dad said. "They have warm memories, which they treasure and keep. A guy might let a detail slide off the story, because it has to be pretty significant to be stored in our memory bank."

"Well put," Mom said. "I always think it's our Mary feature. You know how the Bible says, 'Mary kept these things in her heart'? I think that we keep these things in our heart, so that later we can reference them."

7. Grandma's last words were 'Keep the family together.' Do you think we've done this?

"Of course," Mom said, without thinking. "We've kept it together, no matter what. "We've had some very rocky roads, and the burden to keep family together is on our generation." She stopped to think about this for a while.

"Our parents taught us, 'Have respect for each other. You might not always agree, but have respect for each other. You might not be the same Everybody's different.' I remember trying to do that with my family. I remember sitting you kids down and saying to you, 'I want you all to remember that holidays are for family. Don't ever go and spend it with your friends.'"

"I didn't want to!" I said, laughing. "You would say that, but I thought, 'Why would I want to go to someone else's house for Christmas?'"

"In our house, traditions were important," Mom said. "Traditions and holidays can hold families together. When you lose these traditions, the breakdown can start. If you ask someone "Where is your child?" Sometimes they say, 'Well, he's spending the holiday with a friend.' I thought 'That's never going to happen in my family! That's why I was adamant you all spent the holidays with us."

I smiled. "I always loved celebrating Christmas here," I said. "Why would I want to spend it anywhere else?" The Christmas celebrations I grew up with included family, children, tamales, Christmas Carols with a guitar, and family, family, family. For all the years Mario and I lived in South Africa, we only spent two Christmas away from family.

37. Seven Questions—Emily/Emmy

My aunt, Amelia Gonzalez, was born on November 4, 1938, in Fresno, California, the sixth child, and fourth daughter of Ignacio and Juana Gonzalez. She was the first born of the twins, the only babies Grandma delivered at a hospital. Emily was born without blemish or distress, despite Grandma's traumatic labor and delivery. The Great Depression was still dragging on, but when the news of twins reached family and friends, people with cameras showed up to take pictures.

(l to r) Emily and Molly (1939) were often hard to tell apart

Any event surrounding the twins' birth—including the death of Grandma's father, which was kept from her for over a year—didn't seem to be strong enough to pierce the atmosphere of having twins. Emily and Molly were baby number six and seven, separated by only eight years from their eldest sibling. Grandma was busy.

For years, Amelia and Amalia, Emily and Molly, were a matched set, never one without the other. Even our interviews were conducted in tandem, with playful energy bouncing off the walls, the sisters finding strength and humor in each other's stories. As identical twins, their playfulness often felt like an inside joke to everyone else.

1950: posing on the fence at the ranchito Molly (l) and Emily (r)

"When we were young ladies, still living at home, we loved to trick people," Auntie Emmy said. "One time, Molly met this guy, and he asked her out. She said yes, but she didn't tell him that she was a twin. When he came to pick her up, I answered the door, wearing a tee-shirt and old shorts. We had this all planned."

"He had asked me to go to a nice dinner," Auntie Molly said, laughing. "It was kind of a dress-up thing. So, Emmy answered the door, wearing flip flops and shorts and a tee-shirt, he was surprised. He said, 'Aren't you ready?' Emmy looked down at herself and went, 'Oh, wait a minute!' Then she went into the back room and I walked out, all dressed up in a dress and heels. He said, 'Wait! What's going on here?'" My twin aunties guffawed, as if they were reliving the joy of a well-timed practical joke. "He was so confused!" Auntie Emmy said.

"He couldn't understand how I got dressed so fast!" Auntie Molly said, choking on her laughter. I was laughing, too, but not nearly as much as they were. As with most of their stories, it was more fun to listen because of their shared enthusiasm.

Auntie Emmy is the first person I knew who wore a diamond ring. It matched her effervescent and sparkling personality. She wore cute dresses and high heels. She is the only Gonzalez sister who did not physically give birth to children. She married our "handsome uncle," Richard Ward, who resembled Clint Eastwood, and had his ways. Uncle Rich wore jeans, listened to modern music, and loved my Aunt Emmy with his whole heart.

Emily and Richard Ward, married May 24, 1969

Uncle Rich was diagnosed with cancer in his fifties. He died, right after my daughter, Alicia, was born. All the family mourned. Years later, Auntie Emmy started dating Walt, a man who would become her long-term boyfriend. Walt was warm and funny, and our family's new Santa Claus. In 2012, Auntie Emmy and Walt visited Mario and I in South Africa, the only family members who came to visit us in the years we were there.

Emmy and Walt visit the indigenous village in Pilanesberg, South Africa, 2012

By the time I interviewed Auntie Emmy, she'd become a special person to me. During her South African visit, we spoke about deep things. We related to one another as adults. I enjoyed hanging out with her. While there,

Auntie Emmy and Walt visited a game park, where she photographed a lone bull elephant, who appeared out of nowhere and charged their vehicle. When she showed me pictures, my heart stopped.

"Auntie!" I said. "That's so dangerous! How did you get away?"

"I don't know," Auntie Emmy said, laughing. "Walt was driving. Good thing I didn't know how dangerous it was. Isn't that a good picture?"

Not long after their visit, Walt passed away, and Auntie Emmy was left to navigate grief, that appeared out of nowhere, like a charging bull elephant. Somehow, she managed. She was able to see beyond the loss, and find hope again.

More than half of Auntie Emmy's interviews were recorded with Mom or Auntie Molly, but her voice always stood out. Even as a twin, Auntie Emmy could stand out in the world.

***

1. How much of your childhood memories include Grandpa?

"I don't remember interacting with Daddy an awful lot," Auntie Emmy said. "He was more of an authority figure, and the boss of the family. I don't remember many times where he played with us." She remembered something, and smiled. "I do remember a game he played with Molly and I on Sunday mornings. We were little, and up early. We'd both jump into bed with him, and he would be lying down. We wanted to wake him up, and he'd pretend to be sleeping, in the middle of his bed. Molly would get on one side, and I would be on the other. We would raise up his arm, above the covers. It would be lifted up like this, and all of a sudden, he would let it fall." She simulates how Grandpa did this, letting her arm fall to the table with a thud. "He would say, 'Se cayó el poste,' (the post fell down) in a glum voice." She laughed. "We would try to raise his arm back up. It was so heavy that it took both Molly and I, together, just to lift it up. Molly would get on one side and I would get on the other, and together we would struggle to lift his arm up. Then he would say, 'Se levanto el poste,' (the post is raised up) in a happier voice. Then, he would let his arm fall again. He'd say, 'Se cayó el poste,' and we would *laugh*! We played that game for... I don't know how long, but it was fun! That's one thing that I do remember playing with him."

2. What's your favorite childhood memory?

"We played around the ranch a lot," Auntie Emmy said. "Mama used to take us around exploring, to hunt for mushrooms, which we thought was lots of fun. We swam in the canal, and then we'd lie down in the warm sun when we were wet. Of course, we had chores to do—not heavy chores, but some—but I think Molly and I got more playtime than our siblings, because we were the youngest.

"I think my favorite thing we did as a family was listening to the radio. At night, when everything was done, we would all sit in our little living room, huddled around the radio, listening to these programs! That was our entertainment! There was Inner Sanctum, and Red Skelton's show..."

"Red Skelton used to talk like a baby," Auntie Molly said. "We would *laugh*!"

"Yeah, I remember that," Auntie Emmy said. "Daddy's favorite was The Jack Benny Show. It seems funny to think of it now, but we all were together, listening to the same thing, and laughing together at the same parts. It brought us together. Maybe that's why I liked it so much."

3. How did you meet your spouse?

"Rich and I worked together," Auntie Emmy said, smiling. For most of her life, Auntie Emmy worked for Lawrence Livermore National Laboratory, a division of the U.S. Department of Energy. Just over the Altamont pass, "the lab," as people called it, employed many people from Tracy. "I knew Rich for about two years before I was interested in him. He first worked at the Nevada test site, and then he transferred to Lawrence Livermore lab. He started out as a draftsman and then he worked his way up.

"Rich and I always teased one another—it was good-natured teasing—and that became flirting, and it got more serious. At the end of each day, I would make the coffee for the office, in a big urn that held about fifty cups of coffee. I'd have to clean it, then get it ready again for the next morning. It was awkward and heavy, so Rich started filling it with water for me. He was a real gentleman, and I appreciated it so much. He would always show up at my station, very quiet, and ask, 'Are you ready?' I would say, 'Yeah.' One day, as we were making the coffee, I dropped something on the floor, and we stooped down to pick it up at the same time. I thought this was cute, so I looked at him, and when our eyes met...it was like magic!" Auntie Emmy took a moment to rub her arms, covered in goosebumps. "OOOhh! I felt this warm feeling. I thought,

'Whoa! What just happened?'"

After that, Rich and I started going out to lunch together. We started talking about more serious things, and eventually, we started dating. I still think about that chance moment, when we first looked into each other's eyes! To me, it was beautiful and I'll never forget it. It's a warm spot in my heart.

4. When did you decide to get married?

"I was twenty-nine the day I got married," Auntie Emmy said. "That was considered late, for the time. Auntie Millie kept asking me when I was going to get married," she said, laughing.

"Mildred married at seventeen, so by the time I got married, she already had five children!" Auntie Emmy smiled, but grew quiet and looked out the window.

"Rich proposed marriage only a little over a year after he was divorced," she said. "Sometimes I wondered if his proposal came too soon. He and his ex-wife had three other children, and this would always be something in our lives. I knew I wanted to marry Rich, but his first marriage had to be annulled, and that took time. We wanted to get married in the Catholic church. It was very important for me, because I'd been brought up in the Catholic Church, and I was a practicing Catholic. I told Rich that I wanted to continue going to church every Sunday. He agreed.

So, we got married at St. Bernard's in Tracy on May 24, 1969."

Rich and Emily Ward wedding party. Only Uncles as Groomsmen: Smiley, Frank, and Jim. Only Aunties as bridesmaids! (l to r) Mildred, Molly, and Dorothy. The cutest flower girl (me!) and the ring-bearer, who wouldn't dance with me. What was his name?

Auntie's marriage to Uncle Rich came almost ten years after my parents were married. By this time, the family accepted him as a fiancé, provided the Catholic Church was involved. To Grandpa and Grandma, the church was the ultimate authority, and they could either sanctify or forbid a marriage.

5. What was the greatest challenge you had to face in marriage?

"Rich and I were married for nineteen years," Auntie Emmy said. "He was sick for the last seven of those years. He found out he had cancer in 1981, and he died in 1988. He had colon cancer, and it was pretty advanced. The doctor told him, 'You better go home and get your house in order, because you have about three years left. He lived for seven years after that. He worked for a long time, up until he got really sick. He said, 'I don't want you to come home and take care of me. My mother can come and help.' So, his mom came and lived with us, for that last year. The doctors prescribed morphine, for the pain. At that stage, he was sleeping all the time, and really wasn't himself.

"I knew I was going to lose him, so I guess I was prepared for his death. What I really wasn't prepared for was the *impact* of his death. That part was really hard. I was suddenly very lonely. I thought, 'What do people do when they lose their spouse?' I would cry and cry. The uncomfortable part was not being able to control my emotions. When I went back to work, people would come to my desk and tell me how sorry they were. I didn't like that feeling. I was lonely in Livermore, after Rich died. Molly lived in Tracy.

"The year that Rich died, my work sent me on trips," Auntie Emmy said. "I traveled to Switzerland, for work, which was a blessing and a good distraction. Molly joined me there, for our fiftieth birthday. Of course, when I came home, I had to figure out how to live without Rich. I really loved him.

6. You have been blessed with two successful relationships. How did that happen?

"I've been blessed," Auntie Emmy said, smiling. "I was with Rich for nineteen years, and then I met Walt in 1990, when Molly fixed me up with him." Auntie Emmy gave a playful nudge to Auntie Molly, seated next to her. "Walt and I were together until he died, in January of 2014. That's twenty-four years!" She shook her head, in disbelief.

"Those relationships were so different!" Auntie Emmy said. "I was married to one and not married to the other. Their personalities were polar opposites. One was quiet and the other was outgoing. I really loved Rich and we were very close, but I had lots of fun with Walt. He was so outgoing and he brought that out in *me*."

"Because Rich died so long ago, I think I have more memories of Walt that pop into my head. Walt was much more interactive with me than Rich ever was. Rich was very, very reserved. I didn't do as many things with Rich as I did with Walt. I have more memories of traveling, enjoying Walt's company. I had great memories of Rich, and he was one of the best husbands anyone could have, but he liked staying home. Walt helped me live a freer life, and he brought out the friendly, adventurous side of me. It wasn't the most exciting life with Rich. Walt was exciting. The two men were just so opposite.

Auntie Emmy and Walt at the Eiffel Tower, 2012

"Rich and I had a good working relationship, and a lot of the things we had in common had to do with work. I retired in 1998, so I wanted new and exciting things in my life. Retirement is exciting! People sometimes as, 'Isn't retirement boring?' I say, 'No! There's so much to do. I always wonder how I ever had time to work.'

7. Grandma's last words were 'Keep the family together.' Do you think we've done this?

"I think we've done our best," Auntie Emmy said. "Of course, we live in this culture that separates people. We all have cars, and we live far away from each other. Overall, we do our best." Auntie Emmy leaned forward. "Also, as a woman, I've found it's very important to be true to yourself. If you care for people, and believe in God, you'll have enough. There's no reason to be somebody you're not. You'll automatically be a good example for the next generation.

"Family is like a pattern, and I've seen some kids turn out badly, because their parents weren't there for them. Family is the center of life. It's important to pay attention to your family, to care for those around you. You don't have to be radical. You don't have to step on others to be a success. You can be kind. You can care for others, especially for your family, and be yourself.

"Our family has stuck together, and that's unique. I think it has to do with caring for each other and believing in God." Auntie Emmy sits back in her chair and sighs. "The world has changed so much, even in my lifetime. When I look around, I see so many people who are just living for themselves. I know that's not going to make them happy. At least, not for very long."

38. Seven Questions—Molly

Amalia Gonzalez, my Auntie Molly, was born on November 4, 1938, in Fresno, California, the seventh child, and fifth daughter of Ignacio and Juana Gonzalez. Born three hours after her twin, Auntie Molly was pulled from Grandma with forceps, in the hopes that Grandma's life would be saved. No one knew if baby Molly was still alive, and no one expected her to live. She did.

"Poor me," Auntie Molly said, hugging her knees close to herself. "I came out with a bruised face and a pointy head. I wasn't always this beautiful!" She said this, with a pouty face and a child-like voice. We all laughed, a typical response to her humor. Most recorded interviews of Auntie Molly are filled with jokes and laughter. It was her modus operandi when approaching life's most difficult situations. She was convinced that the right amount of silliness would ease the pain. To her, life was serious enough, and most of us took it too seriously.

Emily and Molly, approx. 1943

"I loved being a prankster when I was growing up," Auntie Molly said. "Emmy and I would trick people because we looked so much alike. When we were teenagers, we went to a store and Emmy bought something. She gave the lady forty dollars for a twenty-five-dollar purchase, and then when the lady turned to the register, she went away. I walked up to the register, and the clerk gave me her change!" Auntie Molly laughed, and looked at Auntie Emmy. "I thought, 'Oh, she thinks I'm Emmy,' but I didn't say anything. Instead, I took the change and walked away. When Emmy went back to the sales lady, she said, 'Okay, I'm back for my change." The clerk looked horrified. She said, 'I gave it to you!' Emmy said, 'No, you didn't!' The clerk said 'I just handed it to you!' I couldn't stand back any longer. I came around the corner, laughing, and the clerk just about died. She had a good laugh. It was so much fun to trick people who didn't know we were twins!"

Auntie Emmy interjected, "Especially Molly! She loves being the sly trickster!"

Auntie Molly married Jim Bell, a man I called my favorite Uncle when I was growing up. He was larger-than-life, with a booming voice and strong opinions. This didn't take away from the soft, tender part of him that teared-up at sentimental things. He was a former police officer who became a judge, and later the mayor of Tracy. He brought direction, joy, and structure to our family. Auntie Molly was the perfect balance for his personality.

The Bell Family 1979: Derek, Lisa, Molly and Jim

Together, Uncle Jim and Auntie Molly had two children, Lisa and Derek. They were our closest cousins, since we all grew up in Tracy. Lisa was one year younger than my sister, Colleen. Since Shari and Colleen were born one year apart, the cousins were called "The Three Musketeers."

Auntie Molly was my Godmother, a role in the Catholic tradition that's handled with serious responsibility. To be a Godparent, you must be a "Catholic in good standing," with a life that reflects a holy God. Auntie Molly was the one who convinced me that God had a sense of humor, and laughed whenever possible. Even God didn't take life so seriously.

When I interviewed her, Auntie Emmy and Molly had just celebrated their 80th birthday. Auntie Molly had just been diagnosed with interstitial lung disease, a byproduct of rheumatoid arthritis. Throughout the recordings, she coughed, and stopped to catch her breath. Nevertheless, she thought this book was a fabulous idea.

Emily, Jennie, and Molly at the twins' 80th birthday party

"What do you think about doing a book about the Gonzalez family?" I asked her. "We can start with interviews, and then I piece together your family story."

"Sure!" she said, without thinking. "Let's go!"

And so began the interviews, started in her eightieth year. I collected their words with care and painstaking fervor, as if I were carrying a Fabergé egg in a spoon, across an oil-slick.

To my surprise, Auntie Molly was the most private sister. She didn't readily share about the deepest parts of her heart. The humor might have served as a protective element to her beautiful, tender heart.

***

1. What is your favorite childhood memory?

"We were the babies," Auntie Molly said. "So, our memories are different. Mama worked hard. Back then, there were no modern conveniences. She washed our clothes by hand, and then hung them on the clothesline to dry. Daddy was always out in the fields, or working on projects in the garden.

"Mama cooked the biggest breakfasts, every morning! She insisted we all eat sitting down at the table. Nobody skipped breakfast! If you hadn't come to breakfast, Mama would hand you an egg sandwich on your way out. That was your breakfast. All my life I've been healthy, because that's the most important meal! Emmy and I both were very, very healthy. We would only see the doctor once a year. That is, until I got this arthritis..." Her voice trailed off, as she considered how the rheumatoid arthritis had become a health concern.

"Terry was like our second mom," Auntie Molly said. "She looked after all of us. She educated us about life-things. When we were becoming young women, she's the one who talked to us, not Mama. I was scared of my body changing. I would think, 'What is happening to me?' Terry explained it to us, so calmly, and told us all about the 'facts of life'."

"Terry was very comforting," Auntie Emmy said.

"She made me feel like I didn't have to worry," Auntie Molly said.

2. How did you find your wings, or gain your independence to leave your parents' house?

"When we were in high school, we wanted to be majorettes," Auntie Molly said. "But Daddy wouldn't let us try out. We wanted to do this, since we were kids. Once Jennie and Terry dressed us up as baton majorettes, with painted oat containers around our ankles. They looked like boots."

Emily and Molly as Tracy High majorettes, 1955

"Emmy and I asked Mama if we could try out for majorettes," she said. "That was the beginning of us spreading our wings. Daddy had already told us we couldn't. He said it was too difficult for him to take us to practice and then pick us up."

"He didn't want us showing off, either," Auntie Emmy said. "Being on parade, twirling batons, in our costumes."

"He said no," Auntie Molly said. "But we begged Mama. We said, 'Mama, everyone is saying we should go out for majorettes! They say we'll make it because we're twins. Will you please talk to Daddy for us? You can convince him.' We knew she could talk him into it. She said, 'Let me try.' We waited and waited. We'd ask, 'Mama, did you talk to him?' She'd say, 'Not yet. I need to find the right time.' We finally said, 'Mama, they're going to have try-outs for majorettes tomorrow.' So, she came back to us, and said, 'Alright, he said you can try out.'"

"I don't remember what we said," Auntie Emmy said. "We cried. We were so happy."

"We went to try-outs," Auntie Molly said. "We were the first ones selected to be part of the majorette team. Oh, we were so happy, but when we told Daddy, he was angry. Finally, he said, 'I'll let you do it on one condition. I'll take you to the games, and you have to come back in the car with me. There'll be *no* riding the bus.' Of course, we agreed. We went to the band leader, and told him about Daddy's condition. The band leader said, 'All the majorettes have to ride on the bus with the band. If you can't do this, you can't be a majorette.'"

Auntie Molly let her shoulders drop, dramatically. "We were so brokenhearted. We went back to Daddy, and told him what the band leader said. Daddy was kind of happy, because now he didn't have to bother with it. We'd drop out of majorettes." She sighed, deeply. "Those were very traumatic times for us."

"But Mama convinced him again," Auntie Emmy said. "She talked to him, privately, and encouraged him think about it."

"Daddy came back to us," Auntie Molly said. "He said, 'Okay, you can go on the bus, but I'm going to follow the bus all the way to the game, and follow it all the way home.' That happened once or twice, but then Daddy could see there was no time for funny business on the bus. He ended up feeling more comfortable, because Emmy and I were always together. We looked out for each other."

Emmy and Molly, before a game, in uniform

"That little bit of freedom, when we were majorettes, paved the way for us to spread our wings a little bit more," Auntie Molly said. "Emmy and I took a job, sorting almonds on a conveyor belt, one summer when we were still in high school. We made seventy dollars a week, which was a lot of money for us!"

"Whatever money we got, we always gave to Daddy," Auntie Emmy said. "We helped pay the bills. Jennie was working for the government, and so was Lucy. One of us would make enough for the car payment. One of us would make enough to pay for the living room furniture. One of us would pay toward the electric bill. We were happy to help."

"I didn't feel like I really had freedom until I got my first real job," Auntie Molly said. "I graduated high school, and got my first government job, at the Tracy Defense Depot, in September. I was so happy to work there. It had always been a dream of mine to work there.

"I used to ride the school bus, in grammar school, to New Jerusalem School. Every day, the bus would drive by the depot, make a loop and go by the depot again. I used to say to myself, 'One day I am going to work there as a secretary!' That was my goal.

"Guess what? I worked at the Tracy Defense Depot for thirty-five years, until I retired," Auntie Molly said. She laughed, at the only irony in the memory. "I was never a secretary, though. I started off as a file clerk, and then got elevated to an appointment clerk, which was a little more money, and then I took supervisory positions. I kept advancing, but I never was a secretary. That still counts as a dream come true, doesn't it?"

3. How did you meet your spouse?

"I met Jim at the Tracy Bowl," Auntie Molly said. "We were both in bowling leagues, on different teams. Emmy and I were good bowlers for little gals, and very competitive. Sometimes Emmy bowled better than I did, and other times I'd do better than her.

"Emmy and I kept seeing Jim around. One day, Emmy said, 'Molly have you noticed that guy back there, watching you?' I said, 'No, Emmy, I think he's watching you.' Emmy was always the one people noticed."

"Not always," Auntie Emmy said, smiling.

"Almost always," Auntie Molly said, "Anyway, the next time we bowled he was there. It wasn't creepy at all. He was friendly and everyone seemed to know him, and I felt like he was just a really friendly kind of guy. After the bowling, Emmy and I would always go to the cocktail lounge afterwards. One night, Jim was there with friends, and pretty soon he started talking to us. He bought us a beer, and we got to talking."

"Do you know what I thought of him, Molly?" Auntie Emmy asked. "I thought he seemed older."

"Yeah, he seemed older," Auntie Molly said. "He was six years older than me, but he seemed older. One day, I saw him come in, and he was in his police uniform. I started to think of him differently. He had a way of bringing people close to him, and then *whoom!* He has you. Suddenly, you love everything about him. His personality, his enthusiasm, his humor. Everything."

She's right. Uncle Jim was a charismatic man, larger than life. In Tracy alone, he was a police officer, a traffic justice, a judge, and the mayor. He also sold real estate. He had energy, passion, and enthusiasm. Everyone knew who he was.

"In the cocktail lounge, that night, we made a connection," Auntie Molly said, smiling. "Before that, I had only seen Jim as a friend, not anything romantically. When it was time to go home, he asked if he could take me home. I said, 'No, I'm here with my sister, and we go home together.' So, Jim turned to Emmy and said, 'You don't mind if I take her home, do you?' and Emmy said, 'Of course not!'"

The twins looked at each other and laughed. Auntie Emmy apologized.

"I hadn't even asked Molly if she wanted to ride with him," she said.

"And I thought, 'Oh, well, I guess he can take me home.'" Auntie Molly said. "Emmy drove home in our car, and Jim and I followed her. We both still lived with my parents.

"Anyway, Jim and I started hanging out more. I let him take me home more often. Pretty soon, we were dating, and I introduced him to Mom and Dad. They just *loved* him! He was a policeman, and a big man. He *loved* Mama's food. Mama begged me to marry him. She'd say, 'Mija, he's the one you have to marry! He's the one!'

"But just because Jim was Jim, he wasn't immune to our games, was he, Emmy?" Auntie Molly asked. Auntie Emmy shook her head, smiling mischievously. "Oh no," Auntie Molly said, eyes twinkling. "We couldn't pass up *that* opportunity.

"Because Jim liked Mama's food, he always came over to eat. I told Jim my Spanish speaking parents had a tradition he should learn. It was the proper way to toast with a wine glass. I told him, 'In Spanish, people say, '¡Salud!' like 'Cheers.' When they do that, you're supposed to hold up your glass and say '¡Nicomedes!'" Auntie Molly stopped to laugh. "I didn't tell Jim that Salud and Nicomedes were my sister, Teresa's, Mother-in-law and Father-in-law. We knew that, but he didn't." Auntie Emmy and Auntie Molly started laughing about this. The rest of the story was punctuated with laughter, and coughing.

"I told Jim, 'This is important!'" Auntie Molly said, with a convincing tone. "'You want to impress my parents, don't you?' Jim said, 'Yes, I do. Show me how to do it.' So, I said, 'Next time we get together as a family, someone will lift their glass and say '¡Salud!' That's your chance. You shout, '¡Nicomedes!'"

"And Jim believed this was our tradition," Auntie Emmy said, wiping her eyes.

"Yes, he believed it," Auntie Molly said. "Each time we had dinner, I'd make him practice. I'd say, "Jim, '¡Salud!'" and he would shout, '¡Nicomedes!' with such feeling! Emmy started toasting with him, too. She'd say, 'Jim, ¡Salud!' and he'd shout '¡Nicomedes!' We convinced him he was getting *really* good. I told him, 'If you really want to do it, like they do in Mexico, put heavy emphasis on that first syllable ¡*NIC*-omedes! He did it. He was so proud of himself! Finally, he had so much confidence in himself, we took him to our next family gathering, and he did that." Auntie Molly laughed hard, and coughed as she continued. "At dinner, somebody said, '¡Salud!' and Jim shouted, '¡*NIC*omedes!' The whole family looked at him, and then, busted up laughing. We were all laughing so hard..." Auntie Emmy leaned into Auntie

Molly, and they laughed together.

"We got him so good!" Auntie Molly said, coughing.

"What did he do?" I asked, once we had stopped laughing.

"Oh, at first he was embarrassed," Auntie Molly said. "But then he laughed with us. He knew we got him. By then, he knew what we were like."

This family story, "¡Salud! ¡Nicomedes!" has traveled the world with us. Many of our friends in Africa still toast this way. Now you can, too.

Jim and Molly Bell, married at St. Bernard's Church. Auntie Lucy and Auntie Emmy were bridesmaids. Patty was the flower girl, and our cousin, Jimmy Villaseñor was the Ringbearer.

4. When did you decide to get married?

"It took me a while to figure out that Jim was the one for me," Auntie Molly said. "I liked him a lot, but I still wanted to be free to date other people. Jim had his mind made up. He had me on a pedestal, and he knew I was his wife. He kept trying to convince me that I felt the same about him. I wasn't sure. He wanted marriage, but I wasn't ready. We continued seeing each other, but on and off.

"I dated a few other guys, but didn't feel much for them. None of them made me feel special, like Jim did. I noticed something. When I was with any other date, they didn't treat me like Jim did, and I was always missing Jim. Finally, I came to my senses. I really liked the way I felt about myself when I was with Jim. I didn't want to be with anybody else but Jim.

"I decided to forget about dating and marry Jim. He made me feel very, very special. I don't think I loved him as much when we first got married as

I did later on. Our love just grew and grew and grew. To this day, I think, 'Why did I even *consider* anybody else?' When I was out with anybody else, I thought about Jim. We had a special connection. Very special."

5. How did life change after Uncle Jim died?

"Oh, I can still remember the *absolute shock* of Jim dying!" Auntie Molly said. "We had just come home from spending a nice weekend in Chico. We were with Derek and Jody, and they had just had a baby, our granddaughter, Jada. When we got home, Jim went straight to his chair and sat down. He started watching TV. He always felt a little depressed when we came home to an empty house. He thought, 'Who knows when we'll get to see our kids again?'

"That day, he said, 'I just feel so *down*!' I came in the room and said, 'What about me? Aren't I enough? Don't I fill that family void?' He got up, hugged me, kissed me, and told me I was enough. Still, I could tell it was hard for him. I made him something to eat. I knew eating would make him feel better." She laughed.

"Then, I told him 'I need to get some things in town, I'll be right back.' I stopped by to see Emmy, before I went to do my errands. We talked about the weekend with the kids. As I was driving home, I thought, 'I hope Jim's in a better mood.' When I came home..." Auntie Molly stopped. She tilted her head back, and started to cry. Part of me felt bad for making her retell this story.

"Jim and I had a silly little thing we said when we came home," Auntie Molly said. "We used to say, 'Hi, yourself!' The other would say, 'Hi, yourself!' from wherever we were. So, that day when I walked in, I said, 'Hi, yourself!' No response. I went out back and called, 'Hi, yourself.' Nothing. I thought, 'Where is he?' I went upstairs and found him there. Lying on the floor. It was just such a shock. I looked at him, closely, but for some reason, I was afraid to touch him.

"I was in shock. I must have stayed there, for I don't know how long, before I went to call 911. They gave me directions how to do CPR, but it was already too late. I tried, but nothing happened. The ambulance came, and the paramedics took over. They brought him down the stairs on a stretcher.

Jim had a massive heart attack. After I called 911, I called Emmy. She was immediately in shock, too. She said she would be here, as soon as possible. When the paramedics took Jim outside, the neighbors were all standing around, wanting to see what happened. We're close in this court, and we always check in with each other. The whole thing was just so hard."

"I had to figure out how to live after Jim's death," Auntie Molly said. "Every Saturday and Sunday, Jim would watch golf on TV. I would turn on golf, because just hearing the sound of golf was like having Jim here. It comforted me.

"I started running, and found comfort in that. Auntie Emmy and Lisa would run 5k's and 10k's with me. Then, David and I ran a half-marathon together."

After Auntie Molly spent years grieving the loss of Uncle Jim, she met David, her long-term companion. At first, David was just a plus-one for social gatherings and outings, but they soon developed emotional attachments, and were a couple. David was also quite handy. He helped Auntie Molly with anything she needed around the house, and since he was relatively fit, David started running with her.

"David filled the void of loss of a companion," Auntie Molly said. "I would get really lonesome. Walt knew David, and he introduced us."

Auntie Molly looked at Auntie Emmy and smiled. "Gosh! It's strange to use that language at our age, isn't it? I started dating? That doesn't sound right!"

6. How do you stay so happy? Is there a secret?

"Happiness starts at home," Auntie Molly said. "If you're honest and caring with your partner, that's a good start. I think of how people talk to each other now, and it's sad. When Jim and I were married, we didn't go a lot of places or do a lot of things, but we had fun just being together. We did things here, at home. We loved doing things with our kids! Sometimes, our friends would ask us to go out with them, but Jim and I wouldn't go if the kids weren't invited. Family is the center of happiness.

"If you want to meet your goals, and be satisfied, you need to be determined. You need endurance. You can't give up just because you don't think it's working. Some people think happiness is something that lands on one person, but not on another. Really? Happiness is a choice. You can choose to be happy or choose to be miserable. I distance myself from negative people. I don't want to be around people who make me feel bad about myself. I choose who I'm around. I choose to be happy."

7. Grandma's last words were 'Keep the family together.' Do you think we've done this?

"Yes," Auntie Molly said. "We've had to keep our individual families together, and then keep our extended family together. I think we've tried to do this in the best way we know how.

Everyone is busy. That's the real enemy of togetherness. Being busy is a killer."

I nodded my head wildly, in agreement. This made Auntie Molly laugh and cough, at the same time.

"I always say that this country is the land of *busy*," I said. "Everyone here is so busy, all the time! What about our relationships? What about our health?"

"What about *family*?" Auntie Molly said.

Exactly.

Part Eleven: Dessert

"For a biracial, nothing is more humiliating than this: trying to be half yourself while the other half keeps intervening—and getting caught."
~Stephanie Elizondo Griest, *Mexican Enough*

"Though many respondents expect to see a Hispanic, Latino, or Spanish category on the race question, this question is asked separately because people of Hispanic origin may be of any race(s)."
~The U.S. Census Bureau, on why the 2020 Census doesn't list Hispanic/Latino as a race

---

Molasses Sugar Cookies

¾ cup shortening
1 cup sugar
1 egg
¼ cups molasses
2 cups all-purpose flour
2 tsp. baking soda
½ tsp. salt
½ tsp. ground cloves
½ tsp ground ginger
(extra sugar to roll cookies)

Cream shortening, gradually add 1 cup sugar at medium blender speed until light and fluffy. Add egg and molasses; mix well. In separate bowl, combine flour, soda, salt, and spices; mix well. Add about ¼ of the dry mixture to the creamed mixture, making sure to blend well. Repeat until all the dry ingredients are blended together. Chill dough at least one hour.

Shape into 1-inch balls and roll in sugar. Place 2 inches apart on ungreased cookie sheet. Bake at 375 degrees for 10 minutes. Tops will crack.

Cool on wire rack. Yields 4 ½ dozen (unless kids are visiting). Don't make Snickerdoodles at the same time, because the molasses cookies may get jealous and burn.

39. Third Generation Immigrants

Grandpa and Grandma with some of their grandchildren at their 50th Anniversary Party, 1978. (l to r) Top row: Fidel Villaseñor Jr. (Butchie), Janet Ryan, Steve Ryan, Patty Ryan; 3rd Row: Rocky Gonzalez, Tracy Crow, Don Sutliff, Lorrie Gonzales; 2nd row: Grandpa, Doreen Gonzales, Kathleen (Kathy) Gonzales, Jeannie Gonzales, Debbie Gonzalez, Stephanie (Stevie) Gonzales, Front row: Colleen Ryan, Lisa Bell, Rocky Gonzalez II (Little Rocky, their Great-grandson), Sharon (Shari) Ryan, Derek Bell, Craig Gonzalez, Grandma. [Missing: Anna Villaseñor and James (Jimmy) Villaseñor.]:

The day of my grandparents' 50th wedding anniversary party, my siblings, cousins, and I posed for a formal picture with Grandpa and Grandma. I was fifteen, celebrating with my entire family at the Tracy Inn. Everywhere I looked, cousins, aunts, and uncles were happy. Grandpa wore a tux, and Grandma, a blue, floor-length gown. During the celebration, I read an original poem, a tribute to Grandpa and Grandma.

Take a close look at us. What do you see?

My siblings, cousins, and I are what most sociologists call *third-generation immigrants*: "U.S. born individuals with two U.S.-born parents, but at least one foreign-born grandparent."[21]

Like most of my cousins, I grew up in a suburban house, near parks and schools. I listened to popular music, was influenced by pop culture, and watched *Gilligan's Island* on television. My siblings, cousins, and I didn't know anything about the rigors of farm life, using an outside pump to get drinking water, or using an outhouse. Nope, not us. My cousins and I—all of us born at the tail end of the Baby Boomer generation, or near the beginning of Generation X—had jobs at fast food restaurants, theme parks, or babysitting. This was only if we wanted extra money.

None of our families were wealthy, but none of us were ever hungry. Most of us sat down for dinner at a table each night. Our parents taught us English table manners. In private, we listened to the radio, or watched MTV. We never gave much thought to our culture or assimilation, but many of us chose to identify as white or Caucasian. Like our grandparents and parents, we were caught in the crosshairs of a rapidly changing world. Ours was openly hostile and prejudiced against Mexican-Americans.

Anna, approx. 1958

My cousin, Anna, is my grandparents' eldest grandchild, the firstborn child of Auntie Terry and Uncle Phil. Anna is now a grandmother, but still remembers staying with Grandma and Grandpa one summer, and going grocery shopping.

"While we were shopping, a couple came over to say hello," Anna said. "The lady saw me, and she said, in English, 'You must be Teresa's daughter?' I told her I was. She spoke to Grandma in Spanish, 'Juana, she looks *just like*

---

[21] "The Complexity of Immigrant Generations: Implications for Assessing the Socioeconomic Integration of Hispanics and Asians" by Brian Duncan and Stephen J. Trejo. First published online Nov 12, 2016. doi: 10.1177/0019793916679613

Teresa!' I knew I did. Everyone always said that. As they walked away, the husband and wife were speaking Spanish. He asked her, 'Whose daughter was that?' She said, 'You know Terry? Teresa? She's one of *those Gonzalez girls*...'" She said that part in English. "You know, they're all *so* beautiful? *So* smart, *so* graceful...' She went on and on, talking about Mom and her sisters. I remember that day clearly. It was the first time I heard someone referring to my mom and her sisters as 'those Gonzalez Girls,' like they were one unit, one group."

The third-generation came from "those Gonzalez girls:" women who had high expectations of us. They had the same strict standards that our grandparents did, but they often found themselves fighting against the influence of popular culture. To them, pop-culture represented a flimsy value system.

As a teen, I read Seventeen magazine, where blonde models applied makeup that I would later buy at the drug store with my babysitting money. I was no dummy—I learned that looking good was more important than being smart or even having good manners. Even at school, beauty was a marketable commodity. In those days, Gloria Steinem stood at the helm of what is now called "second-wave feminism," challenging traditional roles and expectations, previously assigned to women. Abortion was declared to be the right of every woman. Working mothers, "latchkey children," and television were realities of our world. These were later blamed for the increase of U.S. divorce rates.

The national question wasn't, "Are you happy?" but, "How much money do you make?" The 80's gave birth to the "me generation," and our collective culture seemed obsessed with personal success, rather than the spirit of cooperation. The belief systems of families and our pop culture were often at war. We, as third-generation immigrants, had inherited capitalism, patriotism, and a desire to succeed—but at what cost?

Grandpa and Grandma remained a solid island in a rising sea of change, but they would often shake their heads when talking about the world around them. They maintained their simple life and cherished memories. For holidays, family weddings, or a funeral, our extended family would come to their place on Lorraine Road. There, every uncle, aunt, and cousin became a big family, greater than ourselves as individuals. We shared Grandma's food as the bonding element that brought us together and held us in place. This is still how we celebrate our ancestral story, our shared culture.

***

Most third-generation immigrants explain their cultural identity in pieces. I usually say, "I'm half-Mexican and half-Irish," but rarely claim to be 100% United States American. Assimilation removed most of my cultural markers—things like traditions, music, art, literature—but the most painful theft was the Spanish language.

I asked my cousins, Lisa and Lorrie, if they ever learned how to speak Spanish.

"Un poquito," Lisa answered. "I understand more than I speak."

"Do you ever feel ripped off of Spanish?" I asked. "Like you were cheated out of your inheritance?"

"I always wish my mom taught me Spanish," Lisa said. "But I don't ever feel spiteful that she didn't." She thought for a minute, then smiled. "I have this theory about why our mothers never taught us Spanish," she said. "I think they wanted to talk about us behind our back, right in front of us, at least that's my theory. Maybe they didn't teach us because they couldn't lose that. They liked talking to Grandma, about us, like that."

"Spanish gave our mothers instant privacy," I said. "It was like a door they shut when they needed privacy. They could say anything, even with kids around."

My cousin, Lorrie, agreed. "I think it was easier for our mothers not to teach us Spanish," she said. "Teaching Spanish is hard work, and we were lazy kids."

"Speak for yourself, Lorrie!" I said, laughing. "You think being lazy is the reason we don't speak Spanish?"

Lorrie shrugged. "I know it's not the *only* reason," she said. "But when I think back on my formative years, I know I didn't take advantage of opportunities to learn the language. How could we have ever known how important it would be to speak another language? I would have embraced it in school, and learned it properly."

As women who have traveled globally, Lorrie and I both recognized the weakness of speaking only one language when most of the world speaks more than one.

"It's embarrassing when I travel," Lorrie said. "In other countries, I know people who speak four or even five different languages, and here I am with my measly little English. I can pick up Spanish words, glue them together, and usually make myself understood, but I never feel comfortable speaking it." She stopped to think. "Maybe I'm still lazy by not pursuing it, right? We can fault our childhoods, but if we really wanted to do something, we'd do it. If we don't, we have to admit, deep down inside, Spanish really isn't that important to us."

A month after our conversation, I started taking Spanish classes again, determined to repatriate this language, even if it takes me a lifetime.

***

The only cultural marker the third generation kept close to us is food, specifically Grandma's recipes. Our ethnic identification belongs more to our parents than to us.

Take another look at the picture at the beginning of this chapter. What do you see? We are third-generation immigrants, the ones who have lost the immigrant sheen, the language of their ancestors, as well as their old-world culture and traditions.

Is this what my grandparents wanted?

40. The Challenge

Me and Grandma, 1983

The day this picture was taken, I told Grandma I wanted a picture with *just* me and her. After spending so much of my life with this woman, I wanted proof that we were close. I still keep this picture in bottom drawer of my jewelry box, one that used to belong to her. It's in the same place I keep the program printed for her funeral, and the Catholic prayer card we were given as a memory of her.

When you have a family patriarch and matriarch, no one can prepare you for their deaths. Grandpa died in October of 1984. Grandma in February of 1992. Grandma's last words, "Keep the family together—don't let it fall apart," still haunt me.

Have we done it?

"Our families have continued growing and expanding," my cousin, Stevie, said. "We're getting married, having children, and our focus turns to our immediate families. It doesn't mean our extended family isn't significant."

"I agree," I said. "But I miss the larger gatherings of aunts and uncles, don't you?"

"I do," Stevie said, smiling. "When Rocky's daughter got married in Elko, Nevada, we went there for the wedding. My family didn't see any of the bigger family until the morning of the wedding. We came downstairs and there was everyone, gathered in the hotel dining room! I was going from table to table, greeting all my aunts and uncles. I kept having to control myself, because it was so touching.

"After the wedding, as I was saying goodbye, I got so emotional. I looked around and wondered if I was seeing my extended family for the last time." Stevie paused, choking with emotion. "To have everyone in the same room seemed so special, so golden...."

"I remember fighting back tears all that day," Stevie said, wiping her eyes. "But I finally gave up and started crying. All I could think was, 'This must be what heaven is like.' When we go home and see our loved ones, it will be like this. All of us together, having a party, a good time. "Right after the wedding, everything changed. Uncle Frank died, and then Daddy got sick..." Stevie's voice trailed off.

She had been right about everything changing. After this, as we saw the older generation leaving, we were powerless to stop it.

***

"We've kept the family together, but in a different sense," my cousin, Doreen, said. "I know the generation before us—your mom, my mom, our aunties—did a better job of keeping us all together. As cousins, we had more activities together, but that was before we moved to Oregon. Now, my sisters and I all live up here, and we have our own families. Things have changed, and distance has played a part. Our family reunions have gotten a little sparser. Even when we lived in San Jose, we were separated from the rest of the family. I think if we had lived in the same general area, we would have seen each other more."

"Our family, too," my sister, Shari said. "Aunt Emmy, Aunt Molly, and Mom were closer together, geographically, so we grew up spending more time with them."

"Mom and her sisters are still really close," my sister, Colleen, said. "They talk on the phone all the time, and send each other letters and email. Family gatherings are still very important to them."

"They make their relationships a priority," my sister-in-law, Mechelle said. "It might stem from their heritage. The Mexican family bond is everything."

"Do you think we've stayed as close, as sisters?" I asked. I always wanted the same kind of closeness that Mom had with her sisters, and often lamented the lack of it.

"I think we're more selfish," Mechelle said, laughing loudly. "We've come into an era where it's all about our own family first. It used to take a village to raise kids, but not anymore. Now, you're supposed to be strong enough to do it by yourself. That's the American way. This belief pulls us away from each other, rather than attracting us to one another."

"I have my own big family," Shari said. "I have four kids and a husband, and I work outside the home. Sometimes I'm just trying to make sure that I'm paying enough attention to all my kids, my husband, and *myself*. I can't take all that on, if our extended family is together enough. I don't want to live with that pressure of, 'Am I enough?' or 'Am I doing enough? I don't feel like we failed Grandma."

Shari brought up a valid point: overcommitment. In our lifetime, the number of women entering the workplace skyrocketed, and now double-income households are the norm. For years, I worked outside the home as my children grew up. Managing time with family was like spinning plates on poles. Something was always crashing to the floor.

I knew Grandma could see the trajectory of American culture, especially the way it was affecting her children and their families. With its hurried lifestyle, everyone driving cars, her kids living far apart, the culture was degrading their chances of family unity. Everything she had done to build a strong family was in danger.

***

"Why are you asking everyone if they kept the family together?" Grandma asks me, uncrossing her ankles and leaning forward in the chair. "What a hard question, mijita!"

"You challenged us, Grandma," I say. "You do remember saying 'Keep the family together,' don't you?"

Grandma smiles and shrugs. "Yes," she says. "But you're doing it."

My eyes fill with tears again. I want so much to hug her, but I can't. I reach for a tissue.

"I'm afraid it's all disappearing," I whisper.

"Don't worry," she says, looking at me. "It's not disappearing. Aún continuamos sobreviviendo." *We continue to survive.*

41. The Way Things Were

Mom and her sisters say the world is changing too fast. They're more than a little surprised at the lack of manners and human kindness these days. When Grandma was alive, she would say the world is getting crazier and crazier every day.

"I'm probably next to go," Auntie Dorothy said, when I interviewed her in 2019. "I already have my plot at the Tracy cemetery. Uncle Frank and I have our gravestone already: a double heart that says *Together Forever* on it, and our name, Gonzalez. One heart has his dates, and the other will have mine, when I go. It even says *Feo and Fea* on it, too." She said, laughing.

I was in awe of her, my beautiful Auntie, talking about death like it was an upcoming vacation. Like a taxi, honking the horn in the driveway. When I left her house that day, it hit me. 'She's going to die one day. They're all going to die.' On the freeway home, I cried. I prayed. I asked God to make me ready. They were getting older, and there's only one way out of this world.

In February of 2020, the first Gonzalez sister died. It wasn't Auntie Dorothy, like she predicted, but the baby of the family, Auntie Molly, my beloved Godmother.

***

In January of 2020, Auntie Molly was in intensive care. Nasal cannulas delivered sufficient oxygen to her lungs. An IV drip, in her arm, kept her hydrated. Interstitial lung disease had taken its toll on her body, and antibiotics were no longer working. Over the course of a year, Auntie Molly had been in and out of the hospital, losing weight as the doctors tried to get her lungs to work properly.

The previous July, my mother, Jennie, had suffered an ischemic stroke that left her dominant right side affected. She spent a whole month in an acute rehab facility, before being released to her home. The day we visited Auntie Molly in ICU, I pushed Mom around in her travel wheelchair. She'd been using a walker pretty well, but moving around the hospital was easier in the wheelchair.

"Jennie, I'm not scared," Auntie Molly said to Mom, calmly holding her sister's hand.

Mom nodded. "Okay, Molly," she said.

"I'm ready," Auntie Molly said. Neither sister seemed too concerned about life or death, only comfort. Not long after this visit, Auntie Molly moved to a long-term care facility, a relatively homey and warm place. We all knew it would be the place she would die.

On the last day of her life, I went with my parents to visit her. Auntie Emmy swabbed her twin's mouth, using a moist lollipop sponge. A Catholic priest administered the Sacrament of the Sick. I whispered goodbye, kissed the top of her head, and went out to buy paper plates and napkins for Auntie Emmy. When I returned, Lisa was there. She and Auntie Emmy were talking, quietly. To respect what little privacy they had left, I said goodbye. About twenty minutes after I left her room, Auntie Molly passed away.

***

I got through the week by having a job to do. I drove to Southern California, to pick up my Aunties, Lucy and Terry, and my cousin Gilbert. They would stay with my parents for the week. My sisters, Colleen and Patty, helped Mom and Dad with the physical needs of hosting.

We're off! Leaving Oxnard with the SoCal family. Front seat: me and Auntie Lucy; back seat: Gilbert and Auntie Terry!

Dad conducted the vigil service and graveside services. He assisted at the funeral. Auntie Terry and Gilbert, being Jehovah's witnesses, joined the family for food at the reception.

People from all over the state came to remember Auntie Molly, including Esther, their cousin, from Fresno, and Joey, el patrón's grandson.

Joey stands with Emily. Front row: Jennie, Terry, Lucy

Weddings and funerals bring families to a central place. They become opportunities to take pictures. Photographs chronicle our lives, so everyone smiled because we were together. We didn't want to spend too much time thinking about the way things were. We celebrated the right now, the life of that moment, and we distracted ourselves with the intoxicating presence of family. We found reasons to laugh with people we hadn't seen in years.

Derek and Lisa, Auntie Molly's children, stand behind: Jennie (Mom), Terry, Emily, and Lucy. I'm kneeling, in front

*Back row (l to r) Esther, Mildred, Dorothy, Dolores (Loli);
front row: Jennie, Terry, Emily, and Lucy*

My favorite picture is of the women who inhabit this story. Not for the photo quality, or the way they're all smiling at the same time, but because they're all together. In the back row, their cousin, Esther, looked stunning in an orchid-color jacket and light hair. Auntie Mildred and Auntie Dorothy pose with their little sister, Loli. For the first time, I can see Grandma Nellie in their smiles. Mom, in her to-go-wheelchair, has perfect hair and lipstick—I've been trained to notice, before I take a picture—and she looks beautiful, as always. Auntie Terry raises her eyebrows, and smiles with a secret happiness. Auntie Emmy, the surviving twin, looks radiant in a black suit and champagne colored blouse. She's determined to get through the day, and enjoy her family around. Auntie Lucy, despite having eaten, still has her lipstick on.

They might ask me later, "How did I look?" I'll answer them honestly: "You look beautiful. You look like home, like my family." These women are the warm heart of our family.

This is the first group picture I've taken where Auntie Molly isn't next to them—but she's there, if you look closely. She's right there among them, with Grandpa and Grandma, and Grandma Nellie, and everyone who went before them.

Grandma Nellie and Grandma, approx. 1983

42. The Baton

In the only interview Doreen collected from Grandma, he talked about a figurative baton, passed from one generation to the next.

"I raised my children," Grandpa said. "Y se fueron muy bien (and they went very well). You are also growing. Some of the grandchildren have married, so, we are proud of this good luck we've lived with. Ahora (now), it's your turn. If you live in the right way and not make a mistake, life's story will continue to be nice for everybody. Not only you, but all of the granddaughters and grandsons." I heard the scrape of a chair against concrete. Grandpa was getting up, and ending the interview. "That's all I can tell," he said. There's a sound of a click— Doreen shutting the tape recorder off.

The abrupt ending to Grandpa's interview might have been symbolic: *Now it's your turn.*

I'm sure Grandpa never meant that he wanted us to live lives that were free of mistakes. He did want us to take responsibly for the mistakes we did make, correct them, and live in a way that matters. His words, "If you live in the right way," sounds like an Old Testament charge, warning the future generations who are entering a new land.

Grandpa's symbolic passing of a baton to the next generation made me reflective. When it's my turn to hand over, have I given my children all they need to continue on in the ways of family? Will they realize the importance of family and traditions? Will they celebrate their ancestors? Their roots? Themselves?

***

At Auntie Molly's funeral At Auntie Molly's funeral, 2020 (l to r): Mario, Rikki (holding Violet) Me, Scarlett, and Vince

Recently, our son, Vince, now in his thirties, took a DNA test, to trace his ethnicity and ancestry. His biological father is adopted, so the DNA test was important to Vince.

"I'm in the sixty-percent range of Irish heritage," Vince said. "Twenty-five percent of Indigenous mixed with Spanish, which would be Mexican. A little bit of Scandinavian, which is probably early Irish, I believe."

The DNA results solved a mystery: Vince's paternal grandmother was Irish-American, which explained Vince's fair skin and green eyes.

"I definitely grew up with pride about my Irish blood," Vince said. "Probably because of Grandpa (Jack Ryan), who was a proud Irish-American. He had Irish art, music, and books."

"Do you feel like you've inherited any kind of heritage from Mexico?" I asked him.

"Not really," he said. "Aside from knowing I'm twenty-five percent Mexican, I don't have a lot of connection to those roots," Vince said. "Sometimes people hear my last name and say, 'Your name is Rodriguez, and you don't speak Spanish? Then you're white.' They say this, this mainly because I don't speak Spanish."

"Do you ever feel ripped-off?" I asked "Like you should speak Spanish?"

"No," Vince said. "Not really. A last name doesn't define you, or your culture."

I felt the stab of this. *He doesn't feel ripped-off? A last name doesn't define you? Really?* The more I thought about this, the more I understood Vince's answer. His recent DNA screening didn't reveal anything about heritage, it just gave him a clearer picture of his ancestral ethnicity.

DNA wasn't able to tell Vince about his ancestral heritage, or the culture he had been given. It couldn't tell him if his ancestors were curious or resourceful. It couldn't say how they survived winters, what foods they ate, if they were prone to depression, or how they cared for their newborn babies. All of these things are heritage, culture, traditions, history. Most of this is passed on through story, and transmitted through people or written records.

Some cultures have these written texts or family records to give to the next generation. All cultures have art, food, music, and the oral tradition. Some of these survive, but some are wiped out. Some cultures have sacred music or texts. These are the things that give us roots, especially when these stories become ours, and we choose to pass them on to the next generation.

"I'm surprised you haven't absorbed more of the Mexican culture," I said. "But that's transmitted through stories and memories."

"And menudo," he said, smiling. I laughed.

Vince still makes menudo. Sometimes he makes it better than I do. For some reason, this satisfies my soul.

***

Clockwise from bottom left: Scarlett, Alannah, Me, Violet

On most Fridays, I drive to see my daughter, Alicia, and her two daughters, Harmony and Alannah, in a Northern California city, only two hours away by car (everything seems closer, after living in Johannesburg). On perfect Fridays, I get to take two of Vince's daughters, Scarlett and Violet, with me for "Fun Fridays." This tradition began as soon as Mario and I returned to the States.

Alicia, a small-business owner, and I have the relationship that most mother-daughters do. We do the mother-daughter dance, a tango through a jungle of issues. Mother-daughter relationships are often the most precious and fragile thing in a woman's life. All the way back to Eve, and her unnamed daughters.

***

Picture on left: 4 Generations, Christmas morning 2019. (Clockwise from left) Alannah, Janet, Mario, Jack, Alicia, Jennie, Harmony. Picture on right: Me and Alicia, 2018.

One Friday, as we hung out on her back porch, I asked Alicia about family.

"Have I done enough to hand you the family baton?" I asked. "Do I encourage you to connect to your roots? Do I give you enough direction about God? Do I encourage you to find your wings? Do I encourage you to visit Grandpa and Grandma? Do I help you connect with family?"

Alicia smiled, and shook her head. "Mom, those are *very* complex questions," she said. "Depending on the day, they have more than one answer." She looked up to the starry sky and exhaled. "You taught me that family wasn't just about me. That was important. You taught me how to stand on my own two feet. I had to do this when you moved to Africa."

For a while, Alicia and I were still. Eventually, we started talking about that life-changing, painful, wonderful time. The stars above us were so numerous, it was like we were in Malawi again. When Mario and I moved to Africa, Alicia came with us. She lived with us there for a year, then chose to come home to the United States. A strong group of friends became her fortified family. The separation was awful, but in retrospect, vitally important.

"I started to get to know myself during that time," Alicia said. "I had to know myself away from you. After that, I was able to have a good relationship with you, but I couldn't have done it without having that time first. You inspired strength and independence. That's what you passed on to me."

"Really?" I asked. "I always think you are much stronger than I am."

"But you taught me the strength of being a mother," she said. "You taught me to get up every day for my kids. To get out of bed and do things with them, and make memories."

"I tried to do that, Alicia," I said. "I really tried my best."

"You did, Mom," she said. "Now you do the same thing with your grandkids."

"What kind of baton have I handed you?" I asked. Unsure how to phrase my question.

She smiled. "A beautiful baton," she said. "You taught me how to recognize things that last," Alicia said. "How to create art, food, music, and well-written words. It's all about art. You do words; I do other media, like painting."

"You're also a wordsmith," I said, smiling.

I thought about Alicia's words long after I left her house. I made a lot of mistakes as a mother—a ton of mistakes, but I did my best. Maybe that was all I was supposed to do.

I look at my children, and their children, and our dubious future, a field of untilled earth that somehow needs us. To paraphrase Grandma, maybe life itself is our reward.

"Aún continuamos sobreviviendo." *We continue to survive.*

***

The fifth generation of my family is remarkably different from the first. Living in California, I see the grandchildren here more than our grandchildren in Kansas, but they all share similar "first-world comforts." On a typical day, during the very complicated beginning of the Covid[19] pandemic, California schools were technically in session, but functioning as hybrids. They had access to books, but school was a different experience.

Scarlett, Alicia, Harmony, and Alannah. Covid-casual school days, September 2020

"On a normal school day, I wake up," Harmony said. The eldest child of our daughter, Alicia, Harmony is a beautiful human, with brains to match. "I get dressed in Alannah's room, and I always manage to wake her up. She gets up and tell me what she dreamed."

"I always dream things," Alannah said, with excited animation. The second child of Alicia, Alannah is usually a burst of energy in a person. "Then I tell my dreams to Harmony."

"Then I get ready in the bathroom," Harmony continued. "I do my hair every day, and then I eat cereal or toast. On rare days, I have a bagel." Harmony nods once, as if she's finished talking.

"Then we get dressed and clean up our rooms," Alannah said. "After breakfast, we head to school, which is in the afternoon now. We wear masks and have special seating."

"I have to wake up early in the night," Scarlett said. The eldest child of our son, Vince, Scarlett is a glowing beam of light—except in the mornings. She made this clear. "My dad is getting ready to go to work," Scarlett said, putting her hands on her hips. "My mom wakes me up, and I do *not* want to get up!" She shook her head in frustration, then added: "My school is on a screen right now."

The girls talked about their schools changing, and the way the pandemic has affected their days. School, for the most part, is the whole world to a child. These children are guaranteed an education, even during a pandemic. No one can deny them their right to an education—not even a parent. My grandmother would have loved any kind of schooling.

Alannah and Harmony showed me their bookshelves of favorite books, collections that they're always being forced to cull. They have clothes, shoes, and toys in abundance. Their rooms are organized with shelves and decorative tubs and baskets.

Scarlett shares a big bedroom her sisters, but the same organization, including tubs, baskets, and labels for everything, are everywhere.

"Your room looks like a toy store," I said to her one day. Scarlett agreed.

"Yeah, I know," she said, sighing. "We have to give more toys away pretty soon. To the poor kids." My daughter-in-law, Rikki, makes regular runs to Goodwill, giving away barely-used toys.

"If someone asks you if we're a close family, what do you say?" I asked Harmony and Alannah.

"Are we talking about Mom's side of the family?" Harmony asked, incapable of balderdash. "Yes, we're a close family."

"I say we are," Alannah said. "We love each other, right? And we get to see you, Grandma, almost every Friday. Sometimes you bring Scarlett and Violet with you."

"Can I say something else about the Rodriguez family?" Harmony asked, holding up her index finger. "My Mom is a future queen and I am a princess."

"Yes, you are," I said, laughing. I had no idea what Harmony meant, but truer words were never spoken.

***

Grandpa teaches me a ranchero chord progression in Oregon, 1982

Our family's heritage is more than our shared DNA, more than a language, and even more than traditions. Our heritage is the strong sense of family, a culture of togetherness. So many questions surround this: Have we kept the family together? Why did our family succeed in this country when others didn't? Is our family moving in the right direction? As Alicia said, *those are very complex questions, and depending on the day, they have more than one answer.* Maybe the answer depends on the person who asks. Maybe most families relate because they understand the challenge of surviving and staying together.

On Día de los Muertos, many Mexican-Americans make ofrendas, or altars, decorated with pictures, flowers, and candles, to remember the treasured members of their families who have passed away. I've never made an ofrenda, because I am a living one. I carry my ancestors in my heart, in my DNA. I'm a museum of memories, filled with their life and experiences.

If I ever did make an ofrenda, it would look a lot like this book. Filled with delicious surprises.

Rosquillas

Crust:

1 cup salad oil
½ cup olive oil
1 cup sugar
1 cup whiskey   1 tsp. anise extract
enough flour to make pie crust
(save some for boards, to roll out dough)

Mix liquids together and then add flour until pie crust consistency is formed.

Filling:

1 can pumpkin
1 jar honey
pinch of cinnamon or nutmeg (if you want)

Cook filling in saucepan, on medium to hot stove. It will be bubbly, so stir until the filling becomes jelly-like. Turn heat to low. Roll dough and cut circles. Don't make them too thin. fill carefully with pie filling. Turn one side of the dough over, and make a turnover. Pinch ends together or seal with fork. Sprinkle tops with sugar if you want. Bake at 375 degrees until golden brown, about 35-40 minutes.

- Don't store in air-tight containers, since the crust gets soft without air.
- Don't store rosquillas where ants can find them—they'll sneak in and ruin them for everybody. This has happened to me.

About The Author

Janet Rodriguez is an author, teacher, and editor living in Northern California. In the United States, her work has appeared in Hobart, Pangyrus, Eclectica, The Rumpus, Cloud Women's Quarterly, American River Review, and Calaveras Station. She is the winner of the Bazanella Literary Award for Short Fiction and the Literary Insight for Work in Translation Award, both from CSUS Sacramento in 2017. Rodriguez has also co-authored two memoirs, published in South Africa. Her short stories, essays, and poetry usually deal with themes involving morality in faith communities and the mixed-race experience in a culturally binary world. She holds an MFA from Antioch University, Los Angeles. She is currently Assistant Editor of Interviews at The Rumpus.

www.ingramcontent.com/pod-product-compliance
Lightning Source LLC
Chambersburg PA
CBHW081333080526
44588CB00017B/2607